To Ida,

with hopes of

continued collaboration

and friendship

many years to come.

Kadriye

"Ercikan and Pellegrino have provided a thorough investigation of how the test-taker response processes influence the validity of score interpretations. By including studies that incorporate new technology with those using more traditional methods, assessment developers can better understand best practices in validity research. This highly readable book offers information that applies to multiple assessment types and purposes."

—**Marianne Perie,** *Director, Center for Assessment and Accountability*
Research and Design, USA

Validation of Score Meaning for the Next Generation of Assessments

Despite developments in research and practice on using examinee response process data in assessment design, the use of such data in test validation is rare. *Validation of Score Meaning for the Next Generation of Assessments* highlights the importance of validity evidence based on response processes and provides guidance to measurement researchers and practitioners in creating and using such evidence as a regular part of the assessment validation process. Response processes refer to approaches and behaviors of examinees when they interpret assessment situations and formulate and generate solutions as revealed through verbalizations, eye movements, response times, or computer clicks. Such response process data can provide information about the extent to which items and tasks engage examinees in the intended ways.

With contributions from the top researchers in the field of assessment, this volume includes chapters that focus on methodological issues and on applications across multiple contexts of assessment interpretation and use. In Part I of this book, contributors discuss the framing of validity as an evidence-based argument for the interpretation of the meaning of test scores, the specifics of different methods of response process data collection and analysis, and the use of response process data relative to issues of validation as highlighted in the joint standards on testing. In Part II, chapter authors offer examples that illustrate the use of response process data in assessment validation. These cases are provided specifically to address issues related to the analysis and interpretation of performance on assessments of complex cognition, assessments designed to inform classroom learning and instruction, and assessments intended for students with varying cultural and linguistic backgrounds.

Kadriye Ercikan is Professor of Measurement, Evaluation, and Research Methodology in the Faculty of Education at the University of British Columbia, Canada, and Vice President of Statistical Analysis, Data Analysis, and Psychometric Research at the Educational Testing Service.

James W. Pellegrino is Liberal Arts and Sciences Distinguished Professor and Distinguished Professor of Education and Co-Director of the Learning Sciences Research Institute at the University of Illinois at Chicago, USA.

Validation of Score Meaning for the Next Generation of Assessments

The Use of Response Processes

**Edited by Kadriye Ercikan and
James W. Pellegrino**

NEW YORK AND LONDON

First published 2017
by Routledge
711 Third Avenue, New York, NY 10017

and by Routledge
2 Park Square, Milton Park, Abingdon, Oxon, OX14 4RN

Routledge is an imprint of the Taylor & Francis Group, an informa business

© 2017 Taylor & Francis

Library of Congress Cataloging-in-Publication Data
A catalog record for this title has been requested

ISBN: 978-1-138-89836-3 (hbk)
ISBN: 978-1-138-89837-0 (pbk)
ISBN: 978-1-315-70859-1 (ebk)

Typeset in Minion Pro
by Apex CoVantage, LLC

Contents

1   Validation of Score Meaning Using Examinee Response Processes for the Next Generation of Assessments

Kadriye Ercikan and James W. Pellegrino

Why This Volume?

The importance of using examinee response processes in validity investigations has been highlighted in the *Standards for Educational and Psychological Testing* (American Educational Research Association et al., 1999, 2014) and emphasized for some time by measurement researchers (Ercikan, 2006; Haertel, 1999; Pellegrino, Chudowsky, & Glaser, 2001). The last decade has seen a growing emphasis on designing and developing assessments that are both informed by and provide information about student cognitive processes in learning as well as test taking while simultaneously considering a range of appropriate measurement models (Chudowsky & Pellegrino, 2003; Leighton & Gierl, 2007; Pellegrino et al., 2001; Wilson & Sloane, 2000). This emphasis has been motivated by multiple developments including: (a) our increased understanding of how students learn (Pellegrino et al., 2001), (b) an emergent emphasis on the importance of complex thinking in disciplinary areas (Schraw & Robinson, 2011), (c) increased attention given to the possible uses of interactive simulations and other dynamic displays as elements of performance assessments, and (d) data collection capabilities made possible by use of technology in testing such as eye tracking (van Gog & Sheiter, 2010) and response time (van der Linden, 2009). This shift in viewing testing as more directly related to constructs associated with learning, cognitive development, and cognitive processing has also impacted investigations of the validity of interpretations of scores relative to such constructs. Several researchers have described and summarized methods for examining the cognitive processes examinees use during test taking to determine whether tasks within a test are tapping the intended knowledge and skills (Baxter & Glaser, 2005; Ercikan & Seixas, 2011; Ferrara & Chen, 2011; Kaliski, France, & Huff, 2011; Magone, Cai, Silver, & Wang, 1994; Messick, 1989; Schnipke & Scrams, 2002). In addition to examining whether tasks captured the intended constructs, research has considered whether different item types (multiple choice versus constructed response) capture similar constructs (e.g., Ercikan et al., 2015, Kaliski et al., 2011), which features of items are related to the difficulty levels of items (Ferrara & Chen, 2011), and how these features affect special student populations such as English language learners and students with disabilities (Abedi, 2014; Sato, 2011; Winter, Kopriva, Chen, & Emick, 2006). In computer-based testing, response time data have been used for capturing rapid guessing as part of examining issues of student engagement and motivation during test taking (van der Linden, 2009; Wise & Kong, 2005).

Investigations of bias and fairness have been expanded to include these newer emphases on understanding examinee response processes during test taking, including whether these processes are comparable for different groups and the possible challenges this poses to interpretations of score meaning. Researchers have examined response processes to determine whether the relative difficulty of items for different groups of examinees is a result of differences in item language in multilingual assessments (Ercikan, Arim, Law, Lacroix, Gagnon, & Domene, 2010; Roth, Oliveri, Sandilands, Lyons-Thomas, & Ercikan, 2013), differences in solution strategies and instructional methods (Lane, Wang, & Magone, 1996), and interactions between item features and student language backgrounds (Winter et al., 2006).

Despite these developments in research and practice on using examinee response process data in assessment design and test validation, research has been limited and the use of such data in test validation is rare, their mention in the joint standards on testing notwithstanding. In particular, only a small number of researchers and practitioners are trained in and are familiar with the methodologies associated with the collection and analysis of such data as part of the validation process. The focus of this book is on validity evidence based on response processes with the goal of highlighting the importance of this rarely used form of validity evidence, while also providing guidance to measurement researchers and practitioners in creating and using such evidence as a regular part of the assessment validation process.

Response Process Data

Response processes refer to the thought processes, strategies, approaches, and behaviors of examinees when they read, interpret, and formulate solutions to assessment tasks. Data on examinee response processes can be gathered and constructed using a variety of methods. These include think-aloud protocols and cognitive interviews that rely on examinees' verbalizations about their own thinking processes. In computer-based testing contexts, data on examinee response processes can also include eye-movement patterns such as fixation duration and fixation sequences, response logs documenting interactions with stimulus materials including which response time as well as which task elements were clicked on, opened, and manipulated. These data collection and generation approaches result in verbal reports or verbalizations, traces of performance/thinking such as steps used in solving problems or error patterns, points of gaze on the computer screen, lengths of time an examinee spends on different aspects of an item, and the extent to which and how examinees utilize resources and information provided by test items.

Response processes can provide information about the extent to which items and tasks engage examinees in the intended ways and whether the inferences involved in creating scores and score meaning are justified. Types of processes that are of particular relevance are: (a) how examinees read and interpret test items, (b) steps they follow and strategies they use in solving problems and responding to test items, (c) knowledge and competencies examinees tap in responding to test items, (d) whether examinees truly engage with items instead of guessing their answers, and (e) how the resources and information provided in the test are utilized.

Contributions of Response Process Data to Validity

The current context for assessment of student achievement is changing in multiple ways including new content standards such as the Common Core Standards in Mathematics and English Language Arts, the Next Generation Science Standards, and new frameworks such as the National Assessment of Educational Progress (NAEP) Technology and Engineering Literacy Framework (TEL), and the content and problem-solving frameworks of the Organisation for Economic Co-operation and Development's Programme for International Student Assessment. These standards and frameworks focus on complex aspects of thinking and reasoning with various types of content as key aspects of the claims to be verified about student competence based upon evidence of student test performance. In many cases, creating the contexts for obtaining such evidence is closely coupled with the design and delivery of technology-based materials and tasks. These developments only serve to highlight growing requirements for evidence of score meaning. In particular, the use of response process data in score meaning validation gains heightened importance as the new generation of assessments increasingly focuses on complex cognitive constructs that involve significant uses of technology as part of stimulus presentation and the response process.

Assessing complex constructs such as those noted above highlights the need for a principled assessment design and validation approach (Ercikan & Oliveri, 2016). In particular, such assessments require taking construct complexity into account across various stages of assessment development such as the design, scaling, reporting, and interpretation of task performance with the challenge of obtaining cognitive validity evidence that goes beyond traditional psychometric analyses of response patterns. An argument-based approach to validity such as that proposed by Kane (2006, 2013) demands a principled approach to delineate intended inferences and requires explicit connections between evidence and score inference and use. Structured around interpretive and validity arguments, this approach to validity both guides the processes of interpreting scores and validating such interpretations. The interpretive argument links performance on the assessment to the intended inferences and interpretation of scores derived from the performance through explicitly stated claims. The validity argument describes the rationales, arguments, and forms of evidence that would support these claims.

The role of validity evidence from response processes is central to validity of score meaning in any assessment. However, such evidence gains heightened importance when claims about scores actually explicitly involve response processes. In many assessments, claims about response processes are integral to interpreting scores. This includes assessments of complex problem solving either individually or collaboratively, where claims are not just based on what examinees produce but the processes they follow as well. In such assessments, the process used, steps followed, and strategies used in deriving the solution are central to making claims about examinee performance the validity of which critically depends on data that documents response processes. With complex tasks it is even possible to consider response process data as part of score derivation and reporting.

Another important role played by response process data is in providing information about constructs assessed by the assessment and potential barriers to examinee performance. Response process data can help examine the degree to which:

- Examinees are reading, understanding and interpreting the tasks in expected ways;
- Examinees are following specific steps, strategies in responding to the task;
- Examinees are engaging in targeted complex thinking;
- Examinees are using the resources such as dictionaries or read-aloud features in expected ways;
- Examinees are spending reasonable amounts of time responding to the task that indicate meaningful engagement with the stimulus materials;
- Examinees at different ability levels or demographic groups are using similar response processes.

These issues are all related to interpretation of score meaning. Similar to other validity evidence, validity evidence based on response processes support interpretive claims "in varying degrees" rather than provide "yes/no" judgments.

Evidence from response processes complements other types of validity evidence such as evidence of standards or curriculum alignment, statistical relationships among tasks, expert judgments about what the tasks are assessing, and relationships with other measurements. It is important to highlight that validity evidence based on response processes can neither replace other forms of validity evidence nor can it be replaced by them. Without response process evidence, interpretation of performance and scores lacks evidence to support the interpretations listed above, such as whether examinees are engaging with the tasks in intended ways and whether the tasks are assessing targeted constructs. Consistency among sources of validity evidence is essential in developing a coherent validity argument. Inconsistency among validity evidence, such as high internal consistency among tasks but lack of evidence that tasks are engaging examinees in intended problem solving, leads to a breakdown of a coherent validity argument. In other words, if we do not have supporting evidence from response processes, other types of evidence have questionable value. When they provide evidence consistent with other sources, validity evidence based on response processes can corroborate other types of validity evidence and provide important insights about the meaning of those other types of validity evidence, for example, factor analytic patterns.

Overview of Contributions from the Chapters in this Volume

The chapters in Part I of this volume discuss conceptual and methodological issues in generating and using response process data to support validity arguments. Kane and Mislevy's chapter opens this section by discussing the framing of validity as an evidence-based argument for the interpretation of the meaning of test scores. It then distinguishes between two important but conceptually different interpretive frames that they label as process-model and trait-model interpretations and discuss the relevance and importance of response process data in validating both types of interpretations (Kane & Mislevy, this volume). This exposition is important because it challenges what might be a tacit assumption that response process data are relevant only to validation of the process-model framing of test score meaning. The next two chapters by Leighton and by Oranje, Gorin, Jia and Kerr then go on to discuss the specifics of different methods of data collection and analysis. Until recently, response process data have been primarily gathered through the collection of think-aloud protocols as part of conducting cognitive laboratory studies of student interactions with assessment tasks. The Leighton chapter describes how verbal reports and protocol analysis used in such data collection efforts can contribute to validating score meaning. The author highlights important distinctions between verbal report and protocol analysis and discusses how each can contribute to validating different performance and score interpretations. During the last decade, as more assessment tasks involved computer presentation and data capture, the use of examinee response process data to validate score meaning has evolved to include nonverbal data such as response time, eye tracking, and computer log files. Chapter 4 by Oranje et al. describes the creation of response process data through response time, eye tracking, and computer log files and discusses how they can be used for validating score meaning, including the types of evidence and arguments they support. Part I ends with a commentary by Wise on the chapters therein, in which he discusses the collection and use of response data relative to issues of validation as highlighted in the joint standards on testing.

The chapters in Part II of the volume constitute a set of examples of the use of response process data in assessment validation, and collectively highlight the importance of validity evidence based on such data. In contrast to the dominant literature on assessment validity that tends to be focused on large-scale assessments of academic achievement, these use cases span multiple contexts and consider multiple student populations. All consider assessments of student learning and thinking whether the assessment content is complex or relatively simple, whether it is used to inform classroom instruction or for large-scale testing contexts, whether the interpretation of scores is derived from automated or human scoring, whether the assessments are original or adapted versions of tests, or whether the validation of score meaning involves regular education students, students with disabilities, or non-native speakers of English. Individually and collectively the emphasis on the use of response process data for validating score interpretations across these very different but important use contexts highlights the unique and necessary insights that can be gained from the collection and analysis of such data. They serve to make the case for increased promotion of the use of such data in score meaning validation. The contributions of the six chapters can be organized in terms of three major sets of issues related to the analysis and interpretation of performance on: (a) assessments of complex cognition (Nichols & Huff; Bejar), (b) assessments designed to inform classroom learning and instruction (DiBello, Pellegrino, Gane, & Goldman;

Tindal, Alonzo, Sáez, & Nese), and (c) assessments intended for students with varying cultural and linguistic backgrounds (Kopriva & Wright; Solano-Flores & Chía).

Assessments of Complex Cognition

Demands for assessments to include complex constructs are often accompanied with the increased use of constructed-response item types. The chapter by Nichols and Huff discusses many of the concerns associated with the design of assessments of complex thinking as well as issues in the scoring, analysis, and interpretation of student performance data. In so doing they highlight the importance of several of the data collection and analysis methods discussed in the chapters in Part I of this volume. They provide an example from the AP History examination of how response process data can be used to inform task design as well as to evaluate not only the meaning of student responses to various types of tasks but also to the processes used by human raters who must score various types of constructed responses. They argue for the value of response process data in the validation of assessments of complex cognition – starting with the design of such assessments and continuing all the way through the scoring and reporting process. In his chapter, Bejar introduces an important set of concerns that have to do with the scoring of complex constructed-response material such as the essays required in many large-scale testing programs like the Graduate Record Examination (GRE). Increasingly, given the scope of these programs and the cost of human scoring, testing programs have turned to the use of automated scoring algorithms to evaluate student responses. The meaning of scores created by automated scoring algorithms is critically tied to the degree to which the scores capture construct-relevant response features and construct-irrelevant variance in the scores is minimized. The meaning, as well as threats to the meaning, of scores derived from automated scoring are discussed by Bejar. The author discusses construct-relevant and construct-irrelevant features of responses and how these features are scored as indicators of the construct. He provides an example of how such an analysis can be conducted as part of the validation process.

Assessments Designed to Inform Learning and Instruction

For over two decades there have been many calls for greater attention to assessments designed to inform the processes of classroom learning and instruction. Despite the fact that the most frequent use of assessment in education is in the context of ongoing teaching and learning, there has been very little research on the design and validation of such assessments. In their Chapter 8, DiBello et al. discuss these concerns and describe a framework for considering evidence regarding the validity of such assessments. They then elaborate on how examinee response processes can contribute to the establishment of a validity argument for instructionally supportive assessments using a case from middle school science assessment. The authors demonstrate that student response process data can be part of a validity argument for assessments designed for diagnostic and formative assessment use, especially when the evidence is combined with other forms of data that collectively consider cognitive, instructional, and inferential components of a validity argument for instructionally supportive assessments.

Similarly Tindal and colleagues discuss the use of curriculum-based assessments in response-to-intervention systems for students with disabilities. A primary goal of these assessments is to provide meaningful information about student performance and progress to inform instruction. Using a case study, the authors demonstrate the relevance and use of response processes from both the student and teacher perspectives to gain insights about student learning. Their case study illustrates how inferences about student learning and actions taken in response to those inferences can be very problematic when the use of response process data was not a major part of the original assessment validation process. Thus, even though students with disabilities may be challenged in providing some of the types of response data obtained through typical methods of the type described in the first part of this volume, it is inappropriate to assume that these students are incapable of providing evidence relevant to score interpretation and use. Their case study is a sobering example of the problems of inference and action that can arise in classroom teaching and learning when the assessments prescribed for use lack some critical interpretive backing.

Assessments Intended for Students with Varying Cultural and Linguistic Backgrounds

An important use of response process data is for providing insights about whether students from special populations are engaging with tasks in expected ways and whether these are comparable to engagement of other students. The Kopriva and Wright chapter discusses a conceptual framework for examining response processes for validating score meaning in the assessment of academic content for non-native speakers. The authors highlight the importance of using response processes for identifying and examining construct-irrelevant barriers. They then discuss how such data was used in the development and validation of an approach known as ONPAR (Online Partnership to Accelerate Research) that attempts to improve the validity of scores by introducing possible solutions to a number of the key problems raised in the literature.

Solano-Flores and Chía provide a systematic framework for examining and delineating response processes in defining the assessment construct, developing assessment design procedures, and piloting assessments in multilingual assessment contexts. The authors discuss how response process studies can help inform assessment design procedures, shed light on the results of differential item functioning studies, and be used to evaluate the assessment translation process. Their discussion is grounded in examples derived from the development and validation of alternative language versions of the large-scale assessments of academic achievement developed by the Smarter Balanced Assessment Consortium.

Part II ends with a commentary by Lane. She first discusses assessment design features that are used to help ensure the assessment of the intended response processes, and consequently, the validity of score meaning. She then provides a brief summary and commentary on the arguments and evidence found in the chapters in this second section relative to the use of response processes as they relate to the design and validation of assessments across the varying use cases.

Moving Forward

During the preparation of this volume the need for data on examinee response processes has grown, in part due to many of the factors identified earlier in this chapter. These include the development of large-scale assessment systems aligned to new academic content standards (e.g., the assessments developed by the Partnership for Assessment of Readiness for College and Careers (PARCC) and the Smarter Balanced Assessment Consortium (SBAC); the launch of the NAEP TEL assessment; and the planned transition of NAEP assessments to technology-based delivery), as well as a call for greater attention to the development of systems of assessment that include high quality classroom-based assessments (e.g., Gordon Commission, 2013a, b; Pellegrino, Wilson, Koenig & Beatty, 2014). Given these and other developments on the horizon, we expect this volume to be valuable to those who are embarking on designing, developing, and validating the next generation of assessments. These include assessments that involve new technologies such as computer-based or game-based assessments, assessments of complex constructs such as complex thinking and reasoning, or collaborative problem solving in various disciplines and domains such as literature, science, mathematics, and history. The volume includes chapters that focus on methodological issues as well as those with focus on applications across multiple contexts of assessment interpretation and use. Therefore, we expect the volume to be of interest and useful for both researchers and measurement professionals working in applied testing settings. We also expect that it will appeal to measurement researchers who are interested in complex fairness issues that may not be easily addressed with current differential item functioning approaches, such as when the populations of interest are diverse (Ercikan & Oliveri, 2013) as well as when dealing with small sample sizes and/or contexts of use beyond typical large-scale assessment programs.

References

Abedi, J. (2014). The use of computer technology in designing appropriate test accommodations for English language learners. *Applied Measurement in Education, 27*(4), 261–272.

American Educational Research Association, American Psychological Association, National Council on Measurement in Education, & Joint Committee on Standards for Educational and Psychological Testing (1999). *Standards for educational and psychological testing.* Washington DC: American Educational Research Association.

American Educational Research Association, American Psychological Association, National Council on Measurement in Education, & Joint Committee on Standards for Educational and Psychological Testing (2014). *Standards for educational and psychological testing.* Washington DC: American Educational Research Association.

Baxter, G. P., & Glaser, R. (2005). Investigating the cognitive complexity of science assessments. *Educational Measurement: Issues and Practice, 17*(3), 37–45.

Chudowsky, N., & Pellegrino, J. W. (2003). Large-scale assessments that support learning: What will it take? *Theory into Practice, 42*(1), 75–83.

Ercikan, K. (2006). Developments in assessment of student learning and achievement. In P. A. Alexander and P. H. Winne (Eds.), American Psychological Association, Division 15, *Handbook of educational psychology* (2nd ed., pp. 929–953). Mahwah, NJ: Lawrence Erlbaum Associates.

Ercikan, K. & Seixas, P. (2011). Assessment of higher order thinking: The case of historical thinking. In G. Shraw and D. H. Robinson (Eds.), *Assessment of higher order thinking skills* (pp. 245–261). Charlotte, NC: Information Age Publishing.

Ercikan, K. & Oliveri, M. E. (2013). Is fairness research doing justice? A modest proposal for an alternative validation approach in differential item functioning (DIF) investigations. In M. Chatterji (Ed.), *Validity, fairness and testing of individuals in high stakes decision-making context* (pp. 69–86). Bingley, UK: Emerald Publishing.

Ercikan, K., & Oliveri, M.E. (2016). In search of validity evidence in support of the interpretation and use of assessments of complex constructs: Discussion of research on assessing 21st century skills. *Applied Measurement in Education, 29*(4), 310–318.

Ercikan, K., Arim, R., G., Law, D. M., Lacroix, S., Gagnon, F., & Domene, J. F. (2010). Application of think-aloud protocols in examining sources of differential item functioning. *Educational Measurement: Issues and Practice, 29*, 24–35.

Ercikan, K., Seixas, P., Lyons-Thomas, J., & Gibson, L. (2015). Cognitive validity evidence for validating assessments of historical thinking. *New Directions in Assessing Historical Thinking*, pp. 206–220. New York and London: Routledge.

Ferrara, S., & Chen, J. (2011). Evidence for the accuracy of item response demand coding categories in think aloud verbal transcripts. Paper presented at the annual meeting of the American Educational Research Association, New Orleans, LA.

Gordon Commission on the Future of Assessment in Education (2013a). *Technical report.* Available: www. gordoncommission.org/publications_reports.html.

Gordon Commission on the Future of Assessment in Education (2013b). *Policy report.* Available: www. gordoncommission.org/publications_reports.html.

Haertel, E. H. (1999). Validity arguments for high-stakes testing: In search of the evidence. *Educational Measurement: Issues and Practice, 18*(4), 5–9.

Kaliski, P., France, M., & Huff, K. (2011). Using think aloud interviews in evidence-centered assessment design for the AP World History Exam. Paper presented at the annual meeting of the American Educational Research Association, New Orleans, LA.

Kane, M. T. (2006). Validation. In R. L. Brennan (Ed.), *Educational measurement* (4th ed., pp. 17–64). Westport, CT: Praeger.

Kane, M. T. (2013). Validating the interpretations and uses of test scores. *Journal of Educational Measurement, 50*(1), 1–73.

Lane, S., Wang, N., & Magone, M. (1996). Gender related differential item functioning on a middle-school mathematics performance assessment. *Educational Measurement: Issues and Practice, 15*(4), 21–27.

Leighton, J., & Gierl, M. (Eds.) (2007). *Cognitive diagnostic assessment for education: Theory and applications.* Cambridge, UK: Cambridge University Press.

Magone, M. E., Cai, J., Silver, E. A., & Wang, N. (1994). Validating the cognitive complexity and content validity of a mathematics performance assessment. *International Journal of Educational Research, 21*(3), 317–340.

Messick, S. (1989). Validity. In R. L. Linn (Ed.), *Educational measurement* (3rd ed., pp. 13–104). New York: American Council on Education and Macmillan.

Pellegrino, J. W., Chudowsky, N., & Glaser, R. (2001). *Knowing what students know: The science and design of educational assessment.* Washington, DC: National Academies Press.

Pellegrino, J. W., Wilson, M., Koenig, J., & Beatty, A. (Eds.) (2014). *Developing assessments for the Next Generation Science Standards.* Washington, DC: National Academies Press.

Roth, W.-M., Oliveri, M. E., Sandilands, D., Lyons-Thomas, J., & Ercikan, K. (2013). Investigating linguistic sources of differential item functioning using expert think-aloud protocols in science achievement tests. *International Journal of Science Education, 35*(4), 546–576.

Sato, E. (2011). Cognitive interviews of English language learners and students with disabilities and features contributing to item difficulty: Implications for item and test design. Paper presented at the annual meeting of the American Educational Research Association, New Orleans, LA.

Schnipke, D. L., & Scrams, D. J. (2002). Exploring issues of examinee behavior: Insights gained from response time analyses. In C. N. Mills, M. Potenza, J. J. Fremer, & W. Ward (Eds.), *Computer-based testing: Building the foundation for future assessments* (pp. 237–266). Mahwah, NJ: Lawrence Erlbaum.

Schraw, G., & Robinson, D. H. (2011). *Assessment of higher order thinking skills. Current perspectives on cognition, learning and instruction.* Charlotte, NC: IAP-Information Age Publishing.

van der Linden, W. J. (2009). Conceptual issues in response-time modeling. *Journal of Educational Measurement, 46*(3), 247–272.

van Gog, T., & Scheiter, K. (2010). Eye tracking as a tool to study and enhance multimedia learning. *Learning and Instruction, 20*(2), 95–99.

Wilson, M., & Sloane, K. (2000). From principles to practice: An embedded assessment system. *Applied Measurement in Education, 13*(2), 181–208.

Winter, P. C., Kopriva, R. J., Chen, C. S., & Emick, J. E. (2006). Exploring individual and item factors that affect assessment validity for diverse learners: Results from a large-scale cognitive lab. *Learning and Individual Differences, 16*(4), 267–276.

Wise, S. L., & Kong, X. J. (2005). Response time effort: A new measure of examinee motivation in computer-based tests. *Applied Measurement in Education, 18*(2), 163–183.

Conceptual and Methodological Issues Associated with Using Examinee Response Process Data to Validate Score Meaning

Part I

Conceptual and Methodological
Issues Associated with Using
Examinee Response Process
Data to Validate Score Meaning

2 Validating Score Interpretations Based on Response Processes

Michael Kane and Robert Mislevy

The most recent edition of the Standards for Educational and Psychological Testing (American Educational Research Association et al., 2014) states: "Validity refers to the degree to which evidence and theory support the interpretations of test scores for the proposed use of tests. . . . The process of validation involves accumulating relevant evidence to propose a sound scientific basis for proposed score interpretations" (p. 11). This chapter addresses lines of validation evidence based on the processes examinees employ in responding to the tasks included in educational tests and the theories that relate these processes to score interpretations.

Traditional standardized tests assign a score to each test taker on a score scale reflecting overall achievement in some domain. While this kind of score interpretation is useful for many purposes, the scores do not tell us much about how the test takers perform the test tasks, and they are not directly helpful in planning instruction. Advances in cognitive theory enable us to examine performance in terms of the knowledge and processes test takers bring to bear, as evidenced by both familiar forms of data such as think-aloud protocols and patterns of response across tasks, and by new forms of data such as digital logs of specific actions and points of gaze on a computer screen. While a number of specific approaches will be mentioned, they share the essential theme of examining how the process data, seen through the lens of cognitive theory at some level, can support, challenge, or enrich proposed interpretations of scores.

The chapter is organized around two broad, albeit overlapping, approaches, which address process-model interpretations and trait interpretations. Process-model interpretations use response data to fit explicit models for some kind of performance (e.g., a procedural model for solving two-digit addition problems). The assessments developed to support this kind of interpretation would consist of tasks that evoke the kind of performance that is accounted for by the model. The tasks, and thus the performances they are designed to elicit, are typically drawn from a narrowly-defined domain associated with the model. The parameters in the measurement model could correspond at some grain size to parameters in the process model (e.g., processes associated with performing single-digit addition, and handling "carries").

A trait is a disposition to behave or perform in some way in some kinds of situations across some range of circumstances. Traits play a particularly large role in personality theory, but we will focus on cognitive traits, involving cognitive competencies. Trait interpretations in education (e.g., reading ability, quantitative reasoning) tend to be associated with broadly defined performance domains (e.g., involving tasks that require reading ability or quantitative reasoning) for which no single, specific process model exists. The trait is thought of as a general ability, but the ability is specified in terms of the kinds of tasks that require the trait; for example, literacy is defined in terms of the ability to make sense of various kinds of printed materials in various ways. Trait assessments involve sampling of tasks from the domain, and scores are interpreted in terms of expected performance in the domain, or in terms of an underlying latent trait that accounts for performance.

Traits typically involve assumptions about how the tasks in the domain are performed and various cognitive processes may be expected to be employed in performing the tasks, although the performances are not modeled in any detail, and the methods used to validate process-model interpretations can be used to evaluate these assumptions. The validity argument for traits is likely to require a more diverse array of evidence than validity arguments for process-model interpretations because broadly defined traits can involve a wide range of tasks. Nevertheless, by developing and evaluating process models for some of these tasks, the trait interpretation can be evaluated by checking on the extent to which test performances depend on appropriate cognitive processes (e.g., in the case of reading assessment, word recognition and syntactical cues), and not on inappropriate processes (e.g., again for reading assessment, prior knowledge or surface cues).

These two kinds of interpretations can be thought of as anchoring the ends of a continuum. Process-model interpretations tend to focus on particular kinds of tasks, the grain size of the analysis tends to be small, involving particular cognitive processes, and the meaning of the scores is, to a large extent, determined by the model. An illustration at this end is Pirolli and Wilson's (1998) multivariate mixture extension of a Rasch model, with its form and its person and task parameters grounded in the Newell-Dennett cognitive framework for goal-directed behavior. Their examples (items from an intelligent tutoring system and Piagetian balance beam problems) use tasks that are tightly defined through particular cognitive theories, and person-parameters that reflect strategies and proficiencies defined in the same theories. Trait interpretations tend to be relatively broad, focusing on performance domains associated with the trait, the grain size tends to be large, focusing on general competencies, and the meaning of the scores is, to a large extent, determined by the performance domain of interest, with cognitive models playing a supporting role rather than a defining role. An illustration is retrospective modeling of traditional reading comprehension tasks, which were used since long before process theories of comprehension existed. Nevertheless, item statistics can now be modeled in terms of features that process theories would predict to affect difficulty (e.g., Gorin & Embretson, 2006). Particular score interpretations will fall at various points along this continuum. Gorin (2006), for example, argues for increased use of cognitive research to design tasks for educational assessments. Users can still interpret test scores in terms of familiar constructs such as analytical reasoning and reading comprehension, but the meaning has stronger theoretical grounding.

The discussions of both process model interpretations and trait interpretations are illustrated with brief examples with a variety of types of data, several of which are treated in more depth in succeeding chapters. The emphasis is on the logic of validation, from the perspective of score interpretation/use arguments (IUAs) (Kane, 1992, 2006, 2013; Mislevy, 2006, 2009). The proposed interpretation of scores is to be explicitly stated as an IUA, and this interpretation/use can be validated by evaluating the coherence and plausibility of the IUA.

An effective strategy for validation can then be systematically implemented. First, the proposed interpretation would be stated as clearly and explicitly as possible (e.g., a trait interpretation or process interpretation). Second, the available evidence relevant to the interpretation and use would be evaluated, and the most questionable assumptions and inferences would be identified. Third, the inferences and assumptions would be evaluated (empirically and/or logically), with an emphasis on the most questionable assumptions. An interpretation that survives all reasonable challenges to its assumptions can be accepted, with an acknowledgment that it may be questioned in the future if new evidence casts doubts on one or more of its components (Cronbach, 1971, 1988; Kane, 1992).

Warrants that Incorporate Response Processes

Interpretation-based validation provides criteria for allocating research effort and in identifying the kinds of evidence needed for validation (Cronbach, 1988). The most relevant evidence is that which can be used to evaluate the main inferences and assumptions in the IUA. The content of the interpretation indicates the evidence needed for validation.

Traditional warrants based on task sampling may still play a role, but they can now be augmented by warrants based on the cognitive structures and activities that are posited to produce the performance. Warrants are backed by theory and experience, which now includes research in cognitive and learning sciences. Interpretations are threatened by alternative explanations, which now include the possibility that performances have been produced by processes other than the ones presumed in the warrant. Validation activities can examine response patterns and additional forms of data, drawn from assessment performances or supplemental studies, to support or rebut these cognitively-motivated alternative explanations.

Process-Model Interpretations

When theory is available to model the performances at some grain size, and scores are to be interpreted in terms of the values of parameters in the model, evidence that a test taker's response patterns are consistent with the model (or that test takers' response patterns are generally consistent with the model) is needed to support the proposed interpretation in terms of the model. Interpretations of this type tend to focus on particular families of tasks and have a fine grain size. Because they can tell us what test takers can and cannot do, they can be particularly useful in formative assessment, and, because they relate processing to features of tasks and examinee actions, they can be particularly useful prospectively in assessment development.

The section on process-model interpretations will first describe production models, as a framework for modeling cognitive processes that has been adapted directly for designing and validating some highly focused assessments, and is useful for understanding psychometric approaches such as cognitive diagnostic modeling that can be used in design, interpretation, and modeling at a somewhat coarser grain size.

Trait Interpretations

A trait interpretation focuses on a target domain of performances and on competencies thought to be involved in the performances. The trait has a dual interpretation; initially, the trait may be defined in terms of expected performance in some target domain (e.g., arithmetic word problems), which may be fairly well defined, and some competencies (e.g., performing arithmetic operations, problem solving) which are not well understood. In these cases, studies of response processes can play an important role in fleshing out the meaning of the trait by developing better understandings of the competencies in terms of process models and in ruling out alternate interpretations. Even if the process theories are not fully detailed or address only some aspects of performance or parts of the assessment, they can illuminate the competencies associated with the trait, and provide evidence that supports or challenges proposed score interpretations.

Validation Based on Process-Model Interpretations

The validity of an interpretation of scores in terms of the value of a theoretical construct depends mainly on the plausibility of the defining theory and the plausibility of the assumed relationship between the scores and the construct (based mainly on empirical checks). In a process-model interpretation, the construct involves the ability to perform certain kinds of tasks, using the procedural processes and knowledge elements in the ways specified by the model. To the extent that a process model and the indicators used to estimate parameters in the model are empirically supported, both the theory and the interpretation of the scores in terms of the model are supported. A theory that survives a range of serious challenges can be accepted, at least presumptively (Cronbach, 1980; Popper, 1965).

In his 1976 article "Psychometric tests as cognitive tasks: A new structure of intellect," John B. Carroll made the case that cognitive models could provide an effective framework for interpreting some test scores. Since then, theoretical interpretations based on cognitive processing models have appeared with increasing frequency, and a range of methods, varying as to data sources and modeling techniques, have since evolved.

This approach holds a close affinity with Cronbach and Meehl's strong program of construct validation, with a theory-based process model as the core of the intended interpretation. A particular application of the argument is characterized by the process model, specifications of task situations, and performance data that are motivated by the process theory and are typically more detailed than test specifications. These data can take the form of additional detail about examinee performance and additional detail about features of tasks with theoretical relationships related to cognitive components and processes.

Validation activities based on a theory-based process model have the following characteristics.

1   At some level of detail, a model is proposed for the knowledge structures and/or activity structures that test takers use to produce task performances. The model provides the core of the IUA for the interpretation, and data can be used to evaluate how well the model accounts for test-taker performance. The validity of the proposed process-model interpretation is supported by evidence indicating that test-taker performance is consistent with the model.

2   The soundness of the proposed process-model interpretation can also be evaluated in terms of operationally-observed data such as item response patterns, and can be extended with supplemental data such as log files and response times (Oranje et al., this volume), or special studies such as think-alouds (Leighton, this volume), video recordings of solution behaviors, eye-tracking, brain-imaging, and physical monitoring.

3   Most operational scores are unidimensional, either overall scores analyzed with classical test theory or obtained through item response theory (IRT). A process model used in validation often involves more-complicated psychometric models that include more information about performance, task features, and/or the proposed processes.

4   Tasks are designed such that the features and the directives activate the targeted cognitive processing, at least in proficient test takers. In some cases, the process model underlying the test specifies processes that less proficient test takers could be using, or it may indicate that some processes are not being employed by lower-scoring test takers.

5   There are enough tasks or portions of extended tasks to investigate patterns of performance across multiple instances of the targeted processing elements.

The five characteristics listed above generally lead to a test that is narrowly focused, in terms of both tasks and test takers. The range of tasks has to be narrow enough so that a model can account for performance on all of the tasks. A test that spans a broad range of content and is administered to a diverse population is unlikely to have an explicit cognitive model for the full range of tasks in the domain, or enough redundancy to estimate the model parameters.

A wide variety of process models can be entertained for modeling responses to educational tests, from the simple learning models of mathematical psychology of the 1950s (Restle & Greeno, 1970) to more-recent neural-network constraint-satisfaction models (e.g., Kintsch & Greeno, 1985) and partially-observed Markov decision process models (e.g., LaMar, 2014). To illustrate the validation thinking that is employed no matter what the particular model or content domain, we will discuss the two approaches that are most widely used in learning and assessment applications. These are production system models and cognitive diagnosis models.

Production System Models

Production systems are the most comprehensive form of contemporary process models (Newell & Simon, 1972). A production system model for a class of assessment tasks approximates the knowledge, activation patterns, and rules that people use to respond to the tasks. Successful applications of production system models match the actual response times, difficulty levels, and learning rates of humans. John Anderson's Adaptive Control of Thought—Rational (ACT-R) model (Anderson, 1996; Anderson, Bothell, Byrne, Douglass, Lebiere, & Qin, 2004) is currently the most widely used production system framework. Its components represent "declarative memory (defined by elements called chunks) and procedural memory (defined by productions), a goal structure for coordinating productions, an activation-based retrieval system, and a scheme for learning new productions" (Lebiere & Anderson, 2008, p. 635).

ACT-R has been applied to problems in domains including air traffic control, computer programming, and language acquisition. Anderson and his colleagues have developed intelligent tutoring systems for computer programming and mathematics (Anderson, Corbett, Koedinger, & Pelletier, 1995). His tutor for LISP programming modeled competence in terms of 325 production rules (Anderson & Reiser, 1985). It also used some 500 "buggy" rules to make sense of students' errors as it parsed their work step by step as likely outcomes of productions.

Production systems like ACT-R work at a very fine grain size, and Characteristic #5 above will usually not be satisfied for operational educational tests. They can nevertheless prove useful in validation in several ways:

Ancillary studies showing that a production system approximates subjects' performance provide backing to interpret scores as summary indicators of the knowledge built into the model. Carpenter, Just, and Shell's (1990) production models for progressive matrices tasks is an example. Their production model contained knowledge of the rules by which progressive matrices tasks are devised, solution strategies, and a hierarchical goal structure for the steps needed to solve a problem. Their best version of the production system, BETTERRAVEN, solved about as many test items as high-scoring college students and produced item percent-correct that correlated 0.9 with those of the students. Moreover, a version called FAIRRAVEN which had fewer rules and a shallower goal stack missed more items, and the ones it missed tended to be those that lower-scoring students also missed more often. Carpenter, Just, and Shell interpreted these findings as support of progressive matrix scores as measures mainly of working memory.

A production system can serve as a framework to scrutinize students' performance, in parsing solution steps, interpreting think-alouds, and informing analyses at a coarser grain size. Carpenter, Just, and Carpenter et al. also tracked subjects' eye movements and collected verbal protocols as they solve matrix tasks. They found in these data that successful solutions were largely consistent with the application of the proposed productions rules for incrementally discovering and verifying the patterns in the tasks. Unsuccessful solutions were either inefficient attempts to carry out such a strategy, or failures to employ any principled strategy.

A production model for a domain specifies how features of tasks elicit particular components of knowledge, procedures, and strategies. The results of studies based on a model thus also inform task development with respect to interfaces, representations, directives, task features, work products, and scoring rules—all to the end of designing tasks whose scores are likely to reflect the intended capabilities. These are validation activities in the design phase of an assessment. Embretson (1998) illustrates their use in the same context of progressive matrices, developing a computer program for generating tasks and modeling responses in terms of the same construction rules that Carpenter, Just, and Carpenter et al. used, and accounting for features that would increase cognitive load.

Cognitive Diagnosis Models

Production systems are comprehensive in that they attempt to approximate all of the key knowledge, procedures, and situation features in a model that accounts for how one could work through a task step by step. They are so comprehensive that they cannot be fit to typical educational tests, with their comparatively fewer tasks and sparser data, and covering an even modestly broad range of content. However, less comprehensive process models that incorporate one or more of the more detailed knowledge, data, or task elements, can sometimes be applied to educational tests. This is so especially when the test has been designed around a process theory that is aligned with such a model (Embretson, 1983, 1998; Leighton & Gierl, 2011; Mislevy, 2006). We will call these cognitive diagnosis models, broadening the term a little from common usage.

This section notes some variations of cognitive diagnosis models that have been applied in test construction and in validation. In all cases, the line of argument for test-score validation is the same: a cognitive theory is proposed at a level more detailed than the construct per se. It is proposed that scores can be interpreted as summary statements about the capabilities described in the theory. The theory makes claims about expected patterns of performance in situations with particular features. A model more detailed in some respect than an overall scoring model can be fit to observable data to provide support or to weaken our confidence in the proposed interpretation.

A historical starting point for this discussion is psychometric models that structure item difficulty (either in terms of correctness or response time) as a function of item features. Theory posits that the knowledge elements and/or processing steps needed to solve items with certain features are more numerous, more advanced, or require more cognitive resources. Finding that the difficulty predictions are consistent with empirical difficulties supports the interpretation of higher scores as demonstrating greater capabilities with respect to these knowledge and processing elements. Early applications of this approach include Suppes and Morningstar's (1972) regression model for arithmetic items' percentage correct in terms of the procedures they required, Sternberg's (1977) regression model for response times for analogy items as a function of four processing steps (encoding, mapping, inference, and application), and Drum, Calfee, and Cook's (1981) study of the task features that predict difficulty in reading comprehension items.

Scheiblechner (1972) and Fischer (1973) extended this idea into IRT with the linear logistic test model (LLTM). Here IRT item difficulty parameters are modeled as functions of item features that are linked to knowledge or processing elements in the solution process. Although less comprehensive than production system models, LLTM models (and the random-weights extension) (Rijmen & De Boeck, 2002) have the advantage of being applicable to a wide range of content domains and psychological theories (e.g., theories for problem solving, reading comprehension, and science inquiry; Leighton & Gierl, 2011). To mention an example, each of the tests in the British Army Recruitment Battery (BARB) consists of items both generated and modeled for each examinee in real time in accordance with such theories (Irvine, 2013). Not only was the process-modeling approach a logistical tour de force in BARB, it simultaneously provided strong evidence for the interpretation of scores.

This basic idea has been extended in several directions. Embretson (1985) brought in distinguishable responses to subtasks of items, and modeled them in terms of multiple cognitive components. The chapters in De Boeck and Wilson (2004) describe extensions such as models with interaction effects for persons and tasks, dynamic effects as testing proceeds, and mixtures of strategy usage. Bejar (this volume) discusses how the approach can be applied to the automated generation of test items. The validity argumentation employs the same logic, but the range of practical applications has been extended in each case. The validity argument for a process-based interpretation needs to evaluate the empirical support for the process model, which provides the core of the IUA for such interpretations, and for the other inferences (e.g., reliability or generalizability, extrapolation to relevant non-test performance domains). As noted earlier, the process model can be evaluated against test-taker response data (from operational uses or tryouts) and through other sources of evidence (e.g., think-aloud protocols).

Cognitive diagnostic models properly address task or task-component responses, modeling them as functions of one or more component abilities that take a small number of values—often just two, for mastery or nonmastery of a skill (Leighton & Gierl, 2007; Nichols, Chipman, & Brennan, 1995; Rupp, Templin, & Henson, 2010). Again tasks are modeled in terms of their features, which are related to skill requirements through a so-called Q-matrix specified by the analyst.

As an example, Katz, Martinez, Sheehan, and Tatsuoka (1998) applied this approach to complex simulation-based architectural design problems, using Tatsuoka's (1983) Rule Space cognitive diagnosis model. They used think-aloud protocols to elicit information at a level of detail that could ground a production system model. The basis of the attributes in their cognitive model was a finely grained taxonomy developed specifically for architectural design, based on a more general theory of Lewis and Polson (1991). To analyze relatively sparse assessment data, however, they collapsed the original production rules into smaller groups of equivalence classes and did not model individual chunks of declarative knowledge. The resulting simplification provided a Q-matrix that could be used to analyze examinee responses at the scale of operational testing. Katz, Martinez, Sheehan, and Tatsuoka used their cognitive diagnosis model for validation in several ways. In one, they coded the verbalizations of a sample of examinees' think-aloud protocols in terms of the attributes coded in the Q-matrix. Seventy-one percent indicated processing consistent with the posited attributes, providing confirmatory evidence that the examinees were working through the design problems in accordance with the more detailed process theory. In another, they examined the differences between attribute classifications (mastery vs. nonmastery) among architecture students, interns, and practicing architects. They found significant differences ($p < .10$) for the "understand" and "solve" attributes, but not the "check" attribute. As an example of implications for task design, if score interpretations are meant to encompass all three attributes, the test could include more tasks with identifiable "check" requirements.

Process-based Validity Evidence for Trait Interpretations

Although great progress has been made in modeling some of the activities involved in learning and in cognitive performance, educational practice still relies on trait interpretations for many purposes (particularly summative assessments). Trait values characterize performance over broad domains (e.g., literacy, achievement in various school subjects), and the goals of schooling are typically described in terms of such broadly defined domains.

The cognitive trait is understood, in large part, in terms of expected performance over some domain of possible performances, the *target domain* for the trait, but this is not defined arbitrarily. Rather, the target domain is defined in terms of performances that are thought to require the competencies associated with the trait. Although performance is expected to vary from task to task, traits are taken to be invariant over some sets of tasks, contexts, and occasions. Messick defined a trait as

> a relatively enduring characteristic of a person—an attribute, process, or disposition—which is consistently manifested to an appropriate degree when relevant, despite considerable variation in the range of settings and circumstances.
>
> Messick, 1970, p. 480

It is the dual conception of traits, as both latent characteristics of test takers and as expected performances over a target domain, that makes them especially useful.

Cognitive traits (e.g., reading ability, quantitative reasoning) can be defined in terms of performance domains (e.g., involving tasks that require reading ability or quantitative ability), or in terms of ability to perform certain kinds of tasks. For example, literacy can be defined in terms of the ability to make sense of various kinds of printed materials in various ways, and quantitative ability can be defined as the ability to solve quantitative problems. We do not generally have process models for most of the tasks in the domain associated with the trait, but we do generally have some ideas about how the tasks are performed (Kane, 2013; Mislevy, Steinberg, & Almond, 2003; Pellegrino, Chudowsky, & Glaser, 2001). By developing and evaluating process models for at least some of the tasks in the domain, the trait interpretation can be evaluated by checking on the extent to which performances on those tasks can be attributed to appropriate cognitive processes (e.g., for reading assessment, word recognition and syntactical cues), and not to inappropriate processes (e.g., for reading assessment, prior knowledge, guessing, or surface cues).

In adopting two complementary definitions of the trait, we make two basic assumptions. First, we assume that a test taker's performance in the target domain can be attributed to the competencies (or latent characteristics), and second, we assume that a test taker's performance on the test tasks can also be attributed to these competencies.

The traits that are of most interest in education tend to be broadly defined. For example, Dwyer, Gallagher, Levin, and Morley (2003) defined quantitative reasoning in terms of being able to solve certain kinds of quantitative problems under certain conditions, but also associated it with skills, such as understanding quantitative information presented in various formats, interpreting and drawing inferences from quantitative information, solving novel quantitative problems, checking the reasonableness of the results, communicating quantitative information, and recognizing the limitations of quantitative methods. Similarly, reading comprehension can be conceptualized in terms of broadly defined domain of performances involving effective interactions with text, and at the same time, it can be thought of as having the cognitive resources needed to perform these tasks (Sabatini, Albro, & O'Reilly, 2012; Sheehan & O'Reilly, 2012).

Although the dual conception of traits as both latent characteristics of test takers and in terms of performances over a target domain introduces some ambiguity, it also introduces some significant opportunities. In particular, we can talk sensibly about traits like quantitative reasoning and literacy in terms of performance domains without fully understanding the cognitive processes involved in the wide range of performances associated with the trait. We have some understanding of the processes involved in the performances based on introspection, on watching others perform the tasks, and on various kinds of systematic investigations, but we are far from having a complete understanding of the processes employed in the performances, and we certainly do not have a formal model of broadly defined traits like quantitative reasoning or literacy. Our understanding of the trait in terms of a performance domain and in terms of our assumptions about processes involved in the performances provide us with a framework for investigating phenomena associated with the trait, for refining our understanding of the trait, and for developing models for the more specific skills involved in the cognitive trait.

For example, we can seek to develop models that account for some specific kinds of performance from the target domain. Although it is not generally possible to develop formal models that will account for the full range of performances in the domain, it is often possible to develop such models for specific kinds of test tasks in the target domain. For example, in investigating quantitative reasoning, we might develop a model for the estimation of areas of irregular figures using approximation methods. Such tasks do not exhaust the meaning of quantitative reasoning, but they are important examples of quantitative reasoning. By developing and evaluating such partial models, we can improve our understanding of the processes involved in effectively estimating areas in general and more particularly, in performing test tasks that require this competency. Think-aloud protocols can provide relatively direct indications of how people perform test tasks (e.g., solving area problems on a test) and non-test tasks (estimating area in real-world contexts) in the target domain.

Validating Trait Interpretations

As is the case for most test-score interpretations, the claims based on trait measures rely on a number of assumptions that merit evaluation. We assume that the tasks included in the test constitute a representative sample of the target domain, or of a significant subset of the target domain. We assume that the test is administered under appropriate conditions and is scored in a way that reflects the intended interpretation of the trait.

Cognitive traits are generally assumed to apply over a range of tasks, contexts, and occasions, and the trait estimates generated by the testing program are assumed, explicitly or tacitly, to be generalizable over samples of tasks, contexts, and occasions. It is further assumed that the trait estimates have implications beyond the testing context, that they tell us something about how test takers will perform in "real-world" situations. Standardized tests typically involve samples of tasks that are limited, or "standardized", in many ways (reading passages of certain lengths on topics that are not too esoteric or specialized, quantitative problems that can be completed in a relative short time without help), but the trait is assumed to apply much more broadly. Test users typically assume that the trait as measured by the test provides an effective and fair basis for some kind of decision; for example, if the test scores are to be used to predict performance in an educational program, it would be important to confirm that the predictions hold up fairly well. All of these assumptions apply to trait measures as much as they do to any test, and all need to be addressed using relevant analyses in order to validate the proposed interpretation and use of the test scores.

Much of the evidence needed for the validity argument can be developed during test development, (e.g., content-related evidence, generalizability/reliability analyses, some criterion-based studies, differential item functioning (DIF) analyses), and this includes process-related evidence as well (e.g., think-aloud studies, eye-tracking, cognitive modeling with more comprehensive performance data). Additional evidence can be collected when the test is operational and data sets with larger sample sizes are available, such as fitting more detailed process-motivated psychometric models to subsets of tasks.

In this section, we will focus on a particular assumption inherent in the interpretation of test scores in terms of cognitive traits, and on the role that process models can play in the evaluation of this assumption. Trait interpretations assume that the test tasks require the cognitive competencies associated with the trait for their successful completion, and the development and evaluation of process models, for at least some test tasks in terms of the cognitive competencies, can provide a particularly effective way to evaluate this core assumption. As Cronbach suggested:

> The job of validation is not to support an interpretation, but to find out what might be wrong with it. A proposition deserves some degree of trust only when it has survived serious attempts to falsify it.
>
> Cronbach, 1980, p. 103

The goal is to develop a convincing validity argument by evaluating the most-plausible challenges to the proposed interpretation and use of the scores.

This approach is consistent with the basic methodology of science. A proposal or conjecture is developed and at least some of the implications of the proposal are spelled out and subjected to empirical evaluation. If the implications of the proposal are confirmed, confidence in the proposal increases, and if some of the implications are contradicted by data, the proposal has to be revised or replaced. Proposals that make specific predictions (as process models can) generate exacting challenges to the proposal, and thereby, can provide strong evidence for or against the proposal. A proposed score interpretation that has survived a number of such challenges, deserves "some degree of trust."

Given their dual interpretation, trait interpretations can be challenged in a number of ways. First, the trait interpretation can be challenged on the grounds that the observed task performances do not require the competencies, or the full range of competencies, associated with the trait. This issue could be addressed to some extent during test development, using expert opinion, think-aloud protocols, and other process studies. These two kinds of evidence can be used in tandem during test development to refine the test tasks. As noted earlier, the methods for collecting data and challenging interpretations in trait-based interpretations come from the same armamentarium as those for validating process-model interpretations. It is not the methodology that distinguishes the two, but rather the nature of the interpretation: tending to be more focused and sharply defined for process-model interpretations, while more general and less well defined for trait interpretations.

A potentially powerful way to investigate whether the test tasks do, in fact, require the competencies associated with the trait is to develop process models for some of the tasks included in the test, and to use these models to make predictions about test-taker performance on the tasks. If the data agree with the predictions, our confidence in our understanding of the competencies associated with the traits, and in the extent to which the test tasks depend on these competencies, increases. If the data do not agree with the predictions, our confidence in our understanding of the competencies, or in the appropriateness of the test tasks, decreases.

Second, the trait interpretation can be challenged on the grounds that different processes are being employed by different examinee groups as they perform the tasks, so the scores do not support the same interpretation across groups. Validation studies addressing this challenge fall under the category of structural lines of evidence, and have been studied in terms of item invariance in multiple-group-factor analyses and differential item functioning in item response theory. However, process data can be employed to investigate this same challenge along the lines that we already discussed. For example, do verbal protocols or eye-tracking studies reveal that males and females are solving tasks using different strategies? Do log files show that students with less computer experience are spending time backtracking when they have misunderstood the computer interface, or not taking advantage of tools or affordances that computer-savvy students are using extensively? Does the same Q-matrix work for students from different cultures? Any such finding, leveraging hypotheses about solution processes and evidenced by process data, can produce confirming or disconfirming evidence for a proposed interpretation.

Third, the trait interpretation can be challenged on the grounds that the scores are not likely to provide a good indication of performance across the target domain as a whole. To the extent that the scores reflect the competencies associated with the trait, as indicated by logical analyses, think-aloud protocol, with other relevant evidence, claims that the test scores provide that a good indication of overall performance in the target domain would be plausible.

A proposed interpretation or use that has undergone a critical appraisal of its coherence and completeness, and of the plausibility of its inferences and assumptions can be accepted as being valid, with the understanding that new evidence could lead to a reconsideration of this conclusion. The availability of a clearly specified interpretation and use makes it easier to "find out what might be wrong with it." Process models that make strong predictions about the results of having various test takers perform various test tasks can provide a powerful way to challenge, and thereby to validate, trait interpretations.

Concluding Remarks

Validation is sometimes presented as a summative activity that occurs at the end of test development or after it, but it is better viewed as an ongoing evaluation that begins with the conceptualization of the intended interpretation and use of the scores and the design of an assessment that would support this interpretation and use, through to empirical studies of how well the assessment performs in practice.

Writing just before Cronbach and Meehl's (1955) watershed formulation of construct validity, Cureton (1951) defined validity in terms of "how well a test does the job it is employed to do" (p. 621). Cronbach and Meehl (1955) advocated that we apply basic scientific methodology to validation, emphasizing then-current theory-based interpretations of constructs within formal axiomatic systems. An alternate, interpretation-based framework for validation began to develop in the latter half of the century (e.g., Cronbach, 1971, 1989; Loevinger, 1957; Messick 1975, 1989), extending to a much broader notion of theories, and more generally, to a wide range of proposed score interpretations. The interpretive framework was further developed with the concepts and structures of evidentiary argument (e.g., Bachman & Palmer, 2010; Kane, 1992, 2006, 2013; Mislevy, 2006, 2009; Shepard, 1993). The same period saw rapid advances in both the sciences of human cognition and the development of digital technologies. Educators have sought to apply emerging understandings of how people acquire and use knowledge—and how it may be exercised and captured—to improve learning, instruction, and, most pertinent to this volume, assessment.

An understanding of test-taker response processes is relevant to almost all interpretations and uses of test scores. When the proposed interpretation involves inferences about response processes (e.g., about use of particular kinds of knowledge or problem-solving techniques, or about traits), evidence indicating that test takers are employing the processes associated with the proposed interpretation supports the validity of that interpretation, while evidence indicating they are employing different processes undermines its validity. For trait interpretations, there is no single process model that the assessment results can be evaluated against, but the evaluation of process is still essential, although it is necessarily more indirect and incremental. The goal here is to show that the test tasks require the competencies associated with the trait and that performance is not unduly influenced by competencies that are not associated with the trait or by extraneous contextual factors.

A great number of theories of human learning and performance have emerged from cognitive psychology, to better understand how people acquire and use knowledge. Many can be applied to improve learning and assessment. More will surely follow. Similarly, a great number of technologies have been developed to extend the range of products and performances that can be exploited to capture ever more detailed and diverse aspects of performance. Again more will surely follow. By all appearances, the framework of assessment interpretation and use arguments will serve to structure our reasoning about process data in validation studies of score interpretation.

It seems fitting to close this discussion of validity argumentation based on process models by returning once again to Lee Cronbach, (1957) who called for a confluence of the two disciplines of scientific psychology—experimental and correlational, as he labeled them—in his 1957 presidential address to the American Psychological Association. As the decades passed, developments in technology, cognitive psychology, validity theory, and assessment design have come together to produce the framework of process data validation outlined above. It can be argued that designing, interpreting, and validating educational assessments, by means of cognitive models for how people acquire and use knowledge, has been moving toward Cronbach's vision, at least in a growing array of applications where sufficiently strong models can be developed (Pellegrino, Baxter, & Glaser, 1999).

References

American Educational Research Association, American Psychological Association, & National Council on Measurement in Education (2014). *Standards for educational and psychological testing*. Washington, DC: American Educational Research Association.

Anderson, J. R. (1996). ACT: A simple theory of complex cognition. *American Psychologist, 51*(4), 355–365.

Anderson J. R., & Reiser B. J. (1985). The Lisp tutor. *Byte, 10*(4), 159–175.

Anderson, J. R., Corbett, A. T., Koedinger, K. R., & Pelletier, R. (1995). Cognitive tutors: Lessons learned. *Journal of the Learning Sciences, 4,* 167–207.

Anderson, J. R., Bothell, D., Byrne, M. D., Douglass, S., Lebiere, C., & Qin, Y. (2004). An integrated theory of the mind. *Psychological Review, 111*(4), 1036–1060.

Bachman, L., & Palmer, A. (2010). *Language assessment in practice: Developing language assessments and justifying their use in the real world.* Oxford, UK: Oxford University Press.

Carpenter, P. A., Just, M. A., & Shell, P. (1990). What one intelligence test measures: A theoretical account of the processing in the Raven Progressive Matrices test. *Psychological Review, 97*(3), 404–431.

Carroll, J. (1976). Psychometric tests as cognitive tasks: A new "structure of intellect." In L. B. Resnick (Ed.), *The nature of intelligence* (pp. 27–57). Hillsdale, NJ: Erlbaum.

Cronbach, L. J. (1957). The two disciplines of scientific psychology. *American Psychologist, 12*(11), 671–684.

Cronbach, L. J. (1971). Test validation. In R. L. Thorndike (Ed.), *Educational measurement* (2nd ed., pp. 443–507). Washington, DC: American Council on Education.

Cronbach, L. J. (1980). Validity on parole: How can we go straight? In W. B. Schrader (Ed.). *New directions for testing and measurement: Measuring achievement over a decade,* No. 5 (pp. 99–108). San Francisco: Jossey-Bass.

Cronbach, L. J. (1988). Five perspectives on validity argument. In H. Wainer, & H. Braun (Eds.), *Test validity* (pp. 3–17). Hillsdale, NJ: Lawrence Erlbaum.

Cronbach, L. J. (1989). Construct validation after thirty years. In R. E. Linn (Ed.), *Intelligence: Measurement, theory, and public policy* (pp. 147–171). Urbana, IL: University of Illinois Press.

Cronbach, L. J., & Meehl, P. E. (1955). Construct validity in psychological tests. *Psychological Bulletin, 52*(4), 281–302.

Cureton, E. E. (1951). Validity. In E. F. Lingquist (Ed.), *Educational measurement* (pp. 621–694). Washington, DC: American Council on Education.

De Boeck, P. & Wilson, M. (Eds.) (2004). *Explanatory item response models: A generalized linear and nonlinear approach.* New York: Springer-Verlag.

Drum, P. A., Calfee, R. C., & Cook, L. K. (1981). The effects of surface structure variables on performance in reading comprehension tests. *Reading Research Quarterly, 16*(4), 486–514.

Dwyer, C. A., Gallagher, A., Levin, J. & Morley, M. E. (2003). *What is quantitative reasoning? Defining the construct for assessment purposes.* Research Report 03–30. Princeton, NJ: Educational Testing Service.

Embretson, S. E. (1983). Construct validity: Construct representation versus nomothetic span. *Psychological Bulletin, 93*(1), 179–197.

Embretson, S. E. (1985). Multicomponent latent trait models for test design. In S. E. Embretson (Ed.), *Test design: Developments in psychology and psychometrics* (pp. 195–218). Orlando, FL: Academic Press.

Embretson, S. E. (1998). A cognitive design system approach to generating valid tests: Application to abstract reasoning. *Psychological Methods, 3*(3), 380–396.

Fischer, G. H. (1973). The linear logistic test model as an instrument in educational research. *Acta Psychologica, 37*(6), 359–374.

Gorin, J. S. (2006). Test design with cognition in mind. *Educational measurement: Issues and practice, 25*(4), 21–35.

Gorin, J. S., & Embretson, S. E. (2006). Item difficulty modeling of paragraph comprehension items. *Applied Psychological Measurement, 30*(5), 394–411.

Irvine, S. H. (2013). *Tests for recruitment across cultures: A tactical psychometric handbook.* Amsterdam: IOS.

Kane, M. (1992). An argument-based approach to validation. *Psychological Bulletin, 112*(3), 527–535.

Kane, M. (2006). Validation. In R. J. Brennan (Ed.), *Educational measurement* (4th ed., pp. 18–64). Westport, CT: Praeger.

Kane, M. (2013). Validating the interpretations and uses of test scores. *Journal of Educational Measurement, 50*(1), 1–73.

Katz, I. R., Martinez, M. E., Sheehan, K. M., & Tatsuoka, K. K. (1998). Extending the rule space methodology to a semantically-rich domain: Diagnostic assessment in architecture. *Journal of Educational and Behavioral Statistics, 23*(3), 254–278.

Kintsch, W., & Greeno, J. G. (1985). Understanding and solving word arithmetic problems. *Psychological Review, 92*(1), 109–129.

LaMar, M. M. (2014). *Models for understanding student thinking using data from complex computerized science tasks*. Doctoral dissertation, University of California, Berkeley.

Lebiere, C., & Anderson, J. R. (2008). A connectionist implementation of the ACT-R production system. Pittsburgh: Carnegie-Mellon University. Downloaded May 8, 2015 from http://act-r.psy.cmu.edu/wordpress/wp-content/uploads/2012/12/234lebiere_and_anderson_93.pdf

Leighton, J. P., & Gierl, M. J. (Eds.) (2007). *Cognitive diagnostic assessment for education: Theory and practices*. Cambridge, UK and New York: Cambridge University Press.

Leighton, J. P., & Gierl, M. J. (2011). *The learning sciences in educational assessment: The role of cognitive models*. Cambridge, UK: Cambridge University Press.

Lewis, C., & Polson, P. (1991, April). Cognitive walkthroughs: A method for theory-based evaluation of user interfaces (tutorial). In Scott P. Robertson, Gary M. Olson, and Judith S. Olson (Eds.), *Proceedings of the Conference on Human Factors in Computing Systems (SIGCHI 91)*.

Loevinger, J. (1957). Objective tests as instruments of psychological theory. *Psychological Reports, Monograph Supplement, 3*, 635–694.

Messick, S. (1970). The criterion problem in the evaluation of instruction: Assessing possible, not just intended outcomes. In M. Wittrock and D. Wiley (Eds.), *The evaluation of instruction: Issues and problems* (pp. 183–202). New York: Holt, Rinehart, and Winston.

Messick, S. (1975). The standard problem: Meaning and values in measurement and evaluation. *American Psychologist, 30*(10), 955–966.

Messick, S. (1989). Validity. In R. L. Linn (Ed.), *Educational measurement* (3rd ed., pp. 13–103). New York: American Council on Education, and Macmillan.

Mislevy, R. J. (2006). Cognitive psychology and educational assessment. In R. L. Brennan (Ed.), *Educational measurement* (4th ed., pp. 257–305). Phoenix, AZ: Greenwood.

Mislevy, R. J. (2009). Validity from the perspective of model-based reasoning. In R. L. Lissitz (Ed.), *The concept of validity: Revisions, new directions and applications* (pp. 83–108). Charlotte, NC: Information Age Publishing.

Mislevy, R., Steinberg, L., & Almond, R. (2003). On the structure of educational assessments. *Measurement: Interdisciplinary Research and Perspectives, 1*(1), 3–62.

Newell, A., & Simon, H. A. (1972). *Human problem solving*. Englewood Cliffs, NJ: Prentice Hall.

Nichols, P. D., Chipman, S. F., & Brennan, R. L. (Eds.) (1995). *Cognitively diagnostic assessment*. Hillsdale, NJ: Erlbaum.

Pellegrino, J. W., Baxter, G. P., & Glaser, R. (1999). Addressing the "two disciplines" problem: Linking theories of cognition and learning with assessment and instructional practice. *Review of Research in Education, 24*(1), 307–353.

Pellegrino, J., Chudowsky, N, & Glaser, R. (Committee on the Foundations of Assessment) (Eds.) (2001). *Knowing what students know: The science and design of educational assessment*. Board on Testing and Assessment, Center for Education, National Research Council, Division of Behavioral and Social Sciences and Education. Washington, DC: The National Academies Press.

Pirolli, P., & Wilson, M. (1998). A theory of the measurement of knowledge content, access, and learning. *Psychological Review, 105*(1), 58–82.

Popper, K. R. (1965). *Conjecture and refutation: The growth of scientific knowledge*. New York: Harper & Row.

Restle, F., & Greeno, J. G. (1970). *Introduction to mathematical psychology*. Oxford, UK: Addison-Wesley.

Rijmen, F., & De Boeck, P. (2002). The random weights linear logistic test model. *Applied Psychological Measurement, 26*(3), 271–285.

Rupp, A., Templin, J., & Henson, R. (2010). *Diagnostic measurement: Theory, methods, and applications*. New York: Guilford Press.

Sabatini, J., Albro, E., & O'Reilly, T. (2012). *Measuring up: Advances in how we assess reading ability*. Lanham, MD: R&L Education.

Scheiblechner, H. (1972). Das lernen und lösen komplexer denkaufgaben. [The learning and solution of complex cognitive tasks.] *Zeitschrift für experimentalle und Angewandte Psychologie, 19*, 476–506.

Sheehan, K. M., & O'Reilly, T. (2012). The case for scenario-based assessments of reading competency. In J. Sabatini, E. Albro and T. O'Reilly (Eds.), *Reaching an understanding: Innovations in how we view reading assessment* (pp. 19–33). Lanham, MD: Rowman & Littlefield Education.

Shepard, L. A. (1993). Evaluating test validity. In L. Darling-Hammond (Ed.), *Review of Research in Education, 19*, 405–450. Washington, DC: American Educational Research Association.

Sternberg, R. J. (1977). Component processes in analogical reasoning. *Psychological Review, 84*(4), 353–378.

Suppes, P., & Morningstar, M. (1972). *Computer-assisted instruction at Stanford, 1966–68: Data, models, and evaluation of the arithmetic programs.* New York: Academic Press.

Tatsuoka, K. K. (1983). Rule space: An approach for dealing with misconceptions based on item response theory. *Journal of Educational Measurement, 20*(4), 345–354.

3 Collecting and Analyzing Verbal Response Process Data in the Service of Interpretive and Validity Arguments[1]

Jacqueline P. Leighton

Imagine being asked a question. You respond. Your answer is interpreted without any regard for your frame of reference, understanding of the question, auxiliary thoughts, fatigue, or the opportunity to clarify your response in light of what you thought you were being asked. Imagine now having your answer to that question lead to a series of inferences about what you know and can do, all without the opportunity to clarify your answer in light of the question, as you understood it. It would be frustrating to say the least and unfair to say the worst.

Next time at a meeting, observe yourself and the nature of the communication that takes place as people exchange ideas. If we were to make high-stakes inferences in our everyday lives about what people did or did not know based solely on their initial answers to questions – without seeking additional information, clarification, or elaboration – we would find ourselves making all kinds of erroneous attributions about what people did or did not know. It is surprising how long it has taken verbal response process data to hit our collective measurement radar but it has indeed – finally.

According to the Standards for Educational and Psychological Testing (American Educational Research Association, et al., 2014), verbal response process data are *one* of the sources of validity evidence gathered to support inferences about what examinees know and can do. However, verbal response process data are still not considered obligatory for safeguarding the validity of inferences made about examinees based on their test scores. This is of concern especially for tests of achievement that often involve inferences about unobservable processes – such as facets of problem solving and depth of comprehension and understanding (i.e., knowledge representation structures). In the absence of response process evidence, inferences about the meaning of test scores, which often depend on unobservable processes, may reflect serious leaps of faith that examinees are indeed solving problems and engaging knowledge representation structures, as expected, in response to items.

Almost all examinee verbal response process data collected in educational measurement studies – including next-generation assessments – for the purpose of test-score validation can be categorized under one of two methods. The two methods of collecting, analyzing, and interpreting these data include *protocol analysis* and *verbal analysis*. As a parenthetical note, the terms protocol analysis and verbal analysis are misnomers as they entail much more than just *analysis*: the two methods involve distinct procedures for collecting, analyzing, and interpreting data. As shown in Figure 3.1, they support different types of claims and inferences about examinee understandings: protocol analysis supports inferences about problem solving, and verbal analysis supports inferences about comprehension and understanding. Thus, protocol analysis and verbal analysis must be used to validate different types of score meaning. The distinction between the methods will be emphasized throughout the chapter.

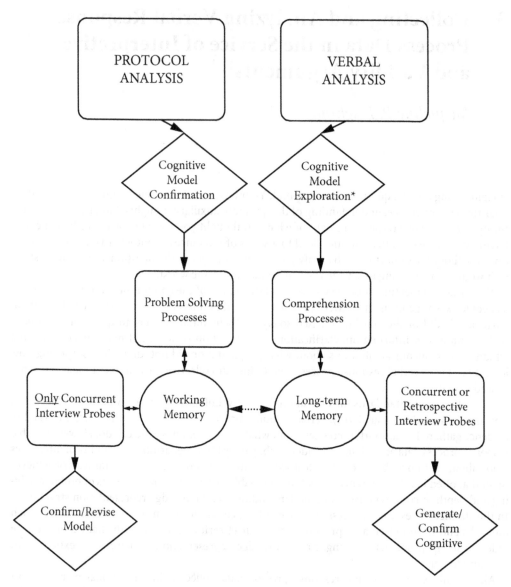

Figure 3.1 Differential measurement objectives for protocol and verbal analyses

Figure note: *Can be in confirmatory mode as well.

Chapter Objective and Outline

In some chapters in this book, verbal response processes are defined and described in relation to their value for validity arguments. The present chapter deals with verbal response process data generated specifically by individuals in the "examinee" role, and focuses primarily on the procedures used to collect, analyze, and interpret these data. However, because the specific procedural details of protocol and verbal analyses have been expounded previously (see Leighton & Gierl, 2007; Leighton, 2009), the present chapter also includes an illustration of how these methods are incorporated in the creation of interpretive and validity arguments. This latter focus provides motivation for distinguishing the methods in the first place.

The chapter is divided into two main sections, followed by a brief discussion of future considerations in the use of these methods. The first section focuses on distinguishing protocol and verbal analyses given their origins, empirical support, and differences in collecting, analyzing, and interpreting data. Examples are used to illustrate points wherever possible. This first section is essential because it provides readers with a glimpse into what makes these methods different. Without this initial section, the second section would make little sense. The second section focuses on ways in which protocol and verbal analyses inform interpretive and validity arguments. The third section focuses on considerations for best practices and areas for future research.

Protocol Analysis Versus Verbal Analysis

Origins

Protocol analysis is a method used to collect, analyze, and interpret verbal responses associated with problem-solving processes (Ericsson & Simon, 1980, 1993). It originates from an early psychological method known as *experimental self-observation*. Experimental self-observation was used by Wilhelm Wundt (1832–1920), the father of modern experimental psychology, to study how highly trained participants described their mental experiences of sensory stimuli. Wundt was highly critical of the conventional view of *introspection* and did not consider experimental self-observation to be introspection.

The cognitive revolution in the 1950s and 1960s encouraged measurement of and inference to mental states (Leahey, 1992). In particular, cognitive scientists (e.g., Newell & Simon, 1972) advanced the idea that people solved problems by creating and searching through an internal *problem space*. The problem space was a type of mental "rat" maze, consisting of an initial state, a goal state, and a set of intermediate states, beyond the initial state, en route to the goal state. To solve problems, people implemented algorithms and heuristics to move incrementally from the initial state to the goal state. The problem space could be externalized on paper, computer, or any learning device for others to observe. Newell and Simon's idea of an internal problem space was first supported with their demonstration that a computer, the General Problem Solver (GPS), could be programmed to apply a series of heuristics to solve well-defined problems or tasks, thus operationalizing the problem space. They also demonstrated that when participants were given problem-solving tasks, they verbalized algorithms and heuristics that were similar to the ones the GPS used to solve the same problems, lending support to the idea that human thinking could be externalized and measured.

As with protocol analysis, verbal analysis owes much of its methodology to the pioneering work of Newell and Simon (1972). However, unlike protocol analysis, which is used to measure problem-solving processes, verbal analysis is used to measure comprehension processes, such as knowledge representational structures defining varying levels of expertise (Chi, 1997, 2006; Jeong, 2013; Leighton & Gierl, 2007). Whereas protocol analysis primarily taps executive processing in working memory, verbal analysis primarily taps storage in long-term memory. Verbal analysis is used to measure response processes that reflect long-term understandings; for example, depth of explanation, elaboration, and justification. Of course "cognition" as it is experienced every day normally includes both memory systems; however, specific aspects of cognition do predominate in distinct memory systems and, thus, protocol and verbal analyses are used to generate evidence and validate claims about distinct types of score meaning.

Empirical Support

Despite Newell and Simon's (1972) empirical findings showing the alignment between human verbalizations and the GPS, many psychologists remained skeptical about participants' ability to verbalize their thinking accurately (e.g., Nisbett & Wilson, 1977; Wilson, 1994; see Leighton, 2004 for a review). In the interest of addressing skeptics, Ericsson and Simon (1993) released a comprehensive "how-to" for performing protocol analysis, and tackled accusations of verbal report inaccuracies by reviewing a series of empirical studies designed to illustrate appropriate procedures (e.g., Dulany & O'Connell, 1963; Frankel, Levine & Karpf, 1970; Schwartz, 1966). For example, in response to Verplanck (1962), who indicated that participants' verbalized rules were disconnected from their actual behaviour in a card-sorting task, the work of Dulany and O'Connell (1963) was presented, showing that participants misunderstood the rules as defined in the original study. When the rules were clarified, participants in all but 11 of the 34,408 trials correctly described the rule governing their card sorting.

Ericsson and Simon (1993) specifically addressed the concerns of Nisbett and Wilson (1977) who, in a particularly critical review paper, indicated that participants generally did not accurately verbalize response processes. Nisbett and Wilson claimed that, instead of verbalizing response processes, participants verbalized subjective impressions or their own naïve theories of why they had responded in particular ways. To address this critique, Ericsson and Simon presented prescribed procedures for collecting accurate response process data that minimized biases and participants' naïve theories, emphasizing that "the accuracy of verbal reports *depends on the procedures used to elicit them* and the relation between the requested information and the actual sequence of heeded information" (1993, p. 27; emphasis added). In 2003, Ericsson again underscored the importance of methods: "In several reviews Herb Simon and I (Ericsson & Simon, 1980, 1993, 1998; Ericsson, 2003) showed that the detailed instructions and the methods to induce participants to give verbal reports influenced the validity and reactivity of collected verbal-report evidence" (p. 2).

As with protocol analysis, there is extensive empirical support for the use of verbal analysis as a method to measure comprehension processes (see Chi, 1997); for example, the mapping of differences in the knowledge representation structures between experts and novices (see Chi, Feltovich, & Glaser, 1981; Leighton & Bisanz, 2003; Vosniadou & Brewer, 1992), identifying components of collaborative interaction (Rummel & Spada, 2005), and testing or piloting survey questions for comprehension (Tourangeau, 1984; Willis, 2005). For example, Chi et al. (1981) investigated individual differences between physics experts and novices in their comprehension of physics tasks, sorting of tasks, and in their explanations of how they would go about responding to the tasks. They found that experts referred to physics principles in their explanations much more than novices, who relied on surface features in their knowledge representations of the tasks.

Procedures to Collect, Analyze, and Interpret Data

Analytical Method

As shown in Figure 3.1, protocol analysis is a *confirmatory method* that involves collecting, analyzing, and interpreting verbal response process data related to problem solving. The main memory location tapped is working memory. The "think-aloud" interview conditions for tapping working memory are not as flexible as most would like them to be. For example, investigators that cite Ericsson and Simon (1993), and go on to employ *cognitive laboratories* believing they are measuring problem solving with retrospective interview probes, often do so incorrectly. Cognitive laboratories often deviate substantially in the data collection, analysis, and interpretive techniques that Ericsson and Simon recommend for measuring problem solving. For example, they strongly recommended concurrent interview probes over retrospective interview probes, and the use of a cognitive model to guide analysis and interpretation of data. Both of these requirements are often not employed in cognitive laboratories. Thus, aside from the superficial similarity that cognitive laboratories require participants to "think aloud", there is actually little similarity between cognitive laboratories and the protocol analysis described by Ericsson and Simon.

In contrast, verbal analysis primarily taps long-term memory and can be used as a *confirmatory* or *exploratory* method. As a confirmatory method, it can be used to test a pre-existing cognitive model of comprehension processes within a specific domain. As an exploratory method it can be used to generate a cognitive model of comprehension processes based on the data revealed by participants' verbalizations.

Data collection

Protocol and verbal analyses involve collection of data using one-to-one interview sessions (however, see Jeong, 2013 and Rummel & Spada, 2005 for *one-to-many* interview sessions to study collaborative interactions in group sessions). During the one-to-one session, the experimenter (or interviewer) asks the participant to verbalize or "think aloud" in response to a task (see Chi, 1997 and Ericsson & Simon, 1993 for specific directives in procedures) while the contents of the session are recorded using audio and/or audiovisual equipment. The participant's recorded verbalizations are then transcribed into a written format, which serves as a *verbal report* of the session. The verbal report can be segmented, reflecting the range of sequential processes used to respond to the task.

Although both protocol and verbal analytical methods involve asking participants to think aloud, these methods differ in the tasks, instructions, and interview probes that are permissible for measuring response processes of interest. First, protocol analysis requires tasks of moderate difficulty that are designed to measure problem solving (see Leighton, 2004 for detailed rationale). Shown in Figure 3.2 is an example of an algebraic math item designed to measure problem solving in primary/elementary students. This item would be an appropriate stimulus for protocol analysis if it was of moderate difficulty for the population of interest; moderate difficulty tasks typically evoke *controlled* processing that can be verbally articulated. Verbal analysis does not require tasks of moderate difficulty; in fact, tasks of almost any difficulty can be used. The difference rests with the type of response process being measured. Because problem solving is narrowly defined as the goal-driven manipulation of information for the purpose of a specific outcome, the tasks that can elicit this form of thinking are limited. In contrast, because comprehension is more broadly defined as the recall and/or elaboration of stored knowledge, the tasks that can elicit this form of thinking are more pervasive given that all participants must do is provide insight into how they understand the content of the task, including reflection on why a task is easy or difficult.

Second, protocol analysis requires instructions to participants at the start of the interview that emphasize the importance of thinking aloud *as they are solving the task*. Verbalization must take place as the task is being solved and not later. Advance notice is given to the participants that, if they stay silent for more than 10 seconds, the request to "keep talking" will be made. The interview probe to "keep talking" is essentially the only probe that is permissible so as to not bias participants

---

Molly is making cupcakes to serve at the school picnic. If the recipe calls for 2 ½ cups of cocoa to serve 4 people, how many cups will she need if 60 children attend the picnic?

(a) 10 cups
(b) 15 cups
(c) 24 cups
(d) 37.5 cups

Figure 3.2 Algebraic Problem Solving Math Item

into explaining or theorizing about their response processes. Again, the key is to capture unadulterated problem solving as it is taking place. Constant verbalizations produce what Ericsson and Simon (1993) call a *concurrent verbal report*. A concurrent verbal report reflects the manipulation of information in working memory. If participants cannot verbalize concurrently, there is no "data capture" showing how participants manipulate information as they solve the task, no evidence of problem solving and no way to substantiate inferences of problem solving. During the delivery of the instructions, it is also recommended that interviewers explicitly indicate they are not experts within the domain to reduce participants' potential performance anxiety (Leighton, 2013).

Although concurrent verbal reports are primary in protocol analysis, *retrospective verbal reports* can also be collected as a secondary source of evidence. Retrospective reports reflect participants' verbalizations *after* they have reached a solution to a task. The timing of data capture is the defining difference between concurrent and retrospective reports. For example, in relation to Figure 3.2, examinees might retrospectively say, "*I solved the problem by setting up an equation and solving for the unknown.*" Although retrospective reports collected immediately after task solution are less open to memory loss and bias, these reports are still problematic in capturing the contents of working memory. For example, the retrospective verbalization "*I solved the problem by setting up an equation and solving for the unknown*" is only a summary of how the participant thinks he or she solved the task and does not reflect the step-by-step processing of information as it is happening. Because retrospective reports capture the contents of long-term memory more than they capture the contents of working memory, they tend to include less direct evidence of problem solving as it occurred. When retrospective reports are collected in these cases, the reports reflect participants' theories about how they think they solved the problem, which may in fact not correspond to what they actually did.

In contrast, both concurrent and retrospective reports are equally permissible in verbal analysis. Task instructions must only emphasize the goal of the verbal reports, namely, that comprehension or understanding is being measured. Interview probes following instructions can be broad in scope, including requests for elaboration (e.g., can you expand on that idea?), explanation (e.g., what did you mean by this?), and speculation (e.g., what do you think others might think of this?). For example, when Leighton and Bisanz (2003) interviewed Kindergarten, Grades 3 and 5 students as well as university students for their comprehension of concepts associated with the ozone layer and ozone hole, they created an interview schedule, shown in Figure 3.3, to probe participants' understanding. They began the interview with "*I am going to ask you some questions about light from the sun. These questions will help me understand what (children/adults) know about sunlight . . .*" Again, the objective was to measure comprehension (the contents of long-term memory); thus any probe that allowed the interviewer to map out participants' knowledge representations was considered fair game.

Data Analysis and Interpretation

Protocol analysis is a confirmatory method. As such, it requires the development of a cognitive model to guide the analysis and interpretation of response processes before verbal reports are even collected from participants. The cognitive model may be purely theoretical; nonetheless, it serves as a *visual hypothesis* of the verbalizations expected. If verbal reports are shown to be consistent with the cognitive model, evidence for the model accrues; if not, the cognitive model is revised to account for the data gathered. For example, shown in Figure 3.4 is a cognitive model of the knowledge and skills a student of moderate ability would be expected to apply to solve the algebraic math item shown in Figure 3.2. The model shows five components: identifying the problem, identifying what is known, making a plan, carrying out the plan, and verifying the answer. In addition to the components, the model reflects a series of temporal relationships, for example, identifying the problem before making a plan. The model thus lays out the components and temporal relationships to guide the coding and analysis of response processes.

Structured Interview: Experimenter Questions (Branch A)

1. *Some people say that you should wear sunscreen or suntan lotion when you are out in the sun. Why do you think some people say that you should do this?*
2. *Why would it be bad for us to be burned by the sun's rays?*
3. *Do all of the sun's rays cause problems or just some of them?*
4. *Do you know what the harmful rays are called?* • *Have you ever heard of ultraviolet (UV) light?* • *Can you tell me what you know about ultraviolet (UV) light?* • *Is there anything else you can tell me about ultraviolet (UV) light?*
5. *Is there anything between us and the sun that surrounds our planet? If yes, what is it called?* • *Have you ever heard of the atmosphere?* • *Can you tell me what you know about the atmosphere?* • *Is there anything else you can tell me about the atmosphere?*
6. *Is there anything between us and the sun that helps protect us from the harmful rays of the sun?* • *Have you ever heard of the ozone layer?* • *Can you tell me what you know about the ozone layer?* • *Is there anything else you can tell me about the ozone layer?*
7. *Is there something about the ozone layer that makes us worry today?* • *Have you ever heard of the ozone hole?* • *Can you tell me what you know about the ozone hole?* • *Is there anything else you can tell me about the ozone hole?*
8. *Why did this ozone hole start?*
9. *Can you tell me what are some of the things that people use that harm the ozone layer?*
10. *Can you tell me what it is about these things that harms the ozone layer?* • *Have you ever heard of CFCs (Chlorofluorocarbons)?* • *Can you tell me what you know about CFCs (Chlorofluorocarbons)?* • *Is there anything else you can tell me about CFCs (Chlorofluorocarbons)?*
11. *Are we the only ones that should protect ourselves from this hole in the ozone layer or are there other things on our planet that should also be protected?*
<u>Note:</u> Category 1: *The Sun and Adverse Consequences (Questions 1, 2, 3, 4)* Category 2: *UV Light (Questions 1, 3, 4)* Category 3: *UV Light and Human Behaviour (Questions 1, 2, 8, 9, 11)* Category 4: *Ozone Composition (Questions 5, 6, 9)* Category 5: *Ozone Destruction (Questions 1, 2, 7, 9, 10)*

Figure 3.3 Structured Interview: Experimenter Questions (Branch A) Used to Elicit Verbal Reports and Conduct Verbal Analysis (see Leighton & Bisanz, 2003)

The next step is to have at least two trained raters evaluate the verbal reports generated in response to the algebraic math item. Raters would be expected to identify and assess the specific verbal utterances that serve as evidence for the model components and temporal relationships. For example, for each of the five components in Figure 3.4, raters could assign a 0 for each verbal utterance that is completely misaligned with the model component, 1 for partial alignment,

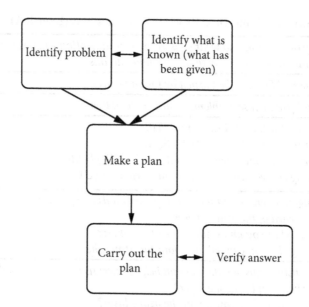

Figure 3.4 Cognitive Model for Algebraic Math Item

or 2 for complete alignment. This reflects an analytical rating scheme, but a holistic one can be used as well – depending on the granularity desired. For example, the whole verbal report produced by a participant in response to the item, including verbalizations for all five components, could be evaluated simultaneously for whether it is completely misaligned, partially aligned or completely aligned with the cognitive model. Irrespective of whether an analytical or holistic rating scheme is used, it is important to calculate the inter-rater reliability of raters' evaluations of verbal reports, e.g., Cohen's kappa coefficient (Cohen, 1968).

An additional point to consider in the collection, analysis, and interpretation of response process data is sample size and representativeness. Sample sizes tend to be small in think-aloud studies because verbal reports are time consuming and labour intensive to collect, analyze, and interpret. All data collection is done one person at a time, and extensive amounts of data are collected from a single individual. Nonetheless, if inferential statistics are used to compare groups of participants, the sample size must be sufficiently large to achieve statistical power. Another key consideration is sample representativeness. In particular, aside from aiming to choose a sample that is reflective of the population to which inferences will be made, including gender and ethnicity, the ability or knowledge-level of participants must be considered. Leighton, Cui, and Cor (2009) illustrate how examinees of varying ability or knowledge levels reveal response processes associated with distinct cognitive models; that is, models showing a different organization of knowledge and skills.

When verbal analysis is used in confirmatory mode, data analysis follows a similar sequence to protocol analysis; namely, the cognitive model under investigation directs the identification, assessment and coding of response processes. Often, however, verbal analysis is used in exploratory mode in order to develop a cognitive model based on the data, and decisions need to be made about how to make sense and interpret verbal utterances. Toward this end, Chi (1997) identifies a series of steps (see also Leighton & Gierl, 2007, p. 165). The most difficult and perhaps consequential step involves the development of a *coding scheme* to categorize features of verbal utterances for interpretation. This coding scheme, often developed in light of the data collected, is a precursor to the generation of a cognitive model of comprehension.

Jeong (2013) offers three analytic strategies for determining the verbal utterances to code. First, utterances can be coded if they reflect *meaningful learning events* related to the objective of interest; for example, utterances that provide an explanation for an answer, or evaluate task difficulty. Second, utterances can be coded to reflect not only the presence of a meaningful learning event (e.g., providing an explanation) but also the *sophistication* of the event; for example, whether the explanation reflects deep structural understanding versus surface-level understanding. Alternatively, explanations can be coded polytomously for quality using an ordinal scale. Third, utterances can be combined and coded as *sequences* of learning events. For example, Leighton and Bisanz (2003) used a coding scheme to evaluate cohesion of comprehension of the ozone layer and ozone hole. Using a two-step coding scheme shown in Figure 3.5, they coded reports initially based on verbalizations to preliminary questions, but then assessed depth and cohesion of understanding based on verbalizations to subsequent questions. This two-step coding scheme shows key knowledge to report in responding to questions about the ozone layer and ozone hole, and can therefore be viewed as the early stages in generating a cognitive model of comprehension.

Protocol and Verbal Analyses in the Service of Interpretive and Validity Arguments

In order for examinees and stakeholders to trust test scores and the inferences (and uses) these scores support, validation of test-based inferences is essential. When employed and incorporated correctly, protocol and verbal analyses can be used to inform the validation of test-based inferences. Kane (2006) identifies two arguments for validation – the interpretive argument, "which specifies the proposed interpretations and uses of test results by laying out the network of inferences and assumption leading from the observed performances to the conclusions and decisions based on the performances" (p. 23) and the validity argument, which "provides an evaluation of the interpretative argument" (p. 23). Protocol and verbal analyses can be used proximally to inform the interpretive argument and, distally, to inform the validity argument.

Interpretive Argument

According to Kane (2006), the interpretive argument for indicators of theoretical constructs includes five major inferences – scoring, generalization, extrapolation, theory-based interpretation, and implication. Although protocol analysis and verbal analysis can be used to inform all five major inferences, these analytical methods are especially useful in informing *theory-based interpretation* of scores. As mentioned previously, protocol and verbal analyses offer methods to identify and analyze problem-solving and comprehension processes, respectively. Consequently, protocol and verbal analyses are used to support *distinct* theory-based interpretations of test scores – distinct because protocol analysis informs theoretical inferences about test scores involving problem-solving processes, and verbal analysis informs theoretical inferences about test scores involving comprehension processes. At this point, it becomes easy to get bogged down with the verbiage associated with "validation-speak" and lose sight of what protocol and verbal analyses essentially "buy us" in terms of validation. In the next section, protocol analysis is used to illustrate how it can inform the interpretive argument. Although a similar illustration of verbal analysis could be made, in the interests of clarity and space, protocol analysis is the focus in order to make use of the problem-solving task shown in Figure 3.2. Furthermore, because protocol and verbal analyses are sufficiently distinct in their methods and response-processing foci (e.g., confirmatory vs. exploratory, reliance on concurrent vs. retrospective interview probes, measurement of problem solving vs. comprehension), an illustration that focuses on one of these methods instead of both may provide a clearer account.

As noted previously, protocol analysis is a method designed to identify, analyze, and interpret response processes underlying observed problem solving. In other words, protocol analysis

Criteria for Evaluating Presence of Models

There are two main parts that need to be considered when deciding whether a students' interview provides sufficient evidence to say that he or she has a "model" of the ozone layer and ozone hole. Part A involves the <u>ozone layer</u> and part B involves the <u>ozone hole</u>.

Preliminary Classification		
Question 1: Is there anything between us and the sun that helps protect us from the harmful rays of the sun?		
Yes	I don't know	No
Question 2: Have you ever heard of the ozone layer? (including—Can you tell me what you know about the ozone layer?)		
Yes	I don't know	No
Question 3: Is there something about the ozone layer that makes us worry today?		
yes	I don't know	No

NO MODEL	PARTIAL MODEL	FULL MODEL
Q1—any response	any response	any response
Q2—any response	any response	"yes"
Q3—"don't know" or "no"	"yes" (partial response)*	"yes" (full response)

Note to Preliminary Classification: Proper judgment requires that one take into consideration any interviewer probes following the response to the question. A partial response is a response that is not a complete idea. This is the case when one reads the transcribed response from the participant's interview and must fill in the blanks as to what the student may mean with such an answer. A full response is a response that conveys a complete idea. There is very little guess work to determine what the sudent means with such an answer.

Final Classification		
Question 4: Have you ever heard of the ozone hole? (including—Can you tell me what you know about the ozone hole?)		
Yes	I don't know	No
Question 5: Why do you think this hole started?		
Because. . . .	I don't know	
Question 6: Can you tell me what are some of the things that people use that harms the ozone layer?		
Yes	I don't know	No
Question 7: Can you tell me what it is about these things that harms the ozone layer?		
Because	I don't know	

Note: Final classification of models with respect to Part B.

NO MODEL	PARTIAL MODEL	FULL MODEL
Q4—any response	any response	any response
Q5—"I don' t know"	partial response	full response
Q6—any response	any response	any response
Q7—"I don' t know" or "no"	partial response	full response

Figure 3.5 Classification/coding scheme for evaluating verbal reports

Adapted from Leighton and Bisanz (2003)

is used to help externalize those unobservable processes associated with test constructs that involve claims about problem solving. Consider again the item shown in Figure 3.2. In reaction to this item, a stakeholder might ask what does algebraic problem solving entail? Experts might invoke Figure 3.4 and answer that it involves a series of response processes such as identifying the problem, identifying what is known (or have been given), making a plan for solving the problem, carrying out the plan, and verifying that the answer makes sense. Each of these response processes (or components) might even involve finer skills; for example, recognizing the unit of the final answer (i.e., cups). But, the stakeholder might ask, how are these response processes measured and verified? Although the cognitive model shown in Figure 3.4 is part of the interpretive argument as it shows how to make sense of observed performance, it requires substantiation or evidence. This is where the verbal report data from protocol analysis come in. Data gathered using protocol analysis can be used to verify that the problem-solving response processes expected to accompany the selection of a correct answer (e.g., as shown in Figure 3.4) do indeed occur, and whether the selection of incorrect answers result from different, misapplied, or faulty response processes. If this is what is found in the data, then this evidence is used to corroborate that correct responses to the item result from the expected algebraic problem-solving processes shown in Figure 3.4.

In principle, protocol analysis could be used to inform the five major inferences of Kane's (2006) interpretive argument – scoring, generalization, extrapolation, theory-based interpretation, and implication. For example, the results of protocol analysis can inform scoring rules such that scores correspond to the facets or components of problem solving as shown in Figure 3.4 and as evidenced in verbal reports (e.g., individual scores for different components involved in algebraic problem solving). Protocol analysis might be used to inform generalization from observed scores to a larger universe of observations if the items that comprise the think-aloud interview materials are representative of the larger universe. Likewise, extrapolation could be informed by protocol analysis to the extent that comparable but higher-level problem-solving tasks are included in the think-aloud interview materials and permit the association of participant response processes to tasks of increasing levels of complexity (e.g., students who respond correctly to algebraic problem solving are also more likely to solve calculus tasks correctly). Implication is informed to the degree that investigators can link or associate participants' response processes to additional outcomes aside from the item, task, or test performance under study. Finally, theory-based interpretation is informed to the degree that the results from protocol analysis provide (a) a reliable and coherent account of the problem-solving processes associated with the test construct, and (b) evidence of expected response processes leading to observed problem-solving performances. In short, results from protocol analysis are relevant in informing the interpretative argument to the extent that test-score interpretations are indeed premised on problem-solving response processes, and the results from verbal reports reveal a reliable link between observed responses arising from specific underlying processes. A similar illustration could be made with verbal analysis, but what needs to be understood is that the intended inference of score meaning would be distinct; verbal analysis is used to support intended score meanings associated with comprehension instead of problem solving.

Validity Argument

Although protocol and verbal analyses directly inform the interpretive argument as these methods help identify the response processes underlying observed item and test performance, these methods, by extension, also inform the overall validity argument. As Kane (2006) points out, the validity argument involves an *evaluation of the interpretive argument*. Thus, the quality of the evidence, originating from protocol and verbal analyses, comprising the interpretive argument is critical to having confidence in the overall validity argument.

The first section of this chapter devoted significant space to delineating the differences between protocol and verbal analyses, and specifically the distinct response processes captured by each method. Readers may wonder what all the fuss is about since in the end both methods simply require participants to think aloud – *what could be so nuanced about that?* Indeed, there is a great deal of nuance and not a semantic difference. The reason for devoting time to reiterating the differences between protocol and verbal analyses rests with the fact that think-aloud interview probes are often and incorrectly used, especially when measuring problem-solving processes. For example, to measure problem-solving processes, a specific memory location (i.e., working/short-term memory) must be tapped during the think-aloud interview with specific probes at specific times (see Ericsson & Simon, 1993); otherwise naïve theories are likely to be measured and this plays directly into the critique of Nisbett and Wilson (1977). To measure comprehension processes, the instructions and timing of probes will be different, as the contents of memory (i.e., long-term) are not as elusive. As noted in the introduction to this chapter, studies and technical reports have been found in some cases to incorrectly cite Ericsson and Simon (1993) in the name of measuring problem-solving processes when, in fact, such processes are not being measured because protocol analysis is not being correctly applied. This undermines the evidence for the interpretive argument and the validity argument.

Best Practices, Further Research, and Conclusion

Caution must be taken when response process data are collected for validation of test-based inferences. Perhaps the most serious consideration is to recognize and understand what type of cognition is being measured and the nature of inferences being validated. A careful consumer of verbal report data would ask the following five basic questions – which provide a focus for best practice.

1   *What are the expected cognitive processing requirements of the items (tasks) serving as stimuli for participants?*
2   *Are the tasks designed to invoke mainly problem-solving processes (e.g., mathematical computation, solving puzzles, combining evidence to generate a conclusion) or knowledge representational structures (e.g., explaining a process or outcome, defending a position, elaborating on why a solution is appropriate)?*
3   *What method is being used to collect the verbal response process data?*
4   *If the tasks are designed to invoke problem-solving processes, has a cognitive model been identified or developed for coding the verbal reports?*
5   *If the tasks are designed to invoke knowledge representational structures, has an interview schedule been developed for asking specific questions during the interview that will guide coding verbal reports?*

Depending on answers to the five questions, researchers can gain confidence in choosing the analytical method that is most appropriate to use to accurately inform the interpretive and validity argument. Without knowing specifics about the kinds of tasks used, what they are designed to measure, what response processes are anticipated to be used to answer the tasks, and what types of procedures have been selected to elicit verbal response process data and analyze it, the evidence is ambiguous to evaluate at best.

Although many testing programs are beginning to collect verbal response process data, there is reason for concern given the rigor required to correctly collect, analyze, and interpret these data. Although research is needed to improve on methods to collect, analyze, and interpret verbal response process data generally for educational measurement studies, at the very least we need to distinguish the methods associated with measuring distinct forms of cognition. In addition, more research is needed on (a) the environmental conditions that arouse emotional reactions from participants during verbalizations and can interfere with working memory function, recall from long-term memory, and possibly lead to social desirable responses; (b) the procedures that will approximate the actual testing conditions for participants; and (c) the appropriate features and levels of difficulty for tasks used to elicit verbal reports (e.g., Leighton, 2013). While the think-aloud interview and corresponding methods of analyses – protocol analysis and verbal analysis – are essential tools for informing the interpretive argument and by extension the validity argument, without proper and rigorous implementation of these methods, the results will be no more useful than those derived from the early days of introspection.

Note

1 Preparation of this chapter was supported by a grant to the author from the Social Sciences and Humanities Research Council of Canada [SSHRC Grant No. 410-2011-0811]. Grantees undertaking such projects are encouraged to express freely their professional judgment. This paper, therefore, does not necessarily represent the positions or the policies of the Canadian Government, and no official endorsement should be inferred.

References

American Educational Research Association, American Psychological Association, & National Council on Measurement in Education (2014). *The Standards for educational and psychological testing.* Washington DC: Author.

Chi, M. T. H. (1997). Quantifying qualitative analyses of verbal data: A practical guide. *The Journal of the Learning Sciences, 6*(3), 271–315.

Chi, M. T. H. (2006). Two approaches to the study of experts' characteristics. In K. A. Ericsson, N. Charness, P. Feltovich, & R. Hoffman (Eds.), *Cambridge handbook of expertise and expert performance* (pp. 21–30). Cambridge, UK: Cambridge University Press.

Chi, M. T. H., Feltovich, P. J., & Glaser, R. (1981). Categorizing and representation of physics problems by experts and novices. *Cognitive Science, 5*(2), 121–152.

Cohen J. (1968). Weighted kappa: Nominal scale agreement provision for scaled disagreement or partial credit. *Psychological Bulletin, 70*(4), 213–220.

Dulany, D. E. & O'Connell, D.C. (1963). Does partial reinforcement dissociate verbal rules and the behaviour they might be presumed to control? *Journal of Verbal Learning and Verbal Behavior, 2*(4), 361–372.

Ericsson, K.A. (2003). Valid and non-reactive verbalization of thoughts during performance of tasks: Towards a solution to the central problems of introspection as a source of scientific data. *Journal of Consciousness Studies, 10* (9–10), 1–18.

Ericsson, K. A., & Simon, H. A. (1980). Verbal reports as data. *Psychological Review, 87*(3), 215–251.

Ericsson, K. A., & Simon, H. A. (1993). *Protocol analysis: Verbal reports as data.* Cambridge, MA: The MIT Press.

Ericsson, K. A., & Simon, H. A. (1998). How to study thinking in everyday life: Contrasting think-aloud protocols with descriptions and explanations of thinking. *Mind, Culture, and Activity, 5*(3), 178–186.

Frankel, F., Levine, M., & Karpf, D. (1970). Human discrimination learning: A test of the blank-trials assumption. *Journal of Experimental Psychology, 85*(3), 342–398.

Jeong, H. (2013). Verbal data analysis for understanding interactions. In C. E. Hmelo-Silver, C.A. Chinn, C. K. K. Chan & A. O'Donnell (Eds.), *The international handbook of collaborative learning* (pp. 168–183). New York: Routledge.

Kane, M. T. (2006). Validation. In R. L. Brennan (Ed.), *Educational measurement* (4th ed., pp. 17–64). Westport, CT: National Council on Measurement in Education and American Council on Education.

Leahey, T. H. (1992). *A history of psychology: Main currents in psychological thought* (3rd ed.). Englewood Cliffs, NJ: Prentice Hall.

Leighton, J. P. (2004). Avoiding misconception, misuse, and missed opportunities: The collection of verbal reports in educational achievement testing. *Educational Measurement: Issues and Practice, 23*(4), 6–15.

Leighton, J. P. (2009). *Exploratory and confirmatory methods for cognitive model development.* Paper presented at the annual meeting of National Council on Measurement in Education (NCME), San Diego, California.

Leighton, J. P. (2013). Item difficulty and interviewer knowledge effects on the accuracy and consistency of examinee response processes in verbal reports. *Applied Measurement in Education, 26*(2), 136–157.

Leighton, J. P., & Bisanz, G. L. (2003). Children's and adults' knowledge and models of reasoning about the ozone layer and its depletion. *International Journal of Science Education, 25*(1), 117–139.

Leighton, J. P., & Gierl, M. J. (2007). Verbal reports as data for cognitive diagnostic assessment. In J. P. Leighton & M. J. Gierl (Eds.), *Cognitive diagnostic assessment for education. Theory and applications* (pp. 146–172). Cambridge, MA: Cambridge University Press.

Leighton, J. P., Cui, Y., & Cor, M. K. (2009). Testing expert-based and student-based cognitive models: An application of the attribute hierarchy method and hierarchical consistency index. *Applied Measurement in Education, 22*(3), 229–254.

Newell, A., & Simon, H. A. (1972). *Human problem solving.* Englewood Cliffs, NJ: Prentice Hall.

Nisbett, R. E., & Wilson, T. D. (1977). Telling more than we can know: Verbal reports on mental processes. *Psychological review, 84*(3), 231–259.

Rummel, N., & Spada, H. (2005). Learning to collaborate: An instructional approach to promoting collaborative problem solving in computer-mediated settings. *The Journal of the Learning Sciences, 14*(2), 201–241.

Schwartz, S. H. (1966). Trial-by-trial analysis of processes in simple and disjunctive concept-attainment tasks. *Journal of Experimental Psychology, 72*(3), 456–465.

Tourangeau, R. (1984). Cognitive science and survey methods: A cognitive perspective. In T. Jabine, M. Straf, J. Tanur, & R. Tourangeau (Eds.), *Cognitive aspects of survey methodology: Building a bridge between disciplines* (pp. 73–100). Washington, DC: National Academy Press.

Verplanck, W. S. (1962). Unaware of where's awareness: Some verbal operants-notates, monents and notants. In C. W. Eriksen (Ed.), *Behavior and awareness: A symposium of research and interpretation* (pp. 130–158). Durham, NC: Duke University Press.

Vosniadou, S., & Brewer, W. F. (1992) Mental models of the earth: A study of conceptual change in childhood. *Cognitive Psychology, 24*(4), 535–585.

Willis, G. B. (2005). *Cognitive interviewing: A tool for improving questionnaire design.* Thousand Oaks, CA: Sage Publications.

Wilson, T. D. (1994). The proper protocol: Validity and completeness of verbal reports. *Psychological Science, 5*(5), 249–252.

4 Collecting, Analyzing, and Interpreting Response Time, Eye-Tracking, and Log Data

Andreas Oranje, Joanna Gorin, Yue Jia, and Deirdre Kerr

The Interplay Between Construct, Task, and Evidence

'Next generation assessments' is an umbrella term that is most commonly understood to describe assessments that do not make (sole) use of multiple choice or basic text entry constructed-response items (e.g., Davey et al., 2015). It also often implies that these assessments take place in some kind of environment that is created with digital technology. Without attempting to represent a complete taxonomy of digital-technology-based item and task types (e.g., Levy et al., 2007), next generation assessments entail tasks that make use of a broader array of stimuli (e.g., audio and video, interactive graphs and tools), response mechanics (e.g., pushing virtual buttons, annotation, drawing, dragging and dropping), and continuous recording (e.g., response and pause time, click, tap or type sequences, tracing of mouse, stylus or finger movements, eye-tracking, facial expressions). The types of tasks and items used in next generation assessments include single stem questions (i.e., a stimulus that is followed by a single question), simulation-based tasks (e.g., a virtual experiment has to be conducted including setting up the experiment, running the experiment, recording findings, and synthesizing results), scenario-based tasks (e.g., one or more virtual environments in which a particular scenario is presented and a problem needs to be solved through argumentation, inquiry, and reflection), and sandbox type tasks (e.g., a virtual space that can be designed with pre-fabricated or newly created objects and system- or user-defined rules to solve one or more questions). In this chapter we will discuss the use of three data types (log data, response time, and eye-tracking) for score validation in the next generation assessments. In the remainder of this section we will discuss terminology including various uses of these types of data. In subsequent sections we will address data collection, coding, and scoring, followed by a discussion of analysis and validation, and a summary in the final section.

The starting point in any assessment should be what claims we want to make and how we structure the evidence to be able to make those claims (Frederiksen & Collins, 1989; Messick, 1994). Developing that evidence structure is greatly facilitated by building cognitively-based assessments, meaning assessing and reporting on the presumed cognitive processes involved in solving and reasoning about a problem (Leighton & Gierl, 2011). This is of course not a new interest, but advances in digital technology open up new possibilities to act on that interest. Starting from a principled design framework – e.g., evidence-centered design (Mislevy et al., 2003) and assessment engineering (Luecht, 2013) – a cognitive model or slice of a model is made explicit and this model is followed through into models of evidence and ultimately items and tasks. These design frameworks have a strong basis in scientific study and require high-frequency iterations between postulating and empirically verifying (cognitive and evidence) models.

As a developing field, there is a lot to be explored, learned, and proven about evidence models before next generation assessments become ubiquitously useful in practice as measurement tools. Data that represent eye-tracking, log data, and response time are often cast in an exploratory light as a largely free addition to the main sources of evidence (i.e., item responses and related work products). The result is that findings from those sources have been very limited representing more digital desert than ocean (DiCerbo & Behrens, 2012) and that the associated effort is anything but free. We argue here and throughout that all data collection, including eye-tracking, log data, and response time, should be governed by purposeful experimentation to answer specific questions. In other words, the design frameworks mentioned above apply equally to this type of data.

In a complex task where we are interested in underlying cognition, the inferential distance between claims and observed behavior can become complex and intricate. Process data, such as log data, eye-tracking, and response time, could shorten this inferential distance in at least five possible ways.

1   *Inference.* Process data can be used in a variety of ways to generate and test inferences about the construct(s) of interest. In principle, log data can entail all input a test taker has provided, including answers to specific questions. For constructs that are complex and process focused and for which an environment may be required that allows for a lot of freedom of movement, sequences of actions (i.e., diagnosing and testing solutions in the right order) may represent critical evidence about that construct.
2   *Design.* Process data can also be used to improve task and item designs including user interfaces, by showing patterns of behavior that may indicate when particular task or environment design features are underused and, possibly, less than intuitive. Often, this type of information can be triangulated through smaller scale think-aloud protocol studies.
3   *Contextual evidence.* Process data may also be used to offer a context to the inferences about the construct(s) of interest. While several different approaches to solving a particular task may lead to correct answers, identifying those approaches might be insightful to inform teaching and learning strategies.
4   *Indicators of engagement.* Most assessments have an implicit assumption about the level of engagement and make inferences based on that. For example, it is assumed that the test taker did their best and, therefore, that the results represent the test taker's maximum performance. Certain types of process data (e.g., eye-focus, concentration) can provide an indicator of the level of engagement.
5   *Data cleaning and filtering.* Process data can help provide evidence about how test takers are engaged with the assessment material. For example, in low-stakes assessments, it might be possible to verify whether someone spent enough time on a task to be able to process the information in a stem or decode a situation. If not, the answer or solution provided by the test taker might be removed from analysis.

'Process data' or 'continuous data' are without doubt misnomers. One could argue that no data is about process other than the meaning that is given to such data and that no data are truly continuous. On the other hand, both terms help set the timed recording of many sequential events clearly apart from assessments that record only correct and incorrect final responses to questions. As we continue to argue, data collection is to be driven by the inferences we want to make and, therefore, the grain size of recording (and analysis) is one of several design elements that determine the confines of the task or environment. At the one extreme are tasks that essentially provide 'guided walks' to the test taker and are therefore relying significantly on the test taker to follow directions, and on relatively narrow data recording. At the other extreme are open spaces that provide minimal guidance and rely on the test taker to discover, with relatively broad data recordings. Techniques such as scaffolding, redirecting, and leveling may fall somewhere in the middle. This, in turn, will affect the types of analysis and validation models that can be used. In the next section we will discuss the particulars of process data in terms of evidence collection, coding, and processing.

Evidence Collection, Coding, and Processing

So far, we have abbreviated log data, response times, and eye-tracking data as process or continuous data. Log data and response times are intertwined as every logged event is associated with a time stamp. As next generation assessments draw on a wider array of technologies, a wider array of input types become available, including biometric (e.g., heart rate, facial expressions) and gesture-based input (e.g., Kinect). The question is how all these types of data are collected, how they are stored, and how they are linked to each other.

Data Collection and Organization

The type and amount of process data that is collected, as well as the way in which it is used, changes dramatically during the development of next generation assessments. We will refer to the four-process delivery architecture (Almond et al., 2002), phases of evidence identification, and evidence aggregation to frame the discussion. The following data collections associated with distinct phases of development can be utilized.

1   *Pre-concept.* During a pre-concept phase, some potential interactions for a task are developed in a relatively low-grade environment, and play testing with one or two members of a target population is conducted between many quick development iterations. Video recording is often used to capture both the screen used to complete the task component as well as the test taker. Participants are encouraged and prompted to think aloud. Formal coding of these data is usually absent and the purpose is to simply find out whether the interactions make sense and whether specific task features work. Cognitive models of task performance are updated as a result of these findings.

2   *Concept.* A single slice of the task or environment is built that includes one instance of all relevant interactions. Testing usually happens in small try-out samples of a dozen or so people and the most extensive log data and/or eye-tracking are collected at this point, given that the number of interactions is still limited. Log data may be supplemented with recorded think-aloud protocols. The data are mostly reviewed in raw form ('telemetry') and coding is developed as evidence identification and aggregation mechanisms are specified. Cognitive models are further updated and at this point a first culling of telemetry will take place.

3   *Production.* Once all interaction specifications are locked down, the task and/or environment is fully built under production standards for user interface, art, logic, software engineering, and the assessment engine. The assessment engine will include hooks into an architecture for data storage, mechanisms to capture select telemetry (i.e., evidence identification), and mechanisms to score and summarize (i.e., evidence aggregation) and, possibly, feed results back into the delivery system. This phase concludes with a larger scale pilot or field test where select log data including response time is captured and coded. The coded data is verified and some additional exploration of (uncoded) telemetry is likely to occur as well during final tuning and pruning of the established structured data. Subsequently, the task itself is fine-tuned in post-production, but no major changes are introduced at this point.

4   *Operational use.* After post-production is completed, the task or environment is released for operational use and fairly narrowly coded log data are collected to inform data cleaning, scoring, and estimation of inferential models. Depending on the situation, some level of less structured telemetry may be maintained to inform occasional updates that are tested and released. This is most likely in lower stakes assessments. In high stakes assessments, tasks are usually retired out of security concerns before updates can or would be made in addition to the fact that updates are undesirable from a comparability and equity point of view.

Each of these phases come with different levels of data collection and analysis needs. However, there are some overarching principles that should be adhered to regardless. Log data often come in the form of individual text or XML files, one for each unique person session. These individual files need to be cleaned and combined into a single complete dataset. Best practices dictate that the final dataset should be stored in a relational database such as SQL, with person names replaced with identification numbers that can be linked to other datasets in the database (e.g., background or demographic survey data, pretest/posttest data, or process data from other tasks). This architecture supports the querying and aggregation of process data into the standard one-row-per-participant format required by most statistical techniques, as well as the combination of the aggregated data with other forms of evidence that have been gathered outside of the educational video game or simulation. Additionally, this architecture supports secondary analyses of the process data, particularly if documentation is incorporated into the data (e.g., identifying each button by name, rather than 'button 286').

Response-time data are generally collected alongside the log data as an attribute of each captured action. Seemingly trivial, the most important component of response-time data capture and processing is time-stamp calibration. Different time mechanisms, time zones, or even internal clocks can compete with each other resulting in unusable data. This is particularly true if an assessment is conducted across different devices and times (e.g., switching tablets or computers across different school days in a multi-day assessment). As with all biometric information, recording eye-tracking requires specialized equipment at the level of precision required for assessment and is currently not suitable for larger scale deployment. That being said, consumer devices continue to become widely equipped with extraordinarily sensitive cameras among other sensors. For now, an eye-tracking study would typically be conducted during the concept phases. At the very basic level and when properly synchronized, these data contain (calibrated) coordinates for specified time intervals that can directly be traced back to a particular point in the assessment and, therefore, a particular point in the log data.

Coding and Scoring Log Data

In the video game industry, evidence of player performance is often collected in log files that record the state of the in-game world every few seconds or even milliseconds. This method of logging is referred to as a 'heartbeat.' At every recorded time point, the heartbeat reports the player's in-game location, character status variables (e.g., percentage of life remaining, current equipment, or available inventory items), and the status of potentially important components of the world (e.g., number and location of undefeated enemies, location of undiscovered items, or general world status such as in-game year, time of day, or turn/round number). These heartbeat logs can record an incredible amount of fine-grained data as players progress through the game.

As mentioned above, these data are often considered to be a gold mine, capable of answering any conceivable research question if run through data mining or machine learning analysis systems. However, application of this logging format to (video)game-based assessments, scenario, or simulation-based assessments is problematic, due to the relatively unstructured nature of the data (Garcia et al., 2011; Romero et al., 2009). It is not a trivial task to extract evidence of player performance on specific educational outcomes from the hundreds or thousands of uncoded, highly specific, low-level variables (telemetry) produced by heartbeat logs. In fact, researchers in this area often find, after the data collection has ended, that the log files are not interpretable. It is for this reason that most studies of educational video games or simulations are forced to report the effects of total time spent on the task or total points earned, rather than exploring the effects of specific problem-solving strategies or identifying different problem-solving methods employed in the task. This is particularly troublesome given that the whole point of recording process data is to examine the manner in which players solve in-game problems and test takers complete tasks. In fact, there are easier and more reliable ways to record time spent and points earned in a game or assessment.

In order to provide actionable, interpretable information about a player's or test taker's proficiency, understanding, or strategic choices, logging decisions must be made (Wang et al., 2015) that will support the collection of direct evidence of these constructs (Chung & Kerr, 2012). Log file design needs to be driven by the inferences one wishes to make, otherwise the evidence that would support those inferences will be drowned out by the reams of noise surrounding actions of importance. Rather than just logging a heartbeat, player and test-taker actions that could provide relevant evidence should be logged (e.g., the player/test taker selects an option, the player/test takers moves a slider, etc.). Additionally, the logs should include relevant information about the state of the in-game world or assessment environment at the time of each action, as opposed to all heartbeat information regardless of relevance. For example, if a task contains two sliders, the value of the non-selected slider should be logged whenever a slider is moved. Inclusion of this context information will allow for the distinction between what would otherwise appear to be two identical actions, but which may have been made for very different reasons or may contain very different evidence about player or test-taker performance or understanding.

It is important to note that the difference between evidence identification and evidence accumulation is not always clear. We would argue that there is no such thing as raw data. Even the most basic log file will have some level of inference associated with it by virtue of selection, capture, and representation. Subsequently, additional layers of evidence are placed into inferential models through transformation of data, scoring (rule-based, machine learning, automated models, human), and aggregation. The type and quality of the inferences that can be made from process data collected in the log files are limited by the logging decisions that were made when the delivery system was designed and populated. Recording 'everything' is unrealistic in terms of the volume of data that would be captured unless a very simple environment is offered with few degrees of freedom for the player or test taker. In other words, a decision has to be made about the character status and world status variables that are important enough to include in both the event log and the heartbeat. Not making that decision up front means that the delivery system programmer will be forced to make them, even though they are typically not made aware of the nature of the inferences that the data are intended to support. This appears to be quite a common problem.

Coding and Scoring Eye-tracking Data

Digital eye-tracking is a technology by which one can trace the location of an individual's visual gaze, which suggests where visual attention and cognitive processing is focused. Eye-tracking has a long history in cognitive psychology, beginning with research on reading, as a means by which attention can be measured as a function of the location, duration, and sequence of eye movements (Just & Carpenter, 1980; Posner, 1980; Rayner, 1998, 2004).

Eye movements are neither smooth nor constant in speed. They can be separated into at least two primary types of activities – saccades and fixations. Saccades are rapid movements of the eyes that are relatively uncontrollable and are present whenever we use our eyes. Fixations are the periods between saccades, when our eyes remain relatively still[1] for about 200–300 milliseconds (ms). The location of an examinee's visual attention is captured as frequently as every 5 ms in terms of x and y coordinates, which define a given point in space, say for example when looking at an assessment item presented on a computer screen for a computer-delivered test. Saccades and fixations must be distinguished from one another, with fixations defining the eye movements of interest for making inferences about where cognitive attention and processing is devoted. Typically, a filter is applied that specifies a threshold to define a fixation – the location of the visual attention in space must remain within a defined space for a given amount of time. These distinct, non-overlapping areas of stimuli are called *areas of interest* (AOIs). The fixation thresholds are user defined and can be changed depending on the nature of the stimulus and/or the types of cognitive processes of interest to the researcher. Generally, the longer and more frequent a fixation is directed to a particular stimulus or element of a stimulus, the deeper and longer the cognitive processing for that element is assumed.

Two aspects of eye-movement data are of particular interest for drawing inferences about examinee cognition – the duration and sequence of visual attention, vis-à-vis the location of the gaze. Longer duration of a fixation implies deeper processing; shorter fixations are associated with shallow processing, or perhaps merely movement of the eye in a scanning/skimming manner. The sequence of eye movements provides greater context about the nature of the cognitive processing given that where an examinee looks before or after a given fixation can reveal how they are using the information they are visually retrieving.

Given the copious amounts of raw data generated, visual displays are often used to represent the duration, location, and sequence of fixations. Two types of displays are commonly used to visualize eye-tracking data, always as an overlay onto the assessment environment. The first is a gaze trail that depicts the location of visual attention with markers indicating each fixation and lines connecting them sequentially (see Figure 4.1). The example here is a reading passage, but could entail any stimulus. The order of fixations is indicated by sequential numbering, though other gaze trails often use other coding schemes, such as different colors for early, middle, or late fixations. Additionally, the duration of each fixation is indicated in these representations as a function of the size of the marker for the fixation (e.g., large circles indicating longer fixations; short circles indicating shorter fixations). Heat maps are two-dimensional graphical representations of data from K-dimensional matrices where the individual values of the matrices are represented as colors of varying intensity. For eye-tracking data, the heat map is overlaid on the experimental stimuli (i.e., an assessment task) to indicate which parts of the assessment demanded more visual attention. Figure 4.2 shows a heat map for the same item shown in Figure 4.1. One can see that more time

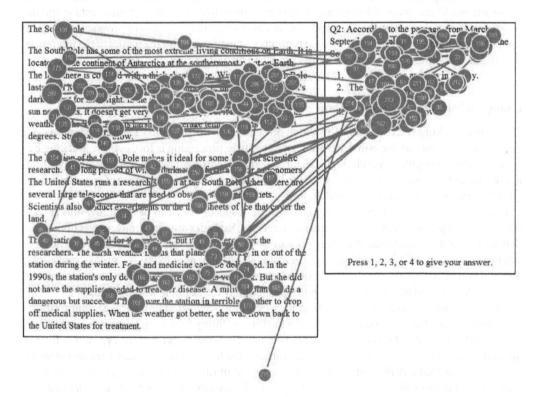

Figure 4.1 A gaze trail for an examinee solving a passage-based multiple-choice reading-comprehension question

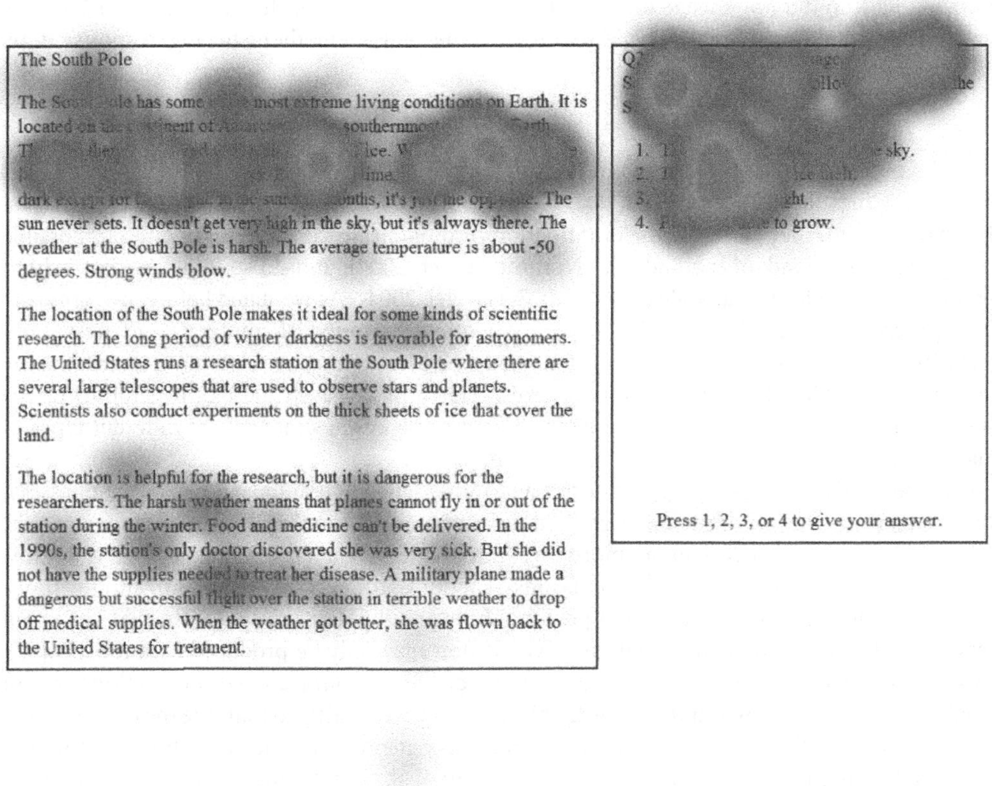

The South Pole

The South Pole has some of the most extreme living conditions on Earth. It is located on the continent of Antarctica, the southernmost point on Earth. The continent is covered in thick ice. When it's dark except for a few summer months, it's just the opposite. The sun never sets. It doesn't get very high in the sky, but it's always there. The weather at the South Pole is harsh. The average temperature is about -50 degrees. Strong winds blow.

The location of the South Pole makes it ideal for some kinds of scientific research. The long period of winter darkness is favorable for astronomers. The United States runs a research station at the South Pole where there are several large telescopes that are used to observe stars and planets. Scientists also conduct experiments on the thick sheets of ice that cover the land.

The location is helpful for the research, but it is dangerous for the researchers. The harsh weather means that planes cannot fly in or out of the station during the winter. Food and medicine can't be delivered. In the 1990s, the station's only doctor discovered she was very sick. But she did not have the supplies needed to treat her disease. A military plane made a dangerous but successful flight over the station in terrible weather to drop off medical supplies. When the weather got better, she was flown back to the United States for treatment.

Press 1, 2, 3, or 4 to give your answer.

Figure 4.2 A heat map for an examinee solving the passage-based multiple-choice reading comprehension question shown in Figure 4.2

was spent by the examinee reading the first paragraph than any other area of the text, and a similar amount of time looking at the question stem and response options. For both heat maps and gaze trails, visual representations can be generated for individuals or for groups, allowing for comparisons of visual attention across different examinees or even subgroups who may be hypothesized to differ in terms of demographics, ability, strategy use, or other meaningful qualitative variable.

Analysis and Validation

In this section, we will discuss how each of the aforementioned process data types is used in analysis and score validation. In reference to the five general uses of process data described earlier (cleaning/filtering, inference, design, engagement, and contextual information) we will focus on the first two.

As argued in the first section, a key character of next generation assessments is greater openness of assessment environments to tap into complex and process-oriented skills (e.g., Gobert et al., 2012). As a result, the range of response behaviors increases alongside the burden on cognitive and evidence models to specify what constitutes evidence. Process data are not only important as evidence of process-oriented constructs themselves, but also to triangulate and give meaning and validity to the overall traits and skills we think we observe. Part of that is excluding information that is to be considered noise, or at the very least, construct irrelevant. Another part is qualifying relevant information such as separating out serious attempts to solve the task from participants who did not engage meaningfully. In the remainder of this section we will discuss analysis and validation intricacies and highlight some analysis methods for log, response time, and eye-tracking data.

Log File Analysis

Because log files record every action taken in the course of solving a problem, rather than just the answer given, they allow for the examination of thought processes that are often impossible to capture using standard methods (Merceron & Yacef, 2004), and do so in a way that is both feasible and cost-effective at scale (Quellmalz & Haertel, 2004). As we stated before, by capturing these process data, log files allow for direct, authentic exploration of complex constructs (Linn et al., 1991). Proper analysis of such data could even be used to improve classroom instruction by allowing for the identification of common errors (Merceron & Yacef, 2004) or by supporting the examination of the relative effectiveness of different pedagogical strategies for different types of students (Romero & Ventura, 2007).

Because log data are more comprehensive and more detailed than most other forms of assessment data, the inclusion of such fine-grained detail presents a number of problems for analysis. Not only do log files usually contain more variables of interest than there are people in the study, but there is often little overlap in the thousands of actions produced by one person and the thousands of actions produced by a second person. Therefore, log data are sparse (in that any given person produces a lot of actions, but any given action may only be produced by a few people), noisy (in that irrelevant actions can vastly outnumber relevant ones, and relevant actions are not usually identifiable a priori), and so large that it is prohibitively costly to examine the data by hand.

Data mining techniques are ideal for automatically identifying and describing meaningful patterns despite the noise surrounding them (Bonchi et al., 2001). This automatic extraction of implicit, interesting patterns from large, noisy datasets can lead to the discovery of new knowledge about how students solve problems in order to identify interesting or unexpected learning patterns and can allow questions to be addressed that were not previously feasible to answer (Romero et al., 2011).

Many data mining techniques have been developed and continue to be developed to analyze log data. Whether dyad/triad analysis, classification and regression trees, canonical regression or machine learning algorithms, all these techniques have in common that they identify and reflect relationships between (groups of) variables and across test takers. In educational settings, cluster analysis is often used to identify sets of test items or types of learners (Castro et al., 2007; Vellido et al., 2011). In these studies, each cluster represents either a group of users with similar behavior patterns or a group of items with similar requirements (Mobasher, et al., 2000). Once the clusters of items or students have been identified, logistic regression is often used to identify the variables that differ between groups (Rodrigo et al., 2008) and dendrograms can be used to visualize the results. Cluster analysis can also be used to identify sets of actions that commonly co-occur (Kerr & Chung, 2012). This process results in the identification of frequent action sets that occur in the course of solving a given problem and which represent distinct, nameable strategies. These strategies can include multiple valid solution strategies, distinct misconceptions, or issues arising from difficulties interacting with the controls.

Response-Time Analysis

A computer delivery platform makes it not just possible, but rather convenient to gather timing information. As a common practice, when the grain size for data collection is determined, logging of time stamps on individual actions occurs automatically. Response time can then be summarized, for example, with regard to the whole test or any part of it (questions, actions, etc.). In this section, we focus our discussion on using response time to support direct and indirect validation of score meaning, noting that there is an extensive literature on test fraud and modeling applications (e.g., Lee et al., 2014; van der Linden & van Krimpen-Stoop, 2003). For a comprehensive review of response-time research see Schnipke and Scrams (2002).

As discussed in the first section, response time can be considered valuable auxiliary information for data cleaning. Missing responses from standardized tests are often assumed to be intentionally omitted and treated as fractionally correct or wrong. If missing responses appear toward the end of a test, they are sometimes treated as if they had not been presented to the respondent. One rather straightforward improvement in treating missing responses is to code missing responses to an item as not presented only if there is also no time spent on that item. In a complex assessment, this translates to coding whether a student has visited a particular area of a task, spent enough time to meaningfully engage, what information was retrieved, and in what order. One type of test-taking behavior that is often studied in the response-time literature is the rapid-guessing behavior. Schnipke and Scrams (1997) classified examinee-item combination as reflecting either solution behavior or rapid-guessing behavior. Generally, rapid-guessing behavior is defined as responses occurring so rapidly that students either do not have time to fully consider the item or do not give their effort. For example, Figure 4.3 shows the response-time distribution of an item in

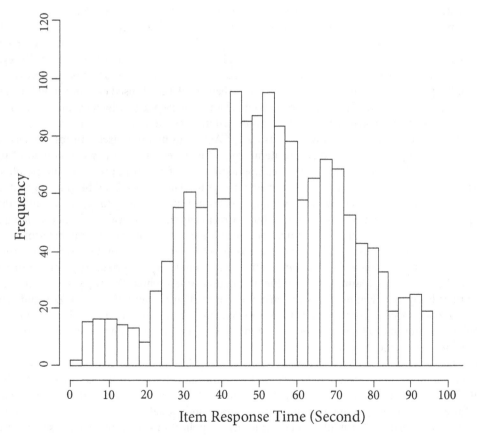

Figure 4.3 The RT distribution for a MCBA item that shows a bimodal pattern (truncated at the 90th percentile of RTs; the gap around 20 seconds could be used as the threshold that separates the two clusters of RTs)

Reproduced with permission from Y.-H. Lee & Y. Jia (2014)

a low-stakes assessment. The gap, which separates the two groups of response times at around 20 seconds, could be considered a threshold for the item that represents the response-time boundary between solution behavior and rapid-guessing behavior (Lee & Jia, 2014). Rapid-guessing behavior in a complex task environment could detect 'WTF' behavior (Wixon et al., 2012), by looking at the extent to which players engage with newly presented information.

Eye-Tracking

A possible barrier to validly interpreting process data is the artificial nature of data collection. In order to obtain evidence from process data about the presence or absence of cognitive processes, behaviors may be elicited as part of the data collection (e.g., verbal utterances, computer clicks) that might require additional, non-targeted cognitive processes. Ideally, opportunities to collect process data could be created without altering the design of assessment tasks, which should primarily optimize fidelity to the problem-solving contexts and procedures defined by the focal constructs. Eye-tracking is one possible solution to this design challenge. To the extent that moment-by-moment information can be captured about where individuals are directing their attention, various strategies that individuals or groups apply can be teased out. Those strategies can then be compared to hypothetical solution strategies that are consistent with theoretical models of focal constructs and implied construct-relevant problem-solving behaviors.

To date, in the context of educational assessment, eye-movement data has primarily been examined as part of the validity argument for score meaning. In a Graduate Record Examination (GRE) Verbal items eye-tracking analysis, Gorin (2006) showed that individuals were able to correctly solve passage-based questions without ever fixating in the passage area of interest (AOI). The eye-movement data in that study confirmed the hypothesis that reading the passage is not necessarily part of the problem-solving process for these tests. Feng et al. (2012) used eye-movement data to test hypotheses about whether item format could change the degree to which examinees actually process the reading passage in a reading comprehension assessment.

While simple analysis of summary statistics for AOIs can be quite useful in testing specific hypotheses regarding score validity and item processing, it leaves out a key component of the eye-movement data that could be quite meaningful in terms of cognitive processes and problem-solving strategies – the sequence of eye movements. Fixation durations could be quite high either because an individual 'looked' at part of a test question one time, for a long time, or it could be that the person looked at that AOI many times, but for relatively short intervals each time, looking at other areas in between. Such patterns might be quite different and quite meaningful in terms of the strategy that examinees use to solve the test questions. One way to incorporate sequence information is via a *transition matrix*. A transition matrix contains the frequency of every possible ordered pair of AOIs – the originating AOI and the destination AOI – which describes what examinees were most likely to look at just before or just after a particular element of the task. Zhu and Feng (2015) applied social network models to eye-movement transition data for middle school mathematics tasks linked to a linear functions learning progression, where higher performing students showed more transitions among fewer AOIs.

Eye-tracking as process data for assessment is slowly gaining traction, with a growing number of studies applying the technology to identify item solution paths or strategies (Gorin, 2006; Ivie et al., 2004; Tai et al., 2006; Zhu & Feng, 2015). Future use of eye-movement data to inform scoring, for example by assigning lower or higher scores to individuals with particular gaze patterns is further off in terms of feasibility, and the number of applications to innovative tasks is still very limited. However, the cost of eye-tracking systems as well as understanding of the data and appropriate psychometric models for analysis are simultaneously becoming less prohibitive in terms of potential for large-scale use in assessment.

Summary

In this chapter, we developed a rationale for the use of log data, response time, and eye-tracking for score validation in next generation assessments. The starting point was to develop the parameters of the space within which next generation assessments are mostly contained. The argument was made that assessments that are typically coined as next generation (i.e., scenario, simulation, and game-based assessments) are typically driven by the interest in and need for information about complex and process-focused constructs. Evidence about such constructs typically not only requires good solutions to problems, but also an evidence trail about how test takers arrive at those solutions from among many possible choices. This implies that the degrees of freedom in terms of movement within next generation assessment tasks and environments is much greater, and that tracking exactly which movements are made becomes critical to the evidence argument. Log, response time, and eye-tracking serve that purpose at different points in a development cycle – from pre-concept to operational release – in addition to informing design, valuing data (e.g., aberrant response treatment), and providing contextual information. Furthermore, the argument was made that while it is attractive and seemingly convenient to collect everything continuously, doing so can serve as an impediment to meaningful analysis. Organizing the data up front in terms of meaningful actions with information about relevant contexts is critical. As no recorded data are truly raw or unstructured, scoring and coding becomes a foundational task that profoundly affects and directs analysis. As much as possible, specific hypotheses that stem from the construct of interest should be built into the tasks/environments and data collection.

Looking ahead, it is difficult to imagine that interest in next generation assessments, including the collection and use of log data, dissipates and meets a similar fate as performance assessments did in the 1990s. Not only are many of society's functions taking place using digital technology, but the ubiquitous use of behavioral data to decipher and predict future patterns has become standard practice in many industries. Adding to that is the desire for reliable assessment of complex, cross-cutting skills in order to predict success in an increasingly complex world. The foremost issue that the assessment industry will have to deal with is building appropriate safeguards for collecting and storing biometrical data. Second, as technology drives an expansion in the range of (naturalistic) modes that are available for assessment, behavioral data will become more specific than is currently the case and, therefore, more informative. With increasingly sensitive detectors, we expect significant leaps in development and validation of cognitive and learning theories, which will ultimately provide robust information for guiding the process of inferences from assessments. This kind of development and validation will require significant investment, well beyond what the assessment world is used to for typical assessments. In the shorter term, the greatest payoff will be in teaching and learning environments that tend to focus on specific contexts and, therefore, for which a smaller initial investment can be made and relatively direct leaning evidence is obtained. In contrast, for large-scale assessments used to monitor on relatively general constructs the payoff will have a much longer term, because a lot still has to be discovered about generalizability, reliability, and construct validity at that level in next generation assessments. Yet, even for those applications we are confident that the value of the information that can be obtained will be well worth it, particularly as the field is trying to build productive connections across formative and summative assessment uses.

Note

1 Although, in the eye-movement literature fixations are typically defined as the time when eyes are still, three types of small movements of the eyes (nystagmus, drifts, and microsaccades) do occur during these relatively stable periods.

References

Almond, R., Steinberg, L., & Mislevy, R. S. (2002). Enhancing the design and delivery of assessment systems: A four process architecture. *The Journal of Technology and Assessment, 5*(1), 1–63.

Bonchi, F., Giannoti, F., Gozzi, C., Manco, G., Nanni, M., Pedreschi, D., & Ruggieri, S. (2001). Web log data warehouses and mining for intelligent web caching. *Data & Knowledge Engineering, 39,* 165–189.

Castro, F., Vellido, A., Nebot, A., & Mugica, F. (2007). Applying data mining techniques to e-learning problems. In L. C. Jain, R. A. Tedman, & D. K. Tedman (Eds.), *Evolution of teaching and learning paradigms in intelligent environment.* Studies in Computational Intelligence Vol. 62 (pp. 183–221). Berlin, Germany: Springer.

Chung, G. K. W. K., & Kerr, D. (2012). *A primer on data logging to support extraction of meaningful information from educational games: An example from Save Patch* (CRESST Report 814). Los Angeles, CA: National Center for Research on Evaluation, Standards, and Student Testing.

Davey, T., Ferrara, S., Shavelson, R., Holland, P., Webb, N., & Wise, L. (2015). *Psychometric considerations for the next generation of performance assessment.* Princeton, NJ: Educational Testing Service.

DiCerbo, K. E., & Behrens, J. (2012). Implications of the digital ocean on current and future assessment. In R. Lissitz & H. Jiao (Eds.), *Computers and their impact on state assessment: Recent history and predictions for the future.* Charlotte, NC: Information Age.

Feng, G., Sabatini, J., O'Reilly, T., Gorin, J. S., Wall, C., Bruce, K., Pillarisetti, S., & Halderman, L. (2012). *Getting students to process texts more deeply in assessments: Tasks type and sequence matter.* Paper presented at the annual meeting of the Society for the Scientific Study of Reading. Montreal, Canada.

Frederiksen, J. R., & Collins, A. (1989). A systems approach to educational testing. *Educational Researcher, 18*(9), 27–32.

Garcia, E., Romero, C., Ventura, S., de Castro, C., & Calders, T. (2011). Association rule mining in learning management systems. In C. Romero, S. Ventura, M. Pechenizkiy, & R. S. J. d. Baker (Eds.), *Handbook of educational data mining* (pp. 93–106). Boca Raton, FL: CRC Press.

Gobert, J., Sao Pedro, M., Baker, R.S., Toto, E. & Montalvo, O. (2012). Leveraging educational data mining for real time performance assessment of scientific inquiry skills within microworlds. *Journal of Educational Data Mining, 15*(4), 153–185.

Gorin, J. S. (2006). Test design with cognition in mind. *Educational measurement: Issues and practice, 25*(4), 21–35.

Ivie, J. L., Kupzyk, K. A., & Embretson, S. E. (2004). *Predicting strategies for solving multiple-choice quantitative reasoning items: An eye tracker study.* Final report of cognitive components study. Princeton, NJ: Educational Testing Service; Lawrence, KS: University of Kansas.

Just, M. A., & Carpenter, P. A. (1980). A theory of reading: From eye fixations to comprehension. *Psychological Review, 87*(4), 329–354.

Kerr, D., & Chung, G. K. W. K. (2012). Identifying key features of student performance in educational video games and simulations through cluster analysis. *Journal of Educational Data Mining, 4*(1), 144–182.

Lee, Y. H., & Jia, Y. (2014). Using response time to investigate students' test-taking behaviors in a NAEP computer-based study. *Large-scale Assessments in Education, 2*(1), 1–24.

Lee, Y. H., Lewis, C., & von Davier, A. A. (2014). Monitoring the quality and security of multistage tests. In D. Yan, A. A. von Davier, & C. Lewis (Eds.), *Computerized multistage testing: Theory and applications* (pp. 285–300). New York, NY: CRC Press.

Leighton, J. P., & Gierl, M. J. (2011). *The learning sciences in educational assessment: The role of cognitive models.* Cambridge, UK: Cambridge University Press.

Levy, R., Behrens, J. T., & Mislevy, R. J. (2007). *A taxonomy of adaptive testing: Opportunities and advantages of online assessment.* Retrieved from www.education.umd.edu/EDMS/mislevy/papers/Taxonomy.doc on October 24, 2014.

Linn, R. L., Baker, E. L., & Dunbar, S. B. (1991). Complex, performance-based assessment: Expectations and validation criteria. *Educational Researcher, 20*(8), 15–21.

Luecht, R. M. (2013). Assessment engineering task model maps, task models and templates as a new way to develop and implement test specifications. *Journal of Applied Testing Technology, 14,* 1–38.

Merceron, A., & Yacef, K. (2004). Mining student data captured from a web-based tutoring tool: Initial exploration and results. *Journal of Interactive Learning Research, 15*(4), 319.

Messick, S. (1994). The interplay of evidence and consequences in the validation of performance assessments. *Educational Research, 23*(2), 13–23.

Mislevy, R. J., Steinberg, L. S., & Almond, R. A. (2003). On the structure of educational assessments. *Measurement: Interdisciplinary research and perspectives, 1*(1), 3–67.

Mobasher, B., Dai. H.-H., Luo, T., Sun, Y. Q., & Zhu, J. (2000). Integrating web usage and content mining for more effective personalization. In K. Bauknecht, S. K. Madria, & G. Pernul (Eds.), *Proceedings of the First International Conference on Electronic Commerce and Web Technologies* (165–176), London, UK: Springer.

Posner, M. I. (1980). Orienting of attention. *Quarterly Journal of Experimental Psychology, 32*(1), 3–25.

Quellmalz, E. S., & Haertel, G. D. (2004). *Use of technology-supported tools for large-scale science assessment: Implications for assessment practice and policy at the state level.* Washington, DC: Center for Education, National Research Council.

Rayner, K. (1998). Eye movements in reading and information processing: 20 years of research. *Psychological Bulletin, 124*(3), 372–422.

Rayner, K. (2004). Future directions for eye movement research. *Studies of Psychology and Behavior, 20*(2), 489–496.

Rodrigo, M. M. T., Anglo, E. A., Sugay, J. O., & Baker, R. S. J. d. (2008). Use of unsupervised clustering to characterize learner behaviors and affective states while using an intelligent tutoring system. *Proceedings of the International Conference on Computers in Education,* 49–56.

Romero, C., & Ventura, S. (2007). Educational data mining: A survey from 1995 to 2005. *Expert Systems with Applications, 33*(1), 135–146.

Romero, C., Gonzalez, P., Ventura, S., del Jesus, M. J., & Herrera, F. (2009). Evolutionary algorithms for subgroup discovery in e-learning: A practical application using Moodle data. *Expert Systems with Applications, 39,* 1632–1644.

Romero, C. Ventura, S., Pechenizkiy, M., & Baker, R. S. J. d. (2011). *Handbook of educational data mining.* Boca Raton, FL: CRC Press.

Schnipke, D. L., & Scrams, D. J. (1997). Modeling item response times with a two-state mixture model: A new method of measuring speededness. *Journal of Educational Measurement, 34*(3), 213–232.

Schnipke, D. L., & Scrams, D. J. (2002). Exploring issues of examinee behavior: Insights gained from response-time analyses. In C. N. Mills, M. Potenza, J. J. Fremer, & W. Ward (Eds.), *Computer-based testing: Building the foundation for future assessments* (pp. 237–266). Hillsdale, NJ: Lawrence Erlbaum Associates.

Tai, R. H., Loehr, J. F., & Brigham, F. J. (2006). An exploration of the use of eye-gaze tracking to study problem-solving on standardized science assessments. *International Journal of Research & Method in Education, 29*(2), 185–208.

van der Linden, W. J., & van Krimpen-Stoop, E. M. L. A. (2003). Using response times to detect aberrant response patterns in computerized adaptive testing. *Psychometrika, 68*(2), 251–265.

Vellido, A., Castro, F., & Nebot, A. (2011). Clustering educational data. In C. Romero, S. Ventura, M. Pechenizkiy, & R. S. J. d. Baker (Eds.), *Handbook of educational data mining* (pp. 75–92). Boca Raton, FL: CRC Press.

Wang, L., Shute, V. J., & Moore, G. (2015). Best practices and lessons learned of stealth assessment. Retrieved December 9, 2015 from http://myweb.fsu.edu/vshute/pdf/IJGCMS.pdf.

Wixon, M., Baker, R. S. J. d., Gobert, J., Ocumpaugh, J., & Bachmann, M. (2012). WTF? Detecting students who are conducting inquiry without thinking fastidiously. Retrieved from www.columbia.edu/~rsb2162/UMAP-WTF-2012-v18R-spacingfixed.pdf on December 9, 2015.

Zhu, M., & Feng, G. (2015). An exploratory study using social network analysis to model eye movements in mathematics problem solving. In Proceedings of the 5th International Learning Analytics and Knowledge Conference (LAK '15). Poughkeepsie, NY: ACM.

5   Commentary I

Validation of Score Meaning in the Next Generation of Assessments

Lauress L. Wise

Introduction

As pointed out in the introductory chapter, there has been considerable recent research on modeling examinee response processes, but use of response process models and data have been primarily limited to assessment test design and development. Models of response processes have rarely been used in validating interpretations of test results for their intended uses. Part I of this volume discusses the use of response models and data to support validity arguments (Kane and Mislevy) and describes verbal (Leighton) and non-verbal (Oranje et al.) response data that may be drawn upon in providing validity evidence.

This commentary chapter begins with a discussion of validation and validity evidence as required by the *Standards for Educational and Psychological Testing* (American Educational Research Association et al., 2015; hereafter referred to as the *Standards*) and then Chapter 2 by Kane and Mislevy on how response models and other response data can be used to clarify the construct being assessed and provide evidence for the validity of intended interpretations. The commentary next turns to discussions of verbal response process data, as described in Chapter 3, and the non-verbal response process data from computer-based testing (CBT) described in Chapter 4, concluding with a summary of considerations for the use of response process models and data in validating the interpretations of test results for their intended uses.

Validating a Test Score Interpretation for its Intended Use

The 2014 edition of the *Standards for Educational and Psychological* Testing (AERA et al., 2015) begins with a discussion of validity and an overarching standard that states:

> Standard 1.0: Clear articulation of each intended test score interpretation for a specified use should be set forth, and appropriate validity evidence in support of each intended interpretation should be provided.
>
> AERA et al., 2014, p. 23

The *Standards* go on to discuss different types of evidence that are appropriate for different types of interpretations and uses. For example, we conduct alignment studies when test scores are interpreted as measures of competence with respect to a specified set of content standards. Alternatively, we conduct predictive validity studies when test scores are interpreted as predictors of a subsequent outcome. One type of evidence described in the *Standards* is less well known and less widely used, specifically evidence regarding response processes. The *Standards* require:

> Standard 1.12: If the rationale for score interpretation for a given use depends on premises about the psychological processes or cognitive operations of test takers, then theoretical or empirical evidence in support of those premises should be provided. When statements about

the processes employed by observers or scorers are part of the argument for validity, similar information should be provided.

AERA et al., 2014, p. 26

In the background section for the validity chapter and the commentary for Standard 1.12, many of the types of response data presented in Chapters 3 and 4 of this volume are discussed.

Use of Response Process Models and Data in Providing Validity Evidence

Response process models and data can support the validity of test score interpretations in two different and important ways. First, response data can be used to identify irrelevant barriers to task performance. A common finding, for example, is that English learners often have trouble with mathematics reasoning questions due to difficulty in understanding the terms used. A question that asks about a "marked down" price may be difficult if a student thinks it means the price is written down, rather than reduced. Cognitive laboratories can be used to understand potential difficulties at the front end (perceptual) of the process that are not related to the intended construct. Demonstrating that scores are free from such irrelevant barriers is an important first step in establishing the validity of intended interpretations of test scores.

A second, and more demanding use of response models occurs when the interpretation is actually about the examinee's response processes. Emphasis on reasoning and problem solving in the Common Core State Standards (www.corestandards.org) and the Next Generation Science Standards (www.nextgenscience.org) reflect an increased focus on the process used by the test taker in responding to an assessment task. Getting to the right answer may not be sufficient evidence that the test taker is engaging in the intended practices. I once had a high school physics instructor who asked us to measure the length and period of a pendulum and use this information to compute the gravitational constant on some fictional planet. I might have been able to get an answer without going through the intended derivation if I had simply memorized the Earth's gravitational constant, but that would not have provided evidence that I understood the process of deriving an answer. It turned out the Earth's gravitational constant was not the intended answer anyway. The pendulum was made of steel and the instructor had hidden a magnet in the base of the pendulum, leading to an apparently larger gravitational constant.

Part I of this volume begins with a detailed discussion by Kane and Mislevy (Chapter 2) of the use of response process models in interpretations of assessment results and in the validation of these interpretations for their intended uses. They distinguish between process-model interpretations and trait interpretations, although the distinction is more a matter of degree.

Models explaining how test takers perform tasks or answer questions are invaluable for understanding underlying cognitive processes. For establishing validity, however, it is critical that we begin with a detailed specification of the interpretation to be validated. For example, Kane and Mislevy reference the work of Carpenter, Just, and Shell (1990) in modeling how test takers solve progressive matrix problems. A key question is if the interpretation of scores involves *whether* the test taker can solve these problems or *how* the test taker goes about solving them. Are interpretations of *whether* the test taker can solve these problems used to predict success in some future outcome or is information on *how* the examinee goes about solving the problems used to provide individual or aggregate diagnostic feedback? Both the intended interpretation and the intended use of this interpretation are important.

The distinction between merely getting the right answer (the outcome) or executing an appropriate process for getting to the answer (the process) has been the subject of a long-running dispute. When "show your work" problems were introduced, many objected to giving any credit for wrong answers, no matter how well students understood and followed a correct process.

Increasingly, however, we are concerned not just with outcomes as demonstrations of knowledge and competence, but also with the process used to produce these outcomes. As noted above, the Common Core State Standards and the Next Generation Science Standards both emphasize the importance of problem solving and reasoning skills. Problem solving and reasoning are clearly processes, not outcomes. In other areas, such as writing, it is an open question whether evaluating the output of the writing process is sufficient. Do we teach outcomes or processes? A student may receive feedback that his or her essay is deficient because the essay itself has weak or missing topic sentences, or the student may be taught, as part of the writing process, to begin each paragraph with a topic sentence and then fill in supporting information.

Back in the 1980s, the U.S. Army Research Institute launched a major effort to measure and to predict performance across a wide range of military jobs (Campbell & Knapp, 2001). For a broad sample of jobs, key job tasks were identified and performance measures were developed for a sample of 15 tasks for each job. Some of the tasks, such as troubleshooting electronic problems, sound a great deal like tasks that may be important for the next generation of assessments. Developers of performance tasks for educational assessments of the late 1980s and early 1990s were initially quite interested in these task performance measures. At least, they were until they found out that the Army was teaching fairly rigid processes for performing each of these tasks. These processes were often highly contextualized in a way that did not generalize well across tasks. The troubleshooting task, for example, was taught as an unfaltering sequence of steps that involved pulling and testing specific components of the system to be fixed. Different systems had different components and different steps. Learning to troubleshoot one did not prepare the recruit to troubleshoot a different system.

The measures of performance of the job-specific tasks were usually go/no-go checklists used by a trained observer to indicate whether the test taker performed each step in the prescribed process accurately and in the correct order. In other words, the measure indicated whether and how the test taker had memorized and could then perform the intended process. In only a very few cases, such as the grenade toss, did the outcome matter as much as the process used to get to an outcome. Needless to say, this approach did not seem to offer much for educational assessment where belief in rigid processes was far less universal.

Kane and Mislevy (Chapter 2) describe the use of response models and response data in the validation of a range of types of constructs. Their discussion of response models suggests that there is a great deal of work to be done building and testing models of the processes we intend to measure. Early efforts in this direction, such as stochastic learning models (Bush & Mosteller, 1955; Estes, 1950) generated probabilistic fit to examinee responses, but offered few suggestions as to how to teach students to learn better. Response models work reasonably well in relatively well-structured settings. Models of student attempts to solve problems of the Raven Progressive Matrices (Carpenter et al., 1990), a form of concept formation tasks, fit a domain where the stimuli vary along a few, reasonably well-defined dimensions. The space of possible solutions is reasonably delimited. The ability to solve these types of problems may not generalize well to problem solving in less structured situations.

An important point made by Kane and Mislevy is that response process data are important for their potential for disconfirming assumptions of interpretive arguments as much as they are for offering corroborative evidence. Verbal response process data may indicate that a test taker does not understand the question or task; response latencies or eye-tracking data may indicate that the test taker is not engaged in solving the problem. A key consideration, for both trait and problem-solving interpretations, is the extent to which scores generalize across similar tasks. The lack of generalization has been limiting factors in the use of performance tasks (Shavelson, Baxter, & Gao, 1993; Davey, Ferrara, Holland, Shavelson, Webb, & Wise, 2015). A deeper dive into understanding and modeling cognitive factors that may limit generalization across tasks is essential to identifying and reducing barriers to generalization.

Verbal Response Process Data

Leighton (Chapter 3) makes a strong case for the use of verbal response process data to support the validity of test score inferences. The historical development of verbal response process data is described, dating back to Wilhem Wundt and early conceptions of "introspection," along with a discussion of some of the skepticism and criticisms of the use of examinee verbalizations.

The chapter argues for a distinction between protocol analyses and verbal analyses, with the former being used to confirm models for problem-solving tasks and the latter used in a more exploratory mode to study comprehension. However, it is not entirely clear that the two types of verbal response process data are all that distinct. On the one hand, comprehension has to be a concern, even with problem-solving tasks. Verbal response data may be used to assess comprehension of the problem to be solved as well as to indicate how the examinee characterizes and manipulates the problem space. On the other hand, there may be more to responding to other types of tasks and questions than just comprehension. In addition, response models derived from verbal analyses would also benefit from further confirmatory analyses, potentially using further verbal response process data.

Currently, the collection of verbal response process data is slow and costly. Data collection invariably involves one-on-one interviews to keep examinees talking and on topic. The non-verbal response indicators described in Chapter 4 by Oranje et al., including response time, other log data, and perhaps even eye tracking, can be collected during computer administration cheaply and on a large scale. Further, the analysis of verbal response process data is highly qualitative, and involves small sample sizes, making it difficult to subject them to statistical analyses. Changes may be coming, however. Audio recording, possibly including appropriate prompting is entirely feasible – just ask Siri or Cortana, for example – and the tools being developed for automated scoring of many types of examinee responses may be extended for use in the analyses of verbal response process data.

Leighton goes on to lay out important considerations for the collection and analysis of both types of verbal response process data, and provides examples that help clarify uses of verbal response process data. The chapter concludes with a discussion of ways in which verbal response data can be used to support interpretative and validity arguments associated with uses of test scores. The concluding discussion expands on conceptions of validity in the Kane and Mislevy chapter.

One possible and potentially important extension of the use of verbal response process data in validating interpretations of overall performance would be to suggest more detailed information on reasons for lower levels of performance. Exploratory uses of verbal response data could suggest ways of identifying different deficiencies. Such diagnostic information could be useful both in helping individual students and, in the aggregate, expanding and improving curriculum and instruction.

Non-Verbal Response Process Indicators

Chapter 4, by Oranje, Gorin, Jia, and Kerr, describes a rich array of non-verbal indicators that are now being collected, mostly in conjunction with next-generation computer-based testing, and are beginning to be analyzed to provide information on test takers' response processes. These include timing and log data and, together with a video recording of examinee's faces during testing, eye-tracking information. The chapter discusses the use of non-verbal response process data at different stages of test development, from pre-concept through operational use. As with verbal response process data, non-verbal response process data may support the validation of test score interpretations indirectly through the identification and elimination of irrelevant barriers to performance or by helping to weed out inappropriate or unmotivated examinee response behaviors. When score interpretations concern the responses themselves, non-verbal response data may be invaluable in building and testing models to support these interpretations.

Of the types of data discussed in Chapter 4, timing data is most often related to construct interpretations when processing speed is a component of these interpretations. Other types of log data, eye tracking, and perhaps also data that tracks other physical movements may or may not relate directly to the interpretation and use being validated. A few brief comments on each of these types of non-verbal response data are offered next, followed by a discussion of the desirability and feasibility of collecting and retaining massive amounts of non-verbal data without connection to specific response process models.

Timing Data

Timing data may be used to identify test takers who are responding too rapidly or, in some cases, too slowly to be believed. Timing data is also a useful component of data forensics efforts to construct indicators of various forms of cheating. Eliminating scores where test-taker engagement is questionable enhances the validity of interpretations of the remaining scores for their intended uses.

Timing data provide more direct evidence to score interpretations involving response speed for constructs such as mathematics fluency (found in CCSS standards for early grade mathematics). In some contexts, processing speed is a consistent difference between novice and expert performance. Shorter response time indicates greater integration of the processes used to interpret and respond to relevant tasks and also a greater degree of automaticity in performing these response tasks. Processing speed may also be modeled as a construct that is separate from but correlated with the cognitive ability that is the primary focus of measurement (van der Linden, 2009; van der Linden & Fox, 2016).

For paper-and-pencil testing, the common practice for assessing processing speed was to include more items than a test taker could possibly answer in a relatively narrow time window. Counts of the number of items answered (correctly) were used as an indicator of processing speeds. When tests are administered by computer, more precise timing data for each item are made available.

Many of the constructs that are measured in current educational assessments do not include elements of processing speed. Thoroughness is rewarded and examinees are often given extra or even unlimited time to complete assigned tasks. In such cases, it is reasonable to ask whether timing data can play any significant role in validating test score interpretations beyond their use in data forensics.

Log Data

Log data include both keystroke information and also data on a variety of other test-taker actions, particularly when touch screens, mouse movement and clicks, or a variety of other input devices are involved. The sequence and timing of log data can also play an important role in data forensics. For CBT, keystroke information can replace erasure analyses with more specific information on when answers were changed and how. Comparisons of the sequence and timing of keystrokes may also be useful in detecting copying. Keystroke logging includes timing information so the preceding discussion of response-time data is encompassed as part of keystroke logging.

A key challenge for the analysis of log data is in grouping keystroke and other information into larger and more meaningful chunks. An empirical, bottom-up approach through cluster analyses or similar techniques will not always lead to meaningful blocks of data. The challenge in building appropriate indicators is best met by starting with a higher-level model of examinee response processes and then figuring out how to organize the log data to model these processes. For example, in writing assessments, we currently judge the quality of the final product, but have little information on how it was produced. A simple model of the writing process might include the following steps:

1   Planning (the time at the beginning when nothing observable is happening)
2   Outlining (entering text in list format)
3   Drafting (with or without outlining, entering text in paragraphs)
4   Revising and editing (going back over previously entered text, cutting and pasting, and correcting grammar and spelling).

Log data could then be analyzed to indicate the relative amount of time (if any) that the test taker spends on each of the steps and whether they are performed in the expected sequence. This approach would provide an approximate, albeit somewhat simplistic, assessment of the writing process engaged in by each test taker. While there may not be a "preferred" writing process that works best for all students, studies of the relationships of curriculum to writing process and writing process to the quality of the output of the writing process could greatly enhance the use of test results for improving instruction. Further, analyses of writing processes could enhance the use of test results for providing diagnostic information to individual students.

Eye Tracking

Chapter 4 describes and illustrates the type of eye-tracking information that can be collected and suggests some ways of organizing the massive amount of information generated (e.g., heat maps). As with other forms of response process data, information so gathered can be used to detect aberrant response patterns that indicate a lack of understanding or lack of engagement. For instance, failure to look at the question or at some critical part of the textual or graphical information associated with the task would suggest that the test taker's response may not support a valid measurement of the targeted construct. In addition, eye-tracking data may be used during test development to identify areas of ambiguity for some or all test takers, and questions that can be answered without reference to the stimulus material.

Particularly for eye-movement data, there is often not a model for optimal patterns. Some test takers may benefit from reading the question or questions first and then attending to the stimulus material, while others may benefit from processing the stimulus material first. Still others may jump back and forth between questions and text rapidly. With the possible exception of Evelyn Wood Reading Dynamics (www.ewrd.com), we rarely teach eye movement. As with log data, the best approach is to start with higher-level models of alternative approaches to accessing the questions and stimulus materials. Then heat maps and tracking patterns can be constructed to indicate which of the alternate approaches the examinee follows.

Cost-Benefit Trade-Offs

Non-verbal indicators of response processes can involve a huge amount of data. Current educational assessments are typically administered in schools that may have limited storage capacity and limited bandwidth for transmitting data to central servers. Retaining gigabytes of data for each student and transmitting it to a central location could be quite daunting. Many argue for collecting as much information as possible so that we can figure out what to do with it all during subsequent analyses. Others argue that we need a clear rationale and plan for using the data before we commit to collecting and retaining it. The discussion in Chapter 4 provides a good beginning for developing such plans and thus provides some justification for collecting the more massive amounts of data associated with these indicators.

Summary

Part I of this volume argues for the use of response process information in validating the interpretation of test results for their intended use, and describes a wealth of verbal and non-verbal response process data that may be used in doing so. As suggested several times in this commentary, a clear statement of intended interpretations and uses is a necessary first step, along with development of interpretive arguments for how test results support the intended interpretation. Until that is done, the use and value of response process data in validating score interpretations cannot be evaluated.

Analyses of examinee response process data supports validation of test score interpretations for intended uses in two basic ways. First, such analyses may be used to identify sources of construct-irrelevant variance. This creates threats to intended interpretations of scores, and score differences may be due to something other than standing on the intended construct. Several examples are discussed in Part I of this volume. Verbal analyses, through think-alouds, have been used for some time in identifying unintended barriers to optimal performance for some or all test takers. Analyses of verbal response data can identify misunderstandings of the questions or tasks posed to the test taker that limit their ability to demonstrate what they know and can do. Results from such analyses can be used to revise and clarify the tasks posed to the test taker in a way that eliminates the irrelevant barriers.

Another example of the identification of sources of irrelevant variance is through the analyses of response-time data to identify unmotivated examinees who may be responding too rapidly to have attended to the questions and tasks. At the other end, taking a very long time to respond to a particular question (relative to other questions) may indicate difficulty in interpreting the question and task. Elimination of scores for examinees who appear to be unmotivated or are having unusual difficulty will eliminate scores whose interpretation would be questionable due to lack of engagement or difficulties in understanding. Similarly, eye-tracking data may also be used to identify examinees who do not appear to be attending to the questions or tasks posed to them, although this type of analysis is relatively new and not yet well developed.

The second major, and perhaps more central, use of response process data analyses is to support development and testing of models of the intended response process. Analysis of verbal protocol data to model how students solve problems (e.g., Newell, Shaw, & Simon, 1959; Newell and Simon, 1972) has been in use for some time. Models that predict item or task difficulty can be helpful in clarifying and extending the definition of the construct being measured and the interpretation of scores indicating standing on that construct. Some of the types of response data from computer-administered tests, such as eye tracking or keystroke logging, are relatively new and considerable work may be needed to identify intended patterns.

Finally, in many cases it is possible or even likely that different test takers may optimize performance through different processes. For example, the amount of time spent planning, outlining, drafting, and revising an essay may vary across examinees who produce the same quality result. Even so, understanding and modeling the different processes executed by different test takers is a first step to understanding individual differences in the effectiveness of different approaches.

In conclusion, it is important to focus not just on test score interpretations, but also on their intended uses. Educational assessments are used to provide diagnostic feedback to or on individual students, but perhaps the more important use is to suggest the need for and possible approaches to improving curriculum and instruction. Modeling and measuring response processes is critical because what we most readily teach is processes for getting to an outcome rather than the outcome itself.

References

American Educational Research Association, American Psychological Association, National Council on Measurement in Education, & Joint Committee on Standards for Educational and Psychological Testing (2014). *Standards for educational and psychological testing.* Washington DC: American Educational Research Association.

Bush, R. R., & Mosteller, F. (1955). *Stochastic models for learning.* New York: Wiley.

Campbell, J. P., & Knapp, D. J. (Eds.) (2001). *Exploring the limits in personnel selection and classification.* Mahwah, NJ: Lawrence Erlbaum Associates.

Carpenter, P. A., Just, M. A., & Shell, P. (1990). What one intelligence test measures: A theoretical account of the processing in the Raven Progressive Matrices test. *Psychological Review, 97,* 404–431.

Davey, T. Ferrara, S., Holland, P. Shavelson, R. Webb, N. M., & Wise, L. L. (2015). *Psychometric considerations for the next generation of performance assessment.* Princeton, NJ: Educational Testing Service.

Estes, W. K. (1950). Toward a statistical theory of learning. *Psychological Review, 57,* 94–107.

Newell, A., Shaw, J. C., & Simon, H. A. (1959). *Report on a general problem-solving program.* Proceedings of the International Conference on Information Processing. pp. 256–264.

Newell, A., & Simon, H. A. (1972). *Human problem solving.* Englewood Cliffs, NJ: Prentice Hall.

Shavelson, R. J., Baxter, G. P., & Gao, X. (1993). Sampling variability of performance assessments. *Journal of Educational Measurement, 30,* 215–232.

van der Linden, W. J. (2009). Conceptual issues in response-time modeling. *Journal of Educational Measurement, 46*(3), 247–272.

van der Linden, W. J., & Fox, J. P. (2016). Joint hierarchical modeling of responses and response time. In W. J. van der Linden (Ed.) *Handbook of item response theory, volume one: Models.* Boca Raton, FL: Chapman & Hall/CRC Statistics in the Social and Behavioral Sciences.

Part II

Using Examinee Response Process Data to Validate Score Meaning

Applications in Different Assessment Contexts

6   Assessments of Complex Thinking

Paul Nichols and Kristen Huff

What students are expected to learn and on what they are assessed is increasingly being conceptualized as complex. Complex thinking and learning is characterized by the integration of the practices, core concepts, and ideas of a discipline, and by the coordination of these practices, concepts, and ideas flexibly and effectively in the context of both familiar and new problems. The conceptualization of thinking and learning as complex is exemplified by standards in mathematics (National Governors Association Center for Best Practices & Council of Chief State School Officers, 2010a), English language arts (National Governors Association Center for Best Practices & Council of Chief State School Officers, 2010b), technology and engineering literacy (National Assessment Governing Board, 2013) and science (NGSS Lead States, 2013). For example, the Next Generation Science Standards (NGSS) describes the kind of thinking that science education should foster as "three-dimensional"—the intertwining of the practices through which scientists and engineers do their work, the key crosscutting concepts that link the science disciplines, and the core ideas of the science disciplines. Learning is described in terms of progressively more-sophisticated understanding characterized by the application of interwoven practices, concepts, and ideas (NGSS Lead States, 2013).

The characterization of thinking and learning as complex raises challenges for the validation of results in educational and psychological assessment. Validation is an investigation into the validity of the inferences we want to make about student performance given the intended purpose and use of the assessment, and validity theory provides a conceptual framework to guide validation practice (Newton & Shaw, 2014). Whereas assessments may appear to provide technically valid and reliable information for specific purposes, they may not assess thinking and learning at the intended level of complexity (Pellegrino, 2013). For example, a number of writers have suggested that the majority of validity evidence offered to support test score interpretation—that is, the alignment between the test content and the standards the assessment is purported to measure, and correlational analyses among test results and other concurrent measures or criteria (Cizek, Rosenberg, & Koons, 2008)—are insufficient as the only sources of validity evidence (Linn, Baker, & Dunbar, 1991; Messick, 1992; Pellegrino, Wilson, Koenig, & Beatty, 2014; Shute, Leighton, Jang, & Chu, 2016). Support for claims of complex thinking and learning requires evidence that test takers are employing in a coordinated fashion the concepts, practices, and ideas that characterize complex thinking.

In this chapter, we will explore the use of results from studies of cognitive response processes (CRPs) as evidence for claims supporting the interpretation and use of results from assessments of complex thinking and learning. CRPs are the moment-to-moment processes required to think and solve problems, are domain-specific, and change depending on the context of the assessment (Pellegrino, Chudowsky, & Glaser, 2001; Sawyer, 2008). Although difficult to circumscribe, examples of CRPs include metacognition, schemas, strategies, and misconceptions, as well as participatory skills such as collaboration. Identification of the CRPs used by examinees from a variety of performance levels on specific tasks is a key element of evidence for claims that complex thinking has been assessed.

This chapter is organized into three sections. First, we introduce argument-based validation as a way to identify the types of claims that are (a) appropriate for the interpretation and use of scores from assessments of complex thinking, and (b) likely to be supported by evidence from CRP studies. We hypothesize a partial validity argument for the AP World History Exam to demonstrate the claims that may constitute a validity argument used to support the interpretation and use of results from an assessment of complex thinking. Next, we identify for which of those claims results from studies of CRP may fruitfully be used as evidence to support results interpretation and use. We then discuss the evaluation of claims backed by findings about CRP. Finally, we conclude with a set of recommendations that, we hope, will inspire assessment makers to prioritize CRPs in their design and development process for assessments of complex thinking.

Argument-Based Approach to Validity

An argument-based approach to validity offers a framework for organizing the collection and evaluation of evidence to support claims with regard to the interpretation and use of assessment results, including CRP findings (Cronbach, 1988; House, 1980; Kane, 1992, 2006; Shepard, 1993). According to Newton and Shaw (2014; Newton, 2013), an argument-based approach involves (a) specifying the overall claim that the argument is intended to eventually support and, in skeletal form, the sequence of claims that leads to this conclusion; (b) specifying the evidence for these claims; and (c) evaluating the strength of the evidence supporting the claims and, eventually, the strength of the overall argument. Because the available evidence is often incomplete and, perhaps, questionable, the argument is, at best, convincing or plausible (Toulmin, 1958, 2003). Note that we use an argument-based approach to refer to a broad understanding of validation as the process of making and supporting an argument for the interpretation and use of assessment results rather than the particular argument-based approach proposed by Kane (2006) as a validation methodology.

A validity argument for student assessment can be represented by an inter-related network of claims, beginning with an assessment framework and concluding with the inferences, predictions, decisions, and so forth involved in the interpretation and use of assessment results for its given purpose. In a validity argument, the intermediate claims that link the intended targets of measurement (e.g., the learning standards) to the intended inferences and score use are stated explicitly. Rather than a linear sequence, these claims resemble a complex network. See Figure 6.1 for an example of a network of claims for the AP World History Exam (Kaliski, France, Huff, & Thurber, 2011). To illustrate our discussion of the use of CRP, we use an abbreviated validity argument for the interpretation of results from the AP World History Exam. The validity argument intentionally omits important claims, for instance with regard to the use of assessment results, for purposes of brevity and illustration.

The overall claim (claim 1) that the argument is intended to eventually support is that the assessment results represent a student's ability to apply historical thinking skills to historical content. Examples of evidence that might be used to support individual claims are shown in italics. This is a validity argument for an assessment designed and developed using evidence-centered assessment design (ECD) (Ewing, Packman, Hamen, & Clark Thurber, 2010; Kaliski et al., 2011), so the claims include reference to characteristic and variable stimuli (claim 7), performance features (claim 5), and knowledge and skills (claim 10) that might be included in task models. Stimuli include the items, tasks, game challenges, passages, and other stimuli used to elicit performance. They are initially identified in domain analysis and later codified in domain modeling. Claims are made about stimuli, e.g., item X elicits skill Y, or passage A supports eliciting skill B.

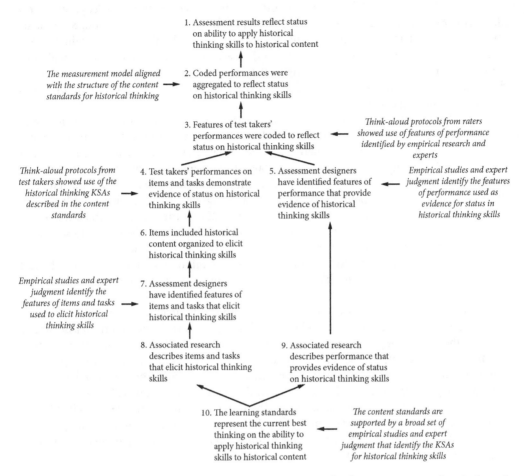

Figure 6.1 The set of claims constituting a partial validity argument for the interpretation of results from the AP World History exam

Cognitive Response Processes as Evidence

Now that we have delineated the claims that constitute an argument supporting the interpretation and use of results from an assessment of a student's ability to apply historical thinking skills to historical content, we can identify for which of those claims results from studies of CRP may fruitfully be used as evidence within a validity argument to support interpretation and use of results from assessments of complex thinking. Results from studies of CRP may be used as evidence to support a number of different claims in a validity argument supporting the interpretation and use of results for assessments of historical thinking or other complex thinking. In this section, we first briefly review several approaches to collecting CRP evidence. Next, we examine the use of results from CRP studies as evidence for several claims in the validity argument for the interpretation of results from the AP World History Exam.

Cognitive Response Process Evidence

Evidence for claims that complex thinking has been assessed may be obtained using a number of approaches including studies of verbal reports, eye movements, and log files. The first approach to the study of CRPs that we examine, verbal reports, results from *think-aloud interviews* (TAIs)

with students. TAIs are useful for identifying the cognitive processes and knowledge structures students employ as they complete a task (e.g., Ercikan, Arim, Law, Lacroix, Gagnon, & Domene, 2010; Leighton, 2004). During a TAI, students are instructed to freely "think aloud" as they engage in a task (e.g., responding to an item from an exam) or as they reflect on the knowledge and skills required by the task. The assumption underlying these methods is that people can be instructed to verbalize their thoughts in a manner that does not react with or alter the sequence or content of the thoughts mediating cognition.

The second approach to the study of CRPs that we examine is the use of eye-tracking information. Eye-tracking studies involve a set of methods used to detect and record the activities of eye movements. The use of eye-tracking methods in the social sciences has proliferated in the last few years (Lai, Tsai, Yang, et al., 2013; Rayner, 2009). Improvements in eye-tracking technology that allow researchers to obtain more accurate data with less intrusive technologies and advances in theory of the relationship between eye behavior and cognitive processes have resulted in an increase in research on eye movements (Mele & Federici, 2012). The degree to which the results of eye-tracking studies are accepted as validity evidence will depend on the degree to which the audience for the validity argument accepts the "eye-mind" assumption of the relationship between eye behavior and cognitive processes. According to the "eye-mind" assumption proposed by Just and Carpenter (1980; see also Mele & Federici, 2012), eye movements provide a dynamic trace of where attention is being directed.

The third approach to the study of CRPs that we examine is the analysis of log files. Log files are the recording of a test taker, player, or other actors' interactions with computerized assessment, games, or other technology-rich environments (Shute et al., 2016). Test takers or other actors in the computerized assessment process, such as raters, who use technology-rich environments leave continuous hidden traces of their activity in the form of log-file records. The theory of the relationship between log-file statements and CRPs proposes that, based on definitions of the CRPs, actions taken by test takers within certain contexts are the result of cognitive processes elicited by the technology-rich environment. For example, spending greater amounts of time solving problems as the problems increase in difficulty is taken as evidence of higher levels of persistence in Physics Playground (Shute & Ventura, 2013).

Learning Standards

Claim 10 states: *The learning standards represent the current best thinking on the ability to apply historical thinking skills to historical content.* In ECD, creating the learning standards by evaluating theories of learning and performance in historical thinking is labeled *domain analysis*, and organizing that information into claims that can inform assessment design is labeled *domain modeling* (Huff, Steinberg, & Matts, 2010; Mislevy & Riconscente, 2006). Results from studies of CRP, along with expert judgment, are often reviewed during domain analysis and summarized in domain modeling. According to Ewing et al. (2010), a critical goal that guided much of the domain analysis was developing a definition of historical competence that moved away from the accumulation of declarative knowledge and toward one that emphasized students' ability to reason with and apply historical thinking skills when engaging with historical content. Conducting the domain analysis involved gathering information from a variety of sources including the latest research on CRPs. The domain analysis was transformed into a domain model by creating claims and evidence from the stimuli and skills identified in the domain analysis. Eventually, assessment framework indicated that the AP World History Exam was to be designed to assess the following nine historical thinking skills:

- Historical argumentation
- Use of evidence

- Historical interpretation
- Historical causation
- Comparison
- Contextualization
- Continuity and change over time
- Periodization
- Synthesis

Item Features

Claim 7 states: *Assessment designers have identified features of items and tasks that elicit historical thinking skills.* Under an ECD approach, assessment developers attempt to engineer intended interpretations and uses of assessment results through the explicit manipulation of features of stimuli, such as items in AP History or game challenges as in Physics Playground, that tend to effectively elicit performances that serve as evidence for the intended targets of measurement. Studies of CRP are often used to inform the identification of these key stimuli features. Typically, CRP studies include rich descriptions of items and tasks employed by researchers to elicit the use of cognitive processes, knowledge structures, strategies, and mental models. Information on the important stimuli features for eliciting evidence of learners' status with respect to the targets of inference can be found in these descriptions of these study materials. Assessment designers can review these studies and link features of these items and tasks to elicitation of evidence with respect to the targets of inference.

For example, Nichols, Ferrara, and Lai (2015), using research on students' use of data to evaluate a scientific explanation, found that identifying data that contains a pattern that is *incompatible* with predictions based on a scientific hypothesis, model, or theory is more demanding than identifying data *compatible* with predictions based on the hypothesis, model, or theory (Bråten, Ferguson, Strømsø, & Anmarkrud, 2014a; Bråten, Ferguson, Strømsø, & Anmarkrud, 2014b; Ferguson, Bråten, & Strømsø, 2012; Sandoval & Millwood, 2005). They used that and other findings to identify stimulus features to design more- and less-complex passages and associated items.

For the AP World History Exam that leveraged ECD in design and development, item features were captured in task models (Hendrickson, Huff, & Luecht, 2010). These task models were derived from claims and evidence identified during domain analysis and summarized in domain modeling. For the subclaim that students could evaluate conflicting historical information, a critical feature was that items had to have at least two elements of historical information that are in conflict. The number of elements in conflict could be fixed (e.g., always 2) or vary (e.g., from 2 to 4).

Test Takers and Items

Claim 4 states: *Test takers' performances on items and tasks demonstrate evidence of status on historical thinking skills.* Results from studies of CRP are probably most often used as evidence for claims that refer to thinking and problem solving of test takers on items and tasks such as claim 4 (Leighton, 2004).

For the AP World History Exam, verbal reports from test takers asked to respond to AP World History items was used as evidence that test takers use historical thinking skills to respond to selected-response items (Kaliski et al., 2011). Verbal report data are transformed into evidence for claims through the laborious process of developing a coding scheme based on hypotheses; coding the data, preferably with more than one rater; analyzing the coded data for patterns; and drawing conclusions about the degree to which the evidence warrants or backs the intended claim.

In the AP World History CRP study (Kaliski et al., 2011), the coding scheme was developed based on a set of hypotheses that were the impetus for the study: (a) the selected-response items developed from an ECD approach were better able to elicit historical thinking skills than selected-response items developed without ECD; (b) items developed from ECD were able to elicit the intended historical thinking skills (e.g., items designed to elicit the historical thinking skill *argumentation* were able to elicit *argumentation* instead of a different historical thinking skill); and (c) different features of items had different impact on the complexity of the item. The coding scheme used for the verbal report data emerged directly from these three categories. For example, the first coding category, "cognitive processes," categorized portions of the verbal reports as any of factual recall, historical thinking skill, guessing, process of elimination, or background knowledge. When the code "historical thinking skill" was chosen, the data were further coded as one or more of the following: historical argumentation, appropriate use of relevant historical evidence, historical causation, patterns of continuity and change over time, and/or periodization. Once data were coded and tabulated, the researchers were able to draw conclusions about each of the stated hypotheses. In each case, the hypothesis was generally supported. In other words, the evidence from the verbal report data was used as warrants and backing to support claims about the construct validity of the assessment.

After the verbal report data were coded, the authors concluded that there was a large degree of alignment between the knowledge and skills the items were intended to assess and the knowledge and skills actually elicited by the items. The new ECD-based items tended to assess particular historical thinking skills as opposed to factual recall. Furthermore, the verbal report data suggested that the items were eliciting complex thinking in that multiple historical thinking skills were elicited by many items. Evidence that a student is interacting with the task using the knowledge and skills that tasks were intended to elicit is referred to as *item construct validity* evidence by Ferrara and colleagues (e.g., Ferrara, Duncan, Perie, et al., 2003; Ferrara, Duncan, Freed, et al., 2004). The consequence of not gathering this evidence for tasks on a particular assessment is that the validity argument for the scores produced by the assessment is threatened. In the words of Leighton: "If test items are being systematically misunderstood, this would mean that (a) the assessment is eliciting content understandings and processes other than what was intended, or (b) the inferences drawn from the scores are inaccurate, or both" (2004, p.8).

Item Writers

In addition, CRP may also be used as evidence for claims about the thinking and problem solving of actors involved in the assessment process other than test takers. These actors include item writers, standard setting panelists, and raters of constructed responses. For example, findings from studies of the CRPs used by item writers may be used as evidence for claims that the items written by these item writers have the characteristic and variable stimuli features described in task models under ECD. A pair of studies by Fulkerson and colleagues (Fulkerson, Nichols, & Mittelholtz, 2010; Fulkerson, Nichols, & Snow, 2011; Nichols & Fulkerson, 2010) illustrates how results from such studies could serve as evidence. In these studies, expert and novice item writers were observed writing innovative items, and their verbal reports analyzed using protocol analysis methods. In the first study, the CRP of experienced item writers was studied as they wrote figural response items in the context of a science scenario. In the second study, the cognitive processes and knowledge structures of experienced and novice item writers were studied as they wrote a four-part scenario and associated items for a science assessment.

These studies found that item writers appear to engage in three phases of problem solving: representation/definition, exploration/operation, and solution (Figure 6.2). These phases were more distinct in the problem-solving activities of more-experienced item writers than less-experienced item writers. The studies also found that novice item writers spend more of their writing time

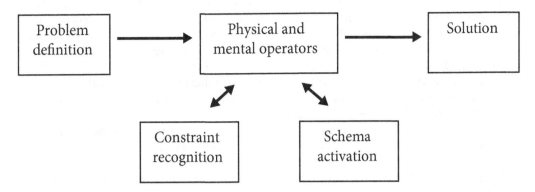

Figure 6.2 Model of item-writing expertise based on cognitive processes

defining the task and evaluating ways to select and sequence assessment content, while expert writers spend more time moving forward in the problem space by developing and sequencing the assessment content so as to elicit relevant student performance. In contrast, expert item writers spent more of their time recognizing, relaxing, and prioritizing constraints stemming from domain-specific stimuli features and/or instructional practices and context-specific nuances that informed the items. Findings that the CRPs of item writers for a particular assessment resembled the thinking of expert item writers would provide evidence for the claim that the items written by these item writers possess the characteristic and variable stimuli features identified in the test blueprint.

Raters of Constructed Responses

Findings from studies of the thinking and problem solving of raters of test takers' constructed responses offer another example of the use of findings from studies of CRPs as evidence for claims about actors involved in the assessment process other than test takers. Findings from studies of the thinking and problem solving of raters of test takers' constructed responses may be used as evidence for claims about the accuracy and consistency of the application of rubrics during the scoring of test-taker responses. In a series of studies by Wolfe (1997, 2006), raters with different levels of experience-scoring essays were asked to think aloud as they scored. The findings from these studies of raters' CRPs suggested that their scoring of essays involved two cognitive frameworks: a framework of writing (i.e., content focus or interpretive framework) and a framework of scoring (i.e., decision-making processes focused on which score to assign to the work sample). Because the frameworks of writing and the frameworks of scoring used by different raters may not be identical, this expanded model accommodates how they could come to different scoring decisions for the same essay.

Wolfe and colleagues classified raters in these studies as "proficient," "intermediate," or "non-proficient," according to whether they had high, medium, or low levels of inter-rater agreement with the scoring rubric. The studies found that proficient raters tended to use an "interpret-then-evaluate" method of scoring whereas intermediate and non-proficient raters tended to use an "interpret-evaluate-interpret-evaluate" method that breaks the scoring task into subtasks. For example, proficient raters would read the text straight through followed by evaluation. Intermediate and non-proficient raters would read part of the text followed by evaluation, then return to reading the text followed by evaluation. Furthermore, the processing actions used by proficient raters were less variable than the processing actions used by the intermediate and non-proficient raters. The proficient raters approached the task of scoring more consistently than the other two groups. In addition, proficient raters were less likely to make an early decision about the quality of an essay than were intermediate and non-proficient raters. Finally, non-proficient raters tended to make a greater number of personal comments about the text and the author than proficient and intermediate raters. Such comments suggest that the non-proficient raters might focus on elements that were not directly pertinent to evaluating the quality of the essay.

In summary, an extensive literature has developed concerning the use of empirical findings and rationales as evidence to support the claims with regard to the interpretation and use of assessment results (Kane 2006, 2013; Messick, 1989). Studies of CRPs—including studies using verbal reports, eye movements, and log files—offer a rich source of empirical findings that can be used as evidence. In this section, we used the AP World History Exam to illustrate the use of findings from studies of CRPs as evidence to support claims in a validity argument. Only verbal reports were offered as evidence to support the validity argument in the case of the AP World History Exam, reflecting the current relative rarity of eye-tracking information and log files as validity evidence in the field of educational and psychological assessment.

Evaluation of Validity Arguments

Under an argument-based approach, evidence is collected and evaluated to support claims with regard to a validity argument for the interpretation and use of assessment results. The evaluation of the validity argument supporting the interpretation and use of scores from an assessment of a complex thinking might employ a number of criteria, including: To what degree is the argument reasonable? To what degree is the argument coherent? And, to what degree is the argument plausible? (Kane, 2006). Evaluation of the argument also includes evaluation of how compellingly each claim is warranted, or supported, by the evidence provided. Claims may be classified as weakly, moderately, or strongly supported or unsupported (Nichols & Lai, 2014).

Ultimately, the quality of the argument is based on the judgment of the evaluator. Consequently, the evaluation is open to the influence of what Messick (1981) describes as the "ideologies" of potential evaluators representing different fields (see also Messick, 1989; Hubley & Zumbo, 2011; Kane, 2001). These ideologies are composed of conventions, practices, and values that tend to be shared by many, but not all, members of a field. The implication for this chapter is that members of different fields may differ in the value they placed on the evidence resulting from CRP studies. These differences across fields even influence the terminology used to construct the validity argument. Drawing on discourse analysis, Hyland (2004, 2009) described the distinctive ways different fields have of presenting and evaluating arguments. "It turns out, in fact, that engineers *show*, philosophers *argue*, biologists *find*, and linguists *suggest*" (Hyland, 2009, p. 11). As such, different evaluators of the validity argument may reach different and sometimes conflicting conclusions.

For example, we speculate that one reason that CRPs may be a relatively rare source of evidence for claims in the *Mental Measurements Yearbook* (Cizek et al., 2008) and the journal *Educational and Psychological Measurement* (Shear & Zumbo, 2014) is that psychometricians may value quantitative data over the more qualitative nature of CRP data. Psychometricians may tend to view the targets of assessment as fundamentally quantitative and believe that studying something scientifically means measuring it (Michell, 2003). This view is exemplified in a number of value statements made throughout the development of the psychometric field. Early in the history of the field, Thorndike (1918) stated: "Whatever exists at all exists in some amount. To know it thoroughly involves knowing its quantity as well as its quality" (p. 16). Later in the development of psychometrics, Spearman (1937, quoted in Michell, 2003) observed, "there is yet another [method] so vital that, if lacking it, any study is thought . . . not to be scientific in the full sense of the word. This further and crucial method is that of measurement" (p. 89). More recently, Petersen, Kolen, and Hoover (1989) defined scaling as "the process of associating numbers with the performance of examinees" (p. 221). This is just a sample from many similar statements found in the psychometric literature.

In the legal field, Sireci and Parker (2006) found no validity studies in the legal field that reported findings from CRP studies as evidence. We speculate that this finding may be because the legal community tends to frame questions of validity within the architecture of existing laws and legal precedent (Sireci & Green, 2000; Sireci & Parker, 2006). This is not to say that courts do not consider psychometric theories and evidence when making a judgment. On the contrary, according to Phillips and Camara (2006), many court cases involving disputes over testing practices have involved the consideration of empirical evidence and expert psychometric testimony. But, since CRP results are almost never used by psychometricians as validity evidence, CRP results are unlikely to be involved in court cases.

In summary, the validity argument is never proven but can be supported to the extent that CRP study results and other evidence support the claims (Kane, 2006; Newton & Shaw, 2014). Alternatively, the validity argument is challenged to the extent that this evidence fails to support claims. The degree to which researchers are comfortable using methodologies and find results convincing from studies of CRPs may depend to some extent on the conventions, practices, and values of the field for which they most closely identify. Nonetheless, studies of CRPs are emerging as an important source of validity evidence, especially when principled approaches to assessment design, such as ECD, are used to design and develop assessments.

Concluding Remarks

In this chapter, we have demonstrated that data resulting from studies of CRPs can be used as compelling evidence to support a variety of claims in a validity argument for assessments of complex thinking. CRP data can be collected from a variety of sources—from verbal reports, eye-tracking, and log files. There are two advantages to this methodological flexibility: first, assessment makers can use the CRP data collection method that is most suitable given the context of the assessment; second, when necessary, multiple forms of CRP data can be used to support different claims in the validity argument (e.g., in a computerized assessment, both log-file data and think-aloud data can be used, when necessary). We also show in this chapter that CRP data are woefully underutilized as evidence to support claims in validity arguments, although both the 1999 and the more-recent 2014 Standards for Educational and Psychological Testing call explicitly for these kinds of evidence. Similarly, the Peer Review Guidance released in 2015 by the U.S. Department of Education also suggests that CRP data be used as evidence to support the validity argument (U.S. Department of Education, 2015). Rather than seeing the collection of CRP data as a burden to be borne after the assessment is operational, we hope that we have persuaded assessment makers that the collection of CRP data early in the assessment design process is an investment in the quality of the assessment program. CRP data can serve as compelling evidence for the validity argument, and, if collected sufficiently early in the design process, can serve a formative role in informing those aspects of the assessment that may need modification to ensure that the intended targets of measurement—complex thinking—are indeed being assessed.

The call for assessments of complex thinking is likely to not abate in the coming years, and assessment designers need the most compelling evidence possible that we are able to assess complex thinking within common constraints, which typically call for shorter exams and short turn-around time between administration and score reporting. Without CRP data, we are at peril of missing the target of measurement if we simply assume that tried-and-true item types (e.g., four-choice selected response) or innovative, technology-enhanced item types are measuring the complex thinking that is in demand and the focus of instruction. With the rise of computerized assessments, which allow for unobtrusive collection of CRP data through log files, and the rise of more principled approaches to assessment design, which value the collection of validity evidence throughout the assessment design process so that the evidence can be used to actually inform the design, it is our hope that we will concurrently witness the rise of CRP studies.

References

Bråten, I., Ferguson, L. E., Strømsø, H. I., & Anmarkrud, Ø. (2014a). Justification beliefs and multiple-documents comprehension. *European Journal of Psychology of Education, 28*, 879–902.

Bråten, I., Ferguson, L. E., Strømsø, H. I., & Anmarkrud, Ø. (2014b). Students working with multiple conflicting documents on a science issue: Relations between epistemic cognition while reading and sourcing and argumentation in essays. *British Journal of Educational Psychology, 83*, 379–395.

Cizek, G. J., Rosenberg, S., & Koons, H. (2008). Sources of validity evidence for educational and psychological tests. *Educational and Psychological Measurement, 68*, 397–412.

Cronbach, L. J. (1988). Five perspectives on validity argument. In H. Wainer & H. Braun (Eds.), *Test validity* (pp. 3–17). Hillsdale, NJ: Lawrence Erlbaum.

Ercikan, K., Arim, R. G., Law, D. M., Lacroix, S., Gagnon, F., & Domene, J. F. (2010). Application of think-aloud protocols in examining sources of differential item functioning. *Educational Measurement: Issues and Practice, 29*, 24–35.

Ewing, M., Packman, S., Hamen, C., & Clark Thurber, F. (2010). Representing targets of measurement within evidence-centered design. *Applied Measurement in Education, 23*(4), 325–341.

Ferguson, L. E., Bråten, I., & Strømsø, H. I. (2012). Epistemic cognition when students read multiple documents containing conflicting scientific evidence: A think-aloud study. *Learning and Instruction, 22*, 103–120.

Ferrara, S., Duncan, T., Perie, M., Freed, R., McGivern, J., & Chilukuri, R. (April, 2003). *Item construct validity: Early results from a study of the relationship between intended and actual cognitive demands in a middle school science assessment.* Paper presented at the annual meeting of the American Educational Research Association, Chicago, IL.

Ferrara, S., Duncan, T. G., Freed, R., Velez-Paschke, A., McGivern, J., Mushlin, S., Mattessich, A., Rogers, A., & Westphalen, K. (April, 2004). *Examining test score validity by examining item construct validity.* Paper presented at the annual meeting of the American Educational Research Association, San Diego, CA.

Fulkerson, D., Nichols, P. D., & Mittelholtz, D. J. (May, 2010). *What item writers think when writing items: Towards a theory of item writing expertise.* Paper presented at the annual meeting of the American Educational Research Association, Denver, CO.

Fulkerson, D., Nichols, P. D., & Snow, E. B. (April, 2011). *Expanding the model of item writing expertise: Cognitive processes and requisite knowledge structure.* Paper presented at the annual meeting of the American Educational Research Association, New Orleans, LA.

Hendrickson, A., Huff, K., & Luecht, R. (2010). Claims, evidence, and achievement-level descriptors as a foundation for item design and test specifications. *Applied Measurement in Education, 23* (4), 358–377.

House, E. R. (1980). *Evaluating with validity.* Beverly Hills, CA: SAGE.

Hubley, A. M., & Zumbo, B. D. (2011). Validity and the consequences of test interpretation and use. *Social Indicators Research, 103*, 219–230.

Huff, K., Steinberg, L., & Matts, T. (2010). The promises and challenges of implementing evidence-centered design in large-scale assessment. *Applied Measurement in Education, 23*, 310–324.

Hyland, K. (2004). *Disciplinary discourses.* Ann Arbor, MI: University of Michigan Press.

Hyland, K. (2009). Writing in the disciplines: Research evidence for specificity. *Taiwan International ESP Journal, 1*, 5–22.

Just, M. A. & Carpenter, P. A. (1980). A theory of reading: From eye fixations to comprehension. *Psychological Review, 87*(4), 329–354.

Kaliski, P., France, M., Huff, K., & Thurber, A. (2011). *Using think-aloud interviews in evidence-centered design for the AP World History exam.* Paper presented at the Annual Conference of the American Educational Research Association, Denver, CO.

Kane, M. T. (1992). An argument-based approach to validity. *Psychological Bulletin, 112*, 527–535.

Kane, M. T. (2001). Current concerns in validity theory. *Journal of Educational Measurement, 38*, 319–342.

Kane, M. T. (2006). Validation. In R. L. Brennan (Ed.), *Educational measurement* (4th ed., pp. 17–64). Washington, DC: The National Council on Measurement in Education & the American Council on Education.

Kane, M. T. (2013). Validating the interpretations and uses of test scores. *Journal of Educational Measurement, 50*(1), 1–73.

Lai, M. L., Tsai, M. J., Yang, F. Y., Hsu, C. Y., Liu, T. C., Lee, S. W. Y., et al. (2013). A review of using eye-tracking technology in exploring learning from 2000 to 2012. *Educational Research Review, 10*(88), 90–115.

Leighton, J. P. (2004). Avoiding misconceptions, misuse, and missed opportunities: The collection of verbal reports in educational achievement testing. *Educational Measurement: Issues and Practice, Winter,* 1–10.

Linn, R. L., Baker, E. L., & Dunbar, S. B. (1991). Complex performance-based assessment: Expectations and validation criteria. *Educational Researcher, 20*(8), 15–21.

Mele, M. L., & Federici, S. (2012). Gaze and eye-tracking solutions for psychological research. *Cognitive Processing, 13*(1 SUPPL).

Messick, S. (1981). Evidence and ethics in the evaluation of tests. *Educational Researcher, 10*(9), 9–20.

Messick, S. (1989). Validity. In R. L. Linn (Ed.), *Educational measurement* (3rd ed., pp. 13–103). New York: Macmillan.

Messick, S. (1992). The interplay of evidence and consequences in the validation of performance assessments. *Educational Researcher, 23*(2), 13–23.

Michell, J. (2003). The quantitative imperative: Positivism, naïve realism and the place of qualitative methods in psychology. *Theory & Psychology, 13,* 5–31.

Mislevy, R. J., & Riconscente, M. M. (2006). Evidence-centered assessment design: Layers, concepts, and terminology. In S. Downing & T. Haladyna (Eds.), *Handbook of test development* (pp. 61–90). Mahwah, NJ: Erlbaum.

National Assessment Governing Board (2013). Technology and Engineering Literacy Framework for the 2014 National Assessment of Educational Progress. U.S. Department of Education.

National Governors Association Center for Best Practices & Council of Chief State School Officers (2010a). *Common Core State Standards for Mathematics.* Washington, DC: Authors.

National Governors Association Center for Best Practices & Council of Chief State School Officers (2010b). *Common Core State Standards for English language arts and literacy in history/social studies, science, and technical subjects.* Washington, DC: Authors.

Newton, P. E. (2013) 'Two kinds of argument?' *Journal of Educational Measurement, 50* (1): 105–109.

Newton, P. E, & Shaw, S. D. (2014). *Validity in educational and psychological assessment.* SAGE. Kindle Edition.

NGSS Lead States. (2013). *Next generation science standards: For states, by states.* Washington, DC: The National Academies Press.

Nichols, P., & Fulkerson, D. (2010). *Informing design patterns using research on item writing expertise (Large-scale assessment technical report 9).* Menlo Park, CA: SRI International.

Nichols, P., & Lai, E. R. (2014, April). *Inclusion of the conventions, practices and values of multiple stakeholders in a validity framework.* Paper presented at the annual meeting of the American Educational Research Association, Philadelphia, PA.

Nichols, P., Ferrara, S., & Lai, E. (2015). Principled design for efficacy: Design and development for the next generation tests. In R. W. Lissitz (Ed.), *The Next Generation of Testing: Common Core Standards, SMARTER-BALANCED, PARCC, and the Nationwide Testing Movement* (pp. 228–245). Charlotte, NC: Information Age Publishing.

Pellegrino, J. W. (2013). Proficiency in science: Assessment challenges and opportunities. *Science, 340,* 320–326.

Pellegrino, J., Chudowsky, N, & Glaser, R. (Committee on the Foundations of Assessment) (Eds.) (2001). *Knowing what students know: The science and design of educational assessment.* Board on Testing and Assessment, Center for Education, National Research Council, Division of Behavioral and Social Sciences and Education. Washington, DC: The National Academies Press.

Pellegrino, J. W., Wilson, M. R., Koenig, J. A., & Beatty, A. S. (Eds.) (2014). *Developing assessments for the Next Generation Science Standards.* Committee on Developing Assessments of Science Proficiency in K-12. Board on Testing and Assessment and Board on Science Education. Washington, DC: National Academies Press.

Petersen, N. S., Kolen, M. J., & Hoover, H. D. (1989). Scaling, norming, and equating. In Linn, R. L. (Ed.), *Educational measurement* (3rd ed.) New York: Macmillan.

Phillips, S. E. & Camara, W. J. (2006). Legal and ethical issues. In R. Brennan (Ed.), *Educational measurement* (4th ed.). Westport, CT: American Council on Education/Praeger.

Rayner, K. (2009). Eye movements and attention in reading, scene perception, and visual search. *Quarterly Journal of Experimental Psychology, 62*(8), 1457–1506.

Sandoval, W. A., & Millwood, K. A. (2005). The quality of students' use of evidence in written scientific explanations. *Cognition and Instruction, 23(1),* 23–55.

Sawyer, R. K. (2008). Optimizing learning: Implications of learning sciences research. In *Innovating to learn, learning to innovate* (pp. 45–65). Paris: OECD.

Shear, B. R., & Zumbo, B. D. (2014). What counts as evidence: A review of validity studies in educational and psychological measurement. In Bruno D. Zumbo, and Eric K. H. Chan (Eds.), *Validity and validation in social, behavioural, and health sciences* (pp. 91–111). New York: Springer.

Shepard, L. A. (1993). Evaluating test validity. *Review of Research in Education, 19,* 405–450.

Shute, V. J., Leighton, J. P., Jang, E. E., & Chu, M.-W. (2016). Advances in the science of assessment. *Educational Assessment, 21*(1), 1–27.

Shute, V. J., & Ventura, M. (2013). *Measuring and supporting learning in games: Stealth assessment.* Cambridge, MA: The MIT Press.

Sireci, S. G., & Green, P. C. (2000). Legal and psychometric criteria for evaluating teacher certification tests. *Educational Measurement: Issues and Practice, 19*(1), 22–31, 34.

Sireci, S. G., & Parker, P. (2006). Validity on trial: Psychometric and legal conceptualizations of validity. *Educational Measurement: Issues and Practice, 25*(3), 27–34.

Spearman, C. E. (1937). Psychology down the ages. 2 vols. London: Macmillan.

Thorndike, E. L. (1918). The nature, purposes, and general methods of measurement of educational products. In S. A. Courtis (Ed.), *The Measurement of Educational Products* (17th Yearbook of the National Society for the Study of Education, Pt. 2., pp. 16–24). Bloomington, IL: Public School.

Toulmin, S. (1958). *The uses of argument.* Cambridge, UK: Cambridge University Press.

Toulmin, S. (2003). *The uses of argument* (updated ed.). Cambridge, UK: Cambridge University Press.

U.S. Department of Education (2015). *U.S. Department of Education Peer Review of State Assessment Systems Non-Regulatory Guidance.* (Washington, DC: Author), available at www2.ed.gov/policy/elsec/guid/assessguid15.pdf.

Wolfe, E. W. (1997). The relationship between essay reading style and scoring proficiency in a psychometric scoring system. *Assessing Writing, 4,* 83–106.

Wolfe, E. W. (2006). Uncovering rater's cognitive processing and focus using think-aloud protocols. *Journal of Writing Assessment, 2,* 37–56.

7 Threats to Score Meaning in Automated Scoring

Isaac I. Bejar

Motivation: Understanding the (Imminent) Problem

The increased use of automated scoring has the potential to enable the benefits of constructed-response formats by reducing the cost of scoring.[1] On one hand, the best evidence regarding the skills students have acquired may not be obtainable with assessments that are limited to selected-response items (Frederiksen, 1984). Incorporating constructed response into tests could make it possible to obtain a better indication of student learning (Lane & Stone, 2006). In addition, the use of constructed responses could serve to convey more clearly to school personnel the full complexity of the standards that students are expected to meet, which may have a positive systemic effect (Bennett, 2010; Messick, 1994). Moreover, there is evidence that teachers adapt their teaching practices to what is perceived to be valued by the assessment, and that they modify their teaching accordingly (Koretz & Hamilton, 2006, p. 552). Therefore, the increased use of constructed-response formats could have a beneficial effect on student learning if the *tasks* used for assessing it are grounded in the *science* of student learning. A further potential benefit is the involvement of teachers in the scoring of constructed responses as a form of professional development (Goldberg, 2012; Heller, Sheingold, & Myford, 1998; Myford & Mislevy, 1995; Nijveldt, Beijaard, Brekelmans, Wubbels, & Verloop, 2009).[2]

While these advantages are fairly compelling, the large-scale use of automated scoring in K-12 presents potential challenges to score meaning because the large volume of responses to be scored encourages reliance on automated scoring as a cost savings measure (Chingos, 2013). The challenge, of course, is to obtain increased efficiency but without sacrificing score meaning, which would be the basis for teacher intervention and effective policy decisions based on aggregate analysis of student performance. To further understand how automated scores are produced and the vulnerabilities that could undermine score meaning, I discuss the anatomy of a scoring engine.

The Anatomy of Automated Scoring

To understand the relationship between score meaning and automated scoring, in this chapter I focus on the scoring of writing samples where automated scoring has a long history and many scoring engines are readily available. Yang, Buckendahl, Juszkiewicz, & Bhola (2002) and Ben-Simon and Bennett (2007) discuss several scoring engines for writing samples. A more extensive and up-to-date discussion of automated scoring of writing can be found in Shermis and Burstein (2013), and a recent special issue of *Assessing Writing* (Elliot & Williamson, 2013). Bejar, Mislevy, and Zhang (2016) discuss automated scoring more generally, including scoring of many other response types, not just textual responses.

We often refer to the software that implements automated scoring as a *scoring engine*. A scoring engine is expensive to develop and, to leverage the investment, multiple assessments need to be supported. To that effect, specific *scoring models* are produced for a given assessment. Scoring engines share a common high-level architecture that consists of two steps. In the nomenclature of evidence-centered design (Bejar et al., 2016; Mislevy, Steinberg, Almond, & Lucas, 2006) these steps are called *feature extraction* and *evidence synthesis*, jointly known as *evidence identification*. Put simply, as seen in Figure 7.1, feature extraction is concerned with the analysis of a response into a set of features or attributes, such as the presence of grammatical errors, appropriate vocabulary, appropriate organization, and so on. In Figure 7.1, the features are generically labeled f_1 to f_{10}. Evidence synthesis refers to a mapping of the features into a score level defined by a scoring rubric. The lower-level features are often combined to define mid-level features (M_1 to M_4, in Figure 7.1). Both of these steps have implications for score meaning.

Developing a scoring engine entails multiple design decisions about the implementation of these two steps that, when done in concert with the design of the assessment (Bennett & Bejar, 1998), results in a far better chance of producing scores that are meaningful, that is, accurately reflecting the levels of proficiencies described by the scoring rubric. When a scoring engine is designed in concert with the rest of the assessment design, the conception of the student knowledge, skills and abilities (KSAs), or proficiencies, and the assumed response processes, flesh out the construct, and inform the design of the scoring engine. Under those conditions, there is a better chance to "build-in" score meaning into automated scores. Once the engine is available, automated scoring becomes a matter of repeatedly applying the scoring engine to each response: a response is read, the features extracted and a score computed based on the features (see below). Under the best of circumstances, the scores that are produced by the scoring engine, and their aggregation into test scores, meet all design expectations. In practice, much can go wrong even under the best of circumstances. Thus, *preserving* score meaning is an important goal once automated scoring is deployed, which

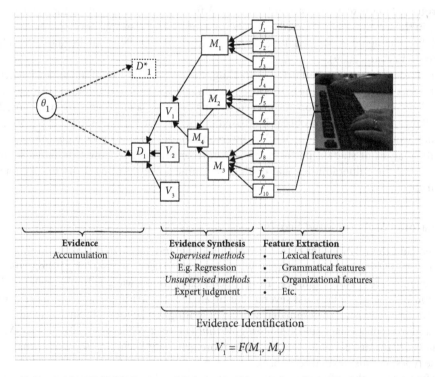

Figure 7.1 Evidence identification consists of feature extraction and evidence synthesis; student proficiency is represented as θ_1, elicited by one or more tasks, D; the scoring of task D_1 is illustrated; evidence accumulation adds up the outcome for multiple tasks into an assessment-level score

is a matter of quality control.[3] As noted by Bejar (2011), quality control in the case of automated scoring is not just detecting an occasional malfunctioning of the software, which is important in its own right, but must be informed by validity considerations. For example, a scoring model is often applied to different instances of a prompt. In such cases, it would be important to corroborate that the scoring engine renders equally meaningful scores for all instances of a prompt. A similar argument applies to subsets of the test-taking population (Zhang, Dorans, Li, & Rupp, 2015).

Ideally, the features at all levels are motivated by the conception of the target construct, which in turn are a function of lower-level features that are applied to the text itself. In practice, the micro-features available for scoring are limited to what is computable from the text, given the state of the art at the time. Unfortunately, certain qualities of writing are not as yet amenable to quantification, for example, argumentation, although progress is inevitable and palpable (Deane, 2013), nevertheless some writers are less optimistic (Perelman, 2014).

When automated scoring is implemented by repurposing an existing scoring engine, there is a potential for a mismatch between the design of the scoring engine and the target construct unless the available lower-level features address all the relevant aspects of performance called for by the target construct, or appropriate features can be added. An unfortunate compromise would be to design the tasks such that they are scorable by the engine as it currently stands and not compensating for the under representation of students' proficiencies in some form.[4]

Another set of decisions in building a scoring engine is how the micro-features are aggregated into mid-level features and the features into a score. Unlike feature extraction, which is highly domain and construct specific, evidence synthesis, is far more generic. It is denoted in Figure 7.1 as a function, F that maps high-level features into a score. However, score meaning also depends on the details of this process. F typically is based on a statistical process, such as regression, or it can be judgmental, or both.

For completeness, *evidence accumulation* (Mislevy et al., 2006) is mentioned in Figure 7.1 and consists of aggregating the evidence from multiple tasks into an assessment-level score by means of standard psychometric models applicable to scoring essays and similar constructed-response item data, which is beyond the scope of this chapter.

Given the foregoing description of the architecture of scoring engines, threats to score meaning could originate in feature extraction, or evidence synthesis. To illustrate these vulnerabilities, I present two examples below. The first example shows results from a study to test the feasibility of artificially increasing automated scores through a lexical strategy that could be effective in "gaming" a scoring engine; the other discusses the effect of a "discourse strategy" that potentially could lead human scorers to overvalue the essay, a tendency that would be inherited by the automated scoring engine possibly inflating the automated scores.

Stumping a Scoring Engine by Obfuscating Mellifluously: Illustrating the Lexical Vulnerabilities of an Automated Scoring Engine

Although the potential vulnerability of automated scoring engines to response strategies has been previously discussed (e.g., Powers, Burstein, Chodorow, et al., 2002), it bears repeating. Powers and colleagues showed that it was possible to "stump" a scoring engine, specifically, e-rater. That is, it was possible for skilled writers to coerce e-rater into producing a higher score than human scorers would assign, by instructing writers on the internal workings of e-rater. Stumping or gaming automated scoring has become of sufficient interest to a lay audience that it has been discussed in the press (Winerip, 2012), in addition to becoming a matter of concern to producers of scoring engines (Higgins & Heilman, 2014; Lochbaum, Foltz, Rosentein et al., 2013).

The vulnerability of the specific scoring engine, e-rater, was studied by Bejar, VanWinkle, Madnani, et al. (2013). They reasoned that the widely available information on the internal workings of e-rater could be used to devise a strategy that would yield higher scores. The high-level features used by e-rater are widely available (Quinlan, Higgins, & Wolff, 2009). Such wide availability is admirable and can be said to be consistent with testing standards (see, e.g., Standard 4.19, p. 91, American Educational Research Association, American Psychological Association, & National Council on Measurement in Education, 2014).

While transparency is consistent with professional standards, when the functioning of the scoring engine is open to examination the potential exists for test takers to successfully increase their scores in a manner that is not construct-relevant. Specifically, the following information about the e-rater engine concerning the role of lexical sophistication in computing the e-rater score is publicly available.

> Two features in e-rater V.2 are related specifically to word-based characteristics. The first is a measure of vocabulary level (referred to as *vocabulary*) based on Breland, Jones, and Jenkins' (1994) Standardized Frequency Index across the words of the essay. The second feature is based on the average word length in characters across the words in the essay (referred to as *word length*).
>
> Attali & Burstein, 2006, p. 11

The characterization of lexical sophistication in the evaluation of writing is justifiable on construct representation grounds (Yu, 2010). Nevertheless, the indicators of lexical quality used in e-rater, namely the frequency of the words and their length, are potentially vulnerable to a construct-irrelevant response strategy (CIRS). To test this idea Bejar et al. (2014) simulated a response strategy using Graduate Record Examination (GRE) essays from the previous edition of the assessment.

The GRE analytical writing section data for the study test was obtained at a time in which test takers responded to two separately-timed analytical writing tasks, a 45-minute issue prompt task and a 30-minute argument task. The issue task requires test takers to state an opinion and support their ideas by use of examples and relevant reasons. The argument task requires test takers to critique an argument. The test assesses the test takers' ability to articulate and support complex ideas, analyze an argument, and sustain a focused and coherent discussion, but not specific content knowledge. The responses are scored on a 1–6 scale based on a scoring rubric that emphasizes two attributes: the quality of the argumentation and the command of written English.

To test the effectiveness of a lexical CIRS, operational GRE data were obtained for eight prompts, four of each type, and scored with the e-rater engine available as of November 2009. The response strategy that was evaluated targeted the two lexical features in e-rater and consists of substituting words in an essay with words that are less frequent and longer, that is, by "obfuscating mellifluously", a phrase used by the press to describe an approach to gaming a scoring engine (Winerip, 2012). Bejar et al. (2014) *simulated* a situation where the test taker would write the essay as usual and would reserve some time to carry out a substitution procedure replacing a portion of the words by longer and less frequently used words. A lexical substitution strategy could easily be detected if everyone substituted the same words. Therefore, the simulation assumed a personalized list. To simulate the strategy, a list of 701 candidate substitutes was carefully constructed from which to draw personalized lists.

To make the strategy cognitively feasible, even for lower-scoring test takers, the number of substitutions was set to be 5 percent of the length of the essay. Since responses can range from 100 to 500 words, the personalized list need not be longer than about 25 words. Importantly, since altering the vocabulary can impact other features, the appropriate corresponding inflected words were substituted. Similarly, the capitalization and punctuation in the essay was preserved in the substitution process.

The results showed that the strategy, for the most part, yielded no gains, but there was a chance between 10 percent and 15 percent of a gain of one or more points (on a six-point scale) for the lower score categories. However, there was also a chance as high as almost 30 percent of a one-point loss for higher-scoring essays. Clearly, the strategy would be effective with some probability but only for low-scoring test takers; the strategy would actually hurt higher-scoring test takers. This is reasonable since the strategy is limited to vocabulary.

The motivation in the Bejar et al. (2014) experiment was not to devise an optimal strategy but rather to illustrate the possibility of a scoring engine's vulnerability to CIRS due to the nature of the features it used. Indeed, devising an optimal strategy would not be simple since it would require access to a sizable corpus of essays to test the strategy, not to mention access to the scoring engine to measure the effect of the strategy. Nevertheless, the possibility exists that such effective strategies could be formulated. A possible protection against such strategies is not to rely entirely on automated scoring. That is, humans could detect a brute-force lexical substitution strategy, or other strategies, and retaining them in the scoring loop would offer a level of protection. Of course, involving humans in the scoring of every essay would limit the cost savings possible with automated scoring. Alternatively, ways of detecting the presence of CIRS by the scoring engine could be developed (Beigman Klebanov & Flor, 2013) to identify just those essays that deserve additional scrutiny.

Discourse Vulnerabilities: Argumentative Babbling

Whereas a lexical substitution strategy could be effective for lower-scoring test takers, the second example I would like to discuss is concerned with a discourse strategy that could be effective in increasing human and automated scores of students that are higher scoring. Specifically, students have been known to attempt gaining a better score by embellishing their essay with what has been called "shell language". This is text that, on the surface, appears relevant in response to a prompt, but in reality it is not responsive to it. For example, consider the following language.

> The argument rests on the assumption that A is analogous to B in all respects. This assumption is weak, since, although there are points of comparison between A and B, there is much similarity as well.

The text would be considered shell unless it is expanded to discuss similarities and dissimilarities between A and B. Although the term shell language originates in an admissions-testing context, it seems applicable more broadly to situations that are increasingly common in K-12 assessments where students are expected to incorporate authentic sources in their written responses. In that context, it is possible to imagine a strategy whereby the sources are mentioned or even quoted, although not necessarily in an appropriate manner.

Both human scoring *and* automated scoring are potentially vulnerable to shell language as a means of obtaining a higher score, and have motivated the development of tools to quantify shell language (Madnani, Heilman, Tetreault, & Chodorow, 2012). Automated scoring is potentially doubly vulnerable to the strategy because the human scores that are used in developing the scoring engine could be inflated *if* humans are vulnerable to the strategy. If so, function *F* will inherit that tendency as well. Under automated scoring, there is the added vulnerability that shell language elongates the text. Even if length is not explicitly used as a scoring feature, it potentially contributes to the scores through other features that are correlated with length (Powers, 2005).

To study the role of shell language in scoring, a means of quantifying shell language is needed. A tool has been developed (Madnani et al., 2012) with that purpose in mind,[5] and has been evaluated and found to work well for its purpose (Bejar et al., 2013). For example, the application of the tool to a large dataset suggested that the use of shell language, as measured by the software tool, is more prevalent in some test taking populations, as well as with GRE argument rather than issue prompts, as had been expected from anecdotal reports. Moreover, Bejar et al. (2016) showed the accuracy of the shell score by showing that the text identified by the software as shell overlapped greatly with the text that two experienced raters classified as shell. (While this example is from an admissions context, a similar investigation could be carried out in a K-12 context where the goal would be to detect references to sources that are not responsive to the task. For example, a task may call for the respondent to take into account two opposing sources. Merely restating the position of the two sources would not merit a higher score and could be considered "shell language".)

Given an automated and objective means to quantify shell, it becomes possible to evaluate the hypothesis that shell language can inflate human scores. Recall that shell language that is accompanied by appropriate analysis, is not considered shell. The shell identification tool developed by Madnani et al. (2012) simply quantifies the text that *potentially* is shell but does not evaluate whether the potential shell is accompanied by appropriate analysis. Nevertheless, given the positive evaluation of the tool by Bejar et al. (2013), there is reason to believe that the tool does identify text that is shell, since it confirmed that students from some regions do engage in that strategy more frequently.

To evaluate whether the presence of shell inflates human scores, Bejar et al. (2013) compared the scores assigned operationally and the scores obtained under more leisurely scoring conditions by highly experienced scorers. Presumably, under more leisurely conditions, raters would not be vulnerable to shell language. Therefore, contrasting operational scores with operational scores as a function of the amount of shell contained in the essays can be informative. Bejar et al. used the shell software tool to compute the amount of shell contained in essays from four prompts that had been first clustered by amount of shell language (three levels) and score level (four levels, by collapsing score 1 and 2, and score 5 and 6). This led to 24 essays, two from each possible combination of factors, for each of the four prompts, or 96 essays altogether.

Two highly experienced raters scored the 96 essays in non-operational mode but otherwise followed the operational scoring process. Although the inter-rater agreement between the two non-operational raters was high with a quadratic-weighted kappa of .82, there were also systematic differences between the two raters. Specifically, there were 11 examples of 3- to 4-point discrepancies out of the 31 discrepancies of one or two points. (Such 3- to 4-point score discrepancies have more consequence for the meaning of scores because there is a qualitative highly construct-relevant distinction, at least for GRE, between the upper half, scores 4 to 6, and the lower half, scores 1 to 3). In an effort to obtain scores as free of error as possible, the discrepancies were adjudicated and annotated by subject matter experts associated with GRE writing measure. Bejar et al. (2013) concluded that raters had been adequately trained to handle the presence of shell. In turn, this suggests that the data used to calibrate e-rater for GRE issue and argument essays are free from the potential effect of inflating scores due to the presence of shell text.

Summary

The increasing adoption of testing formats that go beyond the multiple-choice format is an extremely positive development for educational assessment but does create the operational challenge of scoring all the constructed responses that are subsequently generated. The desire to efficiently score this increasing number of student-constructed responses by using automated scoring is understandable but, given the high stakes associated with school performance, so is the motivation by students and school personnel to obtain high scores. A "perfect storm" could be created unless precautions are taken to detect response strategies that do not reflect and capture the desired evidence of student learning and, instead, are aimed at artificially maximizing the score.

In practice, there are many ways in which the meaning of automated scores under high-stakes testing could be diminished, among them the possibility that students engage in strategies designed to maximize their scores in a construct-irrelevant fashion. The anatomy of a scoring engine and its application was described to point out some of the vulnerabilities of automated scoring to construct-irrelevant response strategies (CIRS). Although the illustrations were limited to one scoring engine and one assessment test—the use of e-rater for the GRE Analytical Writing Measure—I believe the main argument is applicable to other scoring engines. That is, the decomposition of a scoring engine into the evidence identification and synthesis steps is applicable to any scoring engine. And both steps are potentially vulnerable to CIRS.

Two types of vulnerabilities were illustrated. The first example illustrated a case where feature extraction is potentially vulnerable to CIRS. The results suggested that an earlier version of e-rater was, in fact, vulnerable to a response strategy consisting of substituting more-sophisticated vocabulary. The strategy was found to be effective in the sense that the simulation of its application to existing essays led to increases in scores in a fraction of the lower-scoring essays, although the opposite was true for higher-scoring essays.

The second example evaluated the possibility that evidence synthesis could be vulnerable to CIRS. That illustration was based on the widely used evidence synthesis approach of regressing human scores on features extracted by the scoring engine. If human scores were vulnerable to the use of CIRS, the automated scores of essays could be affected in at least two ways. Assume the data used for evidence synthesis contains human scores that are inflated by the presence of CIRS. In that case, subsequent essays scored by the engine could be *under* scored if they do not rely on the same CIRS because the scoring engine has been developed to "value" CIRS. Alternatively, assume the data are free from CIRS, perhaps because they are from a portion of the test-taking population that is not motivated to engage in CIRS. In such a case, essays scored by the engine for test takers motivated to engage in CIRS could be *over* scored through, for example, the lengthening of the essay in a construct-irrelevant fashion.

Implications

In practice, the implications of vulnerabilities in feature extraction and synthesis depend on the role of automated scoring in arriving at the final task-level score. In the case of GRE, automated scoring is used as a check score (Monaghan & Bridgeman, 2005), which means that a human score is compared against the automated score. When the difference exceeds a threshold, a second human scorer is brought in. In this case, even if the automated score is vulnerable to CIRS, it may not present a problem so long as the human scorer is not vulnerable to the strategy, which was shown to be the case in the case of shell language in the GRE context. If, however, the automated score were to be used as the sole score, then the presence of CIRS could erode the meaning of scores unless they are detected by other means.

For example, responses produced at least in part by engaging in CIRS could appear as statistically atypical. Detecting such responses may be possible (Lochbaum et al., 2013). A possible approach is to view atypicality as a case of outlier detection. That is, a response is viewed as a point in a multivariate space defined by the features used by the scoring engine. Essay scores that are very distant from the centroid of that multivariate space are outliers. For example, a longer response is typically produced by a skilled writer. Thus, a long essay with an undue number of misspellings would be atypical and therefore potentially the result of applying an "elongating-the-essay strategy". (Although not publicly documented, univariate outliers are routinely screened for by e-rater but it is still possible for an observation to be a multivariate outlier, even when it is not an outlier with respect to individual features.)

As automated scoring becomes more widely implemented, it will be important to insure that scores are free from CIRS and other variability that would diminish their meaning. While it is important to have quality *control* measures in place with any assessment, quality *assurance* starts much earlier. In discussing quality assurance and control in automated scoring, Bejar (2011) distinguished between *quality defects* and *design defects*. A design defect is permanent until a redesign of the scoring engine addresses the limitation, whereas a quality defect is due to a temporary malfunction of some aspect of the scoring system. The absence of features to address performance aspects that are called for by the construct in scoring engines, such as argumentation, and appropriate reference to sources, is a design defect in that sense. Such construct underrepresentation makes the engine vulnerable to CIRS because the features that are present become even more distant proxies for the aspects of the construct that are not explicitly captured by the features, and potentially can be exploited to produce higher scores by means of CIRS.

Ideally, the design of a scoring engine includes, early on, an evaluation of the vulnerability of the scoring engine to CIRS so that steps can be taken to circumvent the vulnerability from the ground up by, among other things, covering the entire construct. Without a doubt, the automated scoring of textual responses will improve over time as task design and the requirements of judging evidence of student learning become better understood. Until such a time as these improvements prove adequate, quality control measures, including involving human raters in the process as needed is a prudent option.[6]

Acknowledgments

I am grateful to my colleagues, Don Powers and Michael Kane, and to two blind reviewers. Their comments and questions, I believe, have resulted in an improved chapter. I also appreciate the editors' invitation and encouragement.

Notes

1 Putting a price on the human scoring of constructed responses is not a simple matter. There are the fixed costs of developing a system to support the scoring and monitoring of the scoring process, as well as the variable labor costs associated with the compensation of scorers. That is, as the volume of constructed response scoring increases the cost component of human labor costs continues to increase as well. For example, Chingos (2013) estimated that for the Partnership for Assessment of Readiness for College and Careers (PARCC) consortium, scoring represented 75 percent of the cost of delivering the assessment but the cost depended on the assumed volume of responses to be scored. Automated scoring is less labor intensive although the development and maintenance of scoring systems is not trivial. Nevertheless, unlike human scoring, automated scoring should reduce the cost of scoring of each additional response.
2 It is not necessarily the case that the use of automated scoring would preclude the involvement of teachers in scoring. In fact, the use of automated scoring would mean having access to digital representations of performances, such as essays, and other constructed responses, which in principle make it feasible to design more-effective training materials.
3 Quality control is important even in in the process of scoring multiple-choice items as illustrated by the scoring of SAT® answers sheets (Booz Allen Hamilton, 2006). If such a mature scoring technology can occasionally fail, it is reasonable to assume that a more complex and recent technology can also fail.
4 It would be unrealistic, at least currently, to expect that automated scoring can score what humans cannot. That is, it is also the case that the human scoring process has limitations, as was painfully demonstrated by the performance-based assessments of the early 1990s (Stetcher, 2010), and discussions of the cognition of the human rating process (Bejar, 2012).
5 The essence of the approach is to detect text that is *similar* to exemplars of shell language. The measurement of text similarity is a standard natural language method (for an overview, see Gomaa & Fahmy, 2013).
6 For an overview of different ways to combine human and automated scoring, see Zhang (2013).

References

American Educational Research Association, American Psychological Association, & National Council on Measurement in Education (2014). *Standards for educational and psychological testing.* Washington, DC: American Educational Research Association.

Attali, Y., & Burstein, J. (2006). Automated essay scoring with e-rater® V. 2. *The Journal of Technology, Learning and Assessment, 4*(3), 3–30.

Beigman Klebanov, B., & Flor, M. (2013). Word association profiles and their use for automated scoring of essays. *Proceedings of the 51st Annual Meeting of the Association for Computational Linguistics,* (pp. 1148–1158). Sofia, Bulgaria: Association for Computational Linguistics (retrieved from http://aclweb.org/anthology/P/P13/P13-1113.pdf).

Bejar, I. I. (2011). A validity-based approach to quality control and assurance of automated scoring. *Assessment in Education, 18*(3), 319–341.

Bejar, I. I. (2012). Rater cognition: Implications for validity. *Educational Measurement: Issues and Practice, 31*(3), 2–9.

Bejar, I. I., VanWinkle, W., Madnani, N., Lewis, W., & Steier, M. (2013). Length of textual response as a construct–irrelevant response strategy: The case of shell language. Princeton, NJ: ETS (retrieved from www.ets.org/research/policy_research_reports/publications/report/2013/jpnv).

Bejar, I. I., Flor, M., Futagi, Y., & Ramineni, C. (2014). Effect of a construct-irrelevant response strategy (CIRS) on automated scoring of writing. *Assessing Writing, 22,* 48–59.

Bejar, I. I., Mislevy, R. J., & Zhang, M. (2016). Automated scoring with validity in mind. In A. Rupp & J. Leighton (Eds.), *The handbook of cognition and assessment: Frameworks, methodologies, and applications* (pp. 226–246). Hoboken, NJ: Wiley-Blackwell.

Bennett, R. E. (2010). Cognitively based assessment of, for, and as learning (CBAL): A preliminary theory of action for summative and formative assessment. *Measurement: Interdisciplinary Research & Perspective, 8*(2), 70–91.

Bennett, R. E., & Bejar, I. I. (1998). Validity and automated scoring: It's not only the scoring. *Educational Measurement: Issues and Practice, 17*(4), 9–16.

Ben-Simon, A., & Bennett, R. E. (2007). Toward more substantively meaningful automated essay scoring. *Journal of Technology, Learning, and Assessment, 6*(1) (available from www.jtla.org).

Booz Allen Hamilton. (May 26, 2006). *SAT process Review: Answer sheet processing* (retrieved from www.collegeboard.com/prod_downloads/satscoreprocessing/SAT_Process_Review_Final_Report.ppt).

Chingos, M. M. (2013). Standardized testing and the Common Core Standards: You get what you pay for? Washington, DC: Brown Center on Education Policy at Brookings (available from www.brookings.edu).

Deane, P. (2013). Covering the construct: An approach to automated essay scoring motivated by a socio-cognitive framework for defining literacy skills. In M. D. Shermis & J. Burstein (Eds.), *Handbook of automated essay evaluation: Current applications and new directions* (pp. 298–312). New York: Routledge.

Elliot, N., & Williamson, D. M. (2013). *Assessing Writing* special issue: Assessing writing with automated scoring systems. *Assessing Writing, 18*(1), 1–6 (available from www.sciencedirect.com/science/article/pii/S1075293512000517).

Frederiksen, N. (1984). The real test bias: Influences of testing on teaching and learning. *American Psychologist, 39,* 193–202.

Goldberg, G. L. (2012). Judgment-based scoring by teachers as professional development: Distinguishing promises from proof. *Educational Measurement: Issues and Practice, 31*(3), 38–47.

Gomaa, W. H., & Fahmy, A. A. (2013). A survey of text similarity approaches. *International Journal of Computer Applications, 68*(13), 13–18.

Heller, J. I., Sheingold, K., & Myford, C. M. (1998). Reasoning about evidence in portfolios: Cognitive foundations for valid and reliable assessment. *Educational Assessment, 5*(1), 5–40.

Higgins, D., & Heilman, M. (2014). Managing what we can measure: Quantifying the susceptibility of automated scoring systems to gaming behavior. *Educational Measurement: Issues and Practice, 33*(3), 36–46.

Koretz, D., & Hamilton, L. S. (2006). Testing for accountability in K-12. In R. Brennan (Ed.), *Educational measurement* (4th ed., pp. 531–578). Westport, CT: Praeger.

Lane, S., & Stone, C. (2006). Performance assessment. In R. L. Brennan (Ed.), *Educational measurement (4th ed.)* (pp. 387–431). Westport, CT: Praeger.

Lochbaum, K. E., Foltz, P. W., Rosentein, M. B., Derr, M. A., & Farnham, D. (2013). *Detection of gaming in automated scoring of essays with the IEA.* Paper presented at the National Council of Measurement in Education, San Francisco, CA.

Madnani, N., Heilman, M., Tetreault, J., & Chodorow, M. (2012). *Identifying high-level organizational elements in argumentative discourse.* Paper presented at the 2012 Conference of the North American Chapter of the Association for Computational Linguistics: Human Language Technologies, Montreal, Canada (available from www.aclweb.org/anthology-new/N/N12/N12-1003.pdf).

Messick, S. (1994). The interplay of evidence and consequences in the validation of performance assessments. *Educational Researcher, 23*(2), 13–23.

Mislevy, R. J., Steinberg, L., Almond, R. G., & Lucas, J. F. (2006). Concepts, terminology, and basic models of evidence-centered design. In D. M. Williamson, R. J. Mislevy & I. I. Bejar (Eds.), *Automated scoring of complex tasks in computer-based testing* (pp. 49–82). Mahwah, NJ: Lawrence Erlbaum.

Monaghan, W., & Bridgeman, B. (April 2005). E-rater as a quality control of human scores. *R&D Connections*. Princeton, NJ Educational testing Service (retrieved from www.ets.org/Media/Research/pdf/RD_Connec tions2.pdf).

Myford, C. M., & Mislevy, R. J. (1995). Monitoring and improving a portfolio assessment system. Princeton, NJ: Educational Testing Service (retrieved from www.cse.ucla.edu/products/Reports/TECH402.pdf).

Nijveldt, A., Beijaard, D., Brekelmans, M., Wubbels, T., & Verloop, N. (2009). Assessors' perceptions of their judgement processes: Successful strategies and threats underlying valid assessment of student teachers. *Studies in Educational Evaluation, 35*, 29–36.

Perelman, L. (2014). When "the state of the art" is counting words. *Assessing Writing, 21*, 104–111.

Powers, D. E. (2005). "Wordiness": A selective review of its influence, and suggestions for investigating its relevance in tests requiring extended written responses. Princeton, NJ: Educational Testing Service.

Powers, D. E., Burstein, J. C., Chodorow, M. S., Fowles, M. E., & Kukick, K. (2002). Stumping e-rater: Challenging the validity of automated essay scoring. *Computers in Human Behavior, 18*, 103–134.

Quinlan, T., Higgins, D., & Wolff, S. (2009). Evaluating the construct-coverage of e-rater®. Princeton, NJ: ETS.

Shermis, M. D., & Burstein, J. (2013). *Handbook of automated essay evaluation*: New York: Routledge Academic.

Stetcher, B. (2010). Performance assessment in an era of standards-based educational accountability. Stanford, CA: Stanford University, Stanford Center for Opportunity Policy in Education (retrieved from https://scale.stanford.edu/system/files/performance-assessment-era-standards-based-educational-accountability.pdf).

Winerip, M. (2012). Facing a Robo-Grader? Just Keep Obfuscating Mellifluously, *New York Times* (retrieved from www.nytimes.com/2012/04/23/education/robo-readers-used-to-grade-test-essays.html).

Yang, Y., Buckendahl, C. W., Juszkiewicz, P. J., & Bhola, D. S. (2002). A review of strategies for validating computer-automated scoring. *Applied Measurement in Education, 15*(4), 391–412.

Yu, G. (2010). Lexical diversity in writing and speaking task performances. *Applied Linguistics, 31*(2), 236–259.

Zhang, M. (2013). Contrasting automated and human scoring of essays. Princeton, NJ: Educational Testing Service.

Zhang, M., Dorans, N., Li, C., & Rupp, A. (2015). *Differential feature functioning in automated scoring in large-scale assessments.* Paper presented at the 5th Annual Maryland Assessment Conference. College Park, MD.

8 The Contribution of Student Response Processes to Validity Analyses for Instructionally Supportive Assessments

Louis V. DiBello, James W. Pellegrino,
Brian D. Gane, and Susan R. Goldman

Increasing attention is being paid to the need for systems of assessments, with an emphasis on the design and use of assessments intended to function much closer to the processes of teaching and learning (e.g., Gordon Commission, 2013; National Research Council, 2003; Pellegrino, Chudowsky, & Glaser, 2001; Pellegrino, Wilson, Koenig, & Beatty, 2014; Briggs, Diaz-Bilello, Peck, et al., 2015). Thus, there is need for careful consideration of the design and validation of assessments intended for classroom use for both formative and summative purposes. A recent paper by Pellegrino, DiBello, and Goldman (2016) articulates a framework for considering the validity of classroom supportive assessment that includes three components: *cognitive, instructional, and inferential*. The present paper briefly reviews this validity framework, and examines the connections between student response process data and other types of data and evidence that support the validation process.

All three of these validity components – cognitive, instructional, and inferential – relate to response processes elicited as students engage with assessment tasks. Cognitive components of validity are directly related to thinking and reasoning while a student interacts with the stimulus materials and response demands of specific tasks. Whether assessment outcomes are instructionally meaningful depends upon the extent to which student response processes correspond to the intended aspects of knowledge, skill, and performance as specified in standards or curriculum materials. Inferential components of validity depend on an interpretation of the meaning of assessment task scores in terms of student response processes, how well the scoring rubrics and outcome scores capture the underlying cognitive constructs, and effects of measurement and estimation error on interpretations of assessment outcome scores.

The first section reviews key aspects of the validity framework for assessments intended to directly benefit instructors and students (see Pellegrino et al., 2016 for a detailed discussion). To ground the discussion, the second section provides an example of applying this framework to diagnostic assessments from the *Physics Diagnoser* system that focuses on conceptual understanding and reasoning in middle and high school physical science. In particular we interpret student response process data in relation to other sources of data in order to construct a validity argument for the interpretation and use of the assessment outcome results. The paper concludes with a consideration of the need for careful and consistent application of the validity analysis framework, including collection of response process data, in the design of integrated sets of curriculum, and instructional and assessment resources.

Assessment Validity: Argumentation and Evidence

Assessment of student knowledge and proficiency should be construed as a process of reasoning from evidence that is coupled to theories, models, and data on the forms of competence in specific areas of the curriculum and their development through processes of instruction and learning (e.g., Pellegrino et al., 2001). The design of assessments should be guided by several factors, including research and theory about the nature of knowledge in the domain and the intended interpretive use of the results. A principled design process, such as evidence-centered design (e.g., Mislevy & Riconscente, 2006), can help translate theory and research about cognition and learning into an operational assessment that yields evidence aligned with the assessment's intended purpose and interpretive use.

The validity of an assessment for a particular interpretive use depends on features of its design that have been integrated with evidence to back up claims about what an assessment is intended to do along with evidence about how well it actually does so. Just as assessment design has to make clear the evidentiary process of inferring about student proficiencies from scored student performance, multiple forms of evidence are required to support the validity argument for any given assessment intended to function close to classroom teaching and learning.

Multiple Components of Validity

Current, argument-based views of assessment validity espoused by Kane (2006) and others (Haertel & Lorié, 2004; Mislevy, Steinberg, & Almond, 2003), frame test validity as a reasoned argument backed by evidence (e.g., Kane, 2006, 2013) that consists of an interpretive argument, i.e., the propositions that underpin test score interpretation, and the evidence and arguments that provide the necessary warrants for the propositions of the interpretive argument. These contemporary views consolidate aspects of Messick's construct-centered views (Messick, 1989, 1994) of validity as a unified judgment consisting of multiple components that include construct and consequential components of validity related to the interpretive uses of test scores.

For assessment specifically designed to support ongoing classroom teaching and learning, Pellegrino et al. (2016) proposed a specific validity framework that identifies three related components of validity – cognitive, instructional, and inferential – as follows.

1   **Cognitive** – This component of validity addresses the extent to which an assessment taps important forms of domain knowledge and skill in ways that are not confounded with other aspects of cognition such as language or working memory load. Cognitive validity should be based on what is known about the nature of student cognition and understanding in areas of the curriculum such as literacy, mathematics, and science and how it develops over time with instruction to determine what knowledge and skills students are supposed to use and those that they actually do use when interacting with the assessment (e.g., Duschl, Schweingruber, & Shouse, 2007; Kilpatrick, Swafford, & Findell, 2001).
2   **Instructional** – This component addresses the extent to which an assessment is aligned with curriculum and instruction, including students' opportunities to learn, as well as how it supports teaching practice by providing valuable and timely instruction-related information. Instructional validity should be based on evidence about alignment of the assessment with skills of interest as defined by standards and curricula, the practicality and usefulness for teachers, and the nature of the assessment as a guide to instruction (e.g., Black, Harrison, Lee, Marshall, & Wiliam, 2004; Heritage, 2010; Kingston & Nash, 2011; Wiliam, 2007).
3   **Inferential** – This component is concerned with the extent to which an assessment reliably and accurately yields model-based information about student performance, especially for diagnostic purposes. Inferential validity should be based on evidence derived from various analytic methods, including multivariate measurement and statistical inference (e.g., van der Linden & Hambleton, 1997; DiBello, Henson, & Stout, 2015), to determine whether task performance reliably aligns with an underlying conceptual measurement model that is appropriate to the intended interpretive use.

As noted above, these components are identified for the particular assessment context of classroom use. They reorganize classical aspects of validity for best supporting a validity claim about

Table 8.1 Data Collection Activities and Potential Contributions to the Three Components of Validity

Data Collection Activity	Cognitive Validity	Instructional Validity	Inferential Validity
Expert Analyses	How well the design incorporates cognitively critical forms of knowledge and understanding; ethnic and cultural sensitivity review.	How well the design supports and aligns with instructional needs and uses and promotes teacher understanding.	How well the intended constructs are incorporated within the design; appropriateness of scoring rubrics and inferential models.
Student Cognitive Protocol Studies	How well do student engagement with assessment activities and student response processes correspond to design intent? How well do scoring and assessment outcomes reveal actual student thinking, proficiencies and performance; issues regarding linguistic and cultural diversity?	How well do assessment outcomes including test and item scores represent intended student knowledge, thinking and response processes, according to instructional goals and benchmarks? How well do assessment outcomes support teacher decisions and actions?	How well does actual student engagement with assessment activities, both student response processes and work products, support analytic models, including model parameter interpretations, covariance analyses, and relationships to other variables?
Teacher Surveys Teacher Logs Teacher Interviews	How well do teacher interpretations of student outcomes align with design intent of assessment activities? What is revealed about student understandings? What response processes would be expected?	How well do teachers understand and use the assessments and assessment outcomes? How well are differential decisions and actions supported? What was teachers' actual use?	Score report design and usability; teacher knowledge about and use of score reliabilities, item difficulties, expected student responses and variations.
Classroom Observations	How sensitive are assessments to opportunities to learn relative to assessment targets; how does actual instruction support measured proficiencies; how does classroom discourse promote intended student thinking and response processes?	How faithfully do teachers use assessments and what use do they make of assessment outcomes?	How sensitive is assessment performance and statistical and psychometric modeling to variability in instruction and conditions of assessment administration, and classroom uses of assessment outcomes?
Studies of Item and Test Performance	How well do item and test performance work products and scores reflect underlying cognitive processing demands? How well do assessment outcomes at test and item levels reflect underlying cognition and student response processes?	How well do assessment outcomes support instructional needs including formative uses, summative monitoring of progress, and connections to external assessments?	How well do model-based analyses support the intended purpose and use of assessments, including scale score and diagnostic profile reliability, model-data fit and dimensionality, differential functioning for linguistic and ethnic groups, predictive validity, and alignment with other tests?

assessment intended to support instruction and learning at the classroom level. For instance, cognitive validity includes aspects of Messick's construct validity; instructional validity incorporates content and consequential validity; and inferential validity is related to both score reliability and criterion validity. In general the three components overlap. For example, claims about instructional and inferential components of validity depend upon aspects of the cognitive component of validity. In addition, as noted throughout this paper, multiple elements of student response processes are critical forms of evidence for each of the validity components.

Multiple Forms of Evidence

Evidence to support each of these components of validity can come from multiple complementary and convergent sources, as illustrated in Table 8.1. We have intentionally included a range of data sources, including several sources of student response process data, to suggest the breadth and depth of validity analyses that might be conducted with assessments designed to function close to classroom teaching and learning. When well-designed protocols are applied to appropriately constructed assessment arguments, the overlaps among the data and the components enrich and round out the validity argument and evidence.

Each box in Table 1 describes how that particular type of data *might* provide evidence with respect to each component of validity. Whether such data does in fact provide evidence depends on the design of the protocols used for data collection, on identification of subject samples, and on conditions under which assessment data are collected relative to instruction and opportunities to learn. Data collection activities need to be carefully structured so they elicit evidence that is relevant to the validity components of concern to the assessment designer and/or researcher.

A strong validity argument for assessments intended to support classroom teaching and learning depends upon evidence that all three components of validity are high relative to assessment purpose and use. For example, a high Cronbach alpha coefficient only has value if the score reflects instructionally meaningful information. High alignment between the conceptual foundations for an assessment and learning standards will only help teachers if student response processes correspond well with question design and scoring.

We have used this framework to investigate the validity of several instructionally relevant assessments, including: (a) concept inventories that have increasingly come to be used in STEM education settings spanning middle school through university instruction (see e.g., Jorion, Gane, James, et al., 2015); (b) assessment materials embedded within K-8 mathematics curricula (see e.g., Pellegrino et al., 2016). In this chapter, as a concrete illustration of how particular sources of evidence can contribute to multiple components of validity, we discuss our analysis of the *Diagnoser* facet-based diagnostic assessments for middle school and high school physical science instruction (Minstrell, 2001). We utilize evidence derived from three of the sources of data shown in Table 8.1: (a) student cognitive laboratory studies, (b) expert reviews, and (c) statistical analyses of scored student performance.

Application of the Conceptual and Evidentiary Validity Framework to the *Diagnoser* System for Middle School and High School Physical Science

Overview of the Diagnoser *System*

The *Physics Diagnoser* system (available through http://diagnoser.com) integrates key aspects of Newtonian mechanics for multiple middle and high school level physics curricula. The domain *Force and Motion* is organized into three strands: "Description of Motion," "Nature of Forces," and "Forces to Explain Motion," divided into 17 units of instruction (see Table 2). *Diagnoser* instructional units are defined as clusters of identifiable *facets* of desired and problematic thinking

Table 8.2 Three Strands and seventeen clusters within *Diagnoser* Force and Motion

Three Strands of Force and Motion

Description of Motion	Nature of Forces	Forces to Explain Motion
• Position and Distance	• Identifying Forces	• Effects of Pushes and Pulls
• Change in Direction	• Forces Acting at a Distance	• Explaining Constant Speed
• Determining Speed	• Forces as Interactions	• Explaining Changes in 1D Motion
• Average Speed	• Gravitational Forces	• Explaining Changes in 2D Motion
• Change in Speed	• Magnetic Forces	
• Acceleration	• Electric Forces	
	• Electromagnetic	

Source: http://diagnoser.com

(Hunt & Minstrell, 1994; Minstrell, 2001; Minstrell, Anderson, & Li, 2011). The facet clusters provide a conceptual framework for teachers to use to monitor student thinking and to manage classroom dialogue and instructional activities.

Diagnoser includes a set of diagnostic assessments called *question sets* that are tightly integrated into the instructional system and designed to provide information about students' desirable and problematic facets of thinking. The system also includes learning goals, elicitation questions to use in early discussions for a given instructional unit, developmental lessons, and prescriptive activities for teachers to use based on students' diagnostic question set outcomes. The *Diagnoser* system is intended to support an instructional approach called "Building on Learner Thinking" (BOLT) (Minstrell, Anderson, Kraus, & Minstrell, 2008; Minstrell et al., 2011) in which teachers, informed by evidence from the diagnostic question sets about student thinking, pose activities and manage and promote classroom dialogue to help students build on their current thinking.

Diagnoser Facets and Clusters

Each instructional unit is called a *cluster* and is defined as a set of desired and problematic facets of student thinking. The facets and clusters were identified to represent prominent ways that students think about forces and motion, and are based on teaching experience and research conducted by Minstrell and colleagues, and on physics misconceptions research (Minstrell, 1992, 2001). The student's current thinking represents an origination point from which the teacher can help the student progress.

For example, the cluster called "Explaining Constant Speed" within the strand "Forces to Explain Motion" is composed of five specific facets: one goal facet and four problematic facets.

- (DF00 – this is the goal facet) The student knows that when the forces on an object are balanced, the object is either at rest or moving with a constant speed in a straight line.
- (PF30) The student thinks that balanced forces cannot apply to both the constant speed and at rest situations.
- (PF70) The student thinks that if an object is moving at constant speed, there must be an unbalanced force in the direction of motion.
- (PF80) The student believes that if an object is pushed or pulled and it remains at rest, there must be a force keeping it at rest that is larger than the pushing or pulling force.
- (PF90) The student believes that when an object is at rest, some or all of the forces must be zero.

A finer breakdown of the facets is available (see http://diagnoser.com for full details). Facet codes with higher numbers indicate more-serious conceptual problems for students. For instance, PF70, PF80, and PF90 are considered more problematic than PF30. The numerical order is approximate, not a strict linear order among the problematic facets.

The *Diagnoser* question sets, designed to provide diagnostic information about student facets of thinking, are made up primarily of multiple-choice questions in which each response option is linked to a desirable or problematic facet of thinking. Occasionally, a response option is linked to "unknown," indicating that the response should not be considered evidence in favor of any identified facet from the associated cluster. Two sample questions and their facet links from QS1 of the cluster *Explaining Constant Speed* are shown in Figure 8.1.

The question sets are designed to diagnose what kind of student thinking led to the student's particular response. Teachers can view a *Diagnoser* teacher report that summarizes student performance by giving average proportion correct across the class, and proportions of students endorsing each problematic facet. Online resources suggest how teachers can use that information to make instructional decisions, plan activities, and manage classroom dialogue.

Validity Issues for Diagnoser Question Sets

Given the set of interacting instructional and assessment claims relative to the *Diagnoser* system's intended use, we discuss next evidence about the interpretive quality of the facet-based assessments as related to the system's design and intended use – how well the question set outcomes

---

Question Q1

John observed his little sister pushing on a block. Because he was studying forces at school, John wondered about the motion of the block in the situation in which all of the forces on the block were balanced.

Choose the answer below you agree with the most.

- [a] ◉ The block could be going at any constant speed, including being at rest.
- [b] ◉ The bock would have to be at rest.
- [c] ◉ The block would have to be moving at a constant speed.
- [d] ◉ The block would have to be slowing down.

Question Q3

John's sister put the block on a very slippery table and gave it a shove. After she let go, the block slid across the table with an almost **constant speed**.

The block is sliding to the right.

Which statement below best describes the **horizontal forces** on the block as it slides across the table to the right?

- [a] ◉ The force to the right is zero; the frictional force to the left is very small.
- [b] ◉ The force to the right is greater than the frictional force to the left.
- [c] ◉ A force of motion to the right is proportional to the speed.
- [d] ◉ A constant force of motion keeps the block moving to the right.

Figure 8.1 Questions Q1 and Q3 of *Diagnoser* Question Set 1 in the cluster *Explaining Constant Speed*

Source: http://diagnoser.com

Note
The facet codes linked to each response option for Q1 are [a]=DF00, [b]=PF30, [c]=PF80, and [d]=PF70; for Q3 the facet code links to each option are [a]=DF00, [b]=PF70, [c]=PF70, and [d]=PF70.

serve teachers' formative classroom use. In particular, we focus first on cognitive laboratory studies to investigate student response processes directly, and then we briefly discuss other sources of data and how they relate to and support the student response process data. Collectively, our analyses of these data establish an argument for the validity of the *Diagnoser* system relative to its intended purpose and use.

Student response processes are examined directly through cognitive laboratory data about the extent to which the facets linked to response options reflect actual student thinking and responses. We relate the cognitive laboratory findings to other sources of data that reflect on the overall validity of the *Diagnoser* system: (a) how well the facets and clusters align to recognized standards of learning; (b) representativeness of the identified facets within accepted learning goals and problematic student thinking; (c) evidence for the claimed relationships among facets, questions, and response options; and (d) statistical and psychometric properties of scored student responses.

To address the foregoing questions we describe three quite different sources of data and related analyses that focus on the *Diagnoser* question sets: (a) cognitive laboratory studies with students, (b) expert review and alignment studies, and (c) statistical analyses of a large online *Diagnoser* data set. We focus on how these data provide complementary evidence about cognitive, instructional, and inferential components of validity of the diagnostic assessments.

Empirical Evidence of Diagnoser Validity: Cognitive Laboratory Studies

The cognitive laboratory studies directly probed students' response processing as they answered *Diagnoser* questions. The studies sought evidence about how well student thinking corresponds to question design and mapping of question responses to facets (DeBarger, Feng, Fujii, Ructtinger, Harris, & Haertel (2014).

Method and Findings

Sixty middle school students were asked to think aloud as they answered questions from the *Diagnoser* Cluster titled *Explaining Constant Speed*. Student utterances were transcribed and coded by researchers with physics content expertise. Two independent codings were given to student utterances: a Reasoning Code (*facet reasoning* – *FR*, *non-facet reasoning* – *NFR*, or *neither*) and a Match Code (*match* – *M* or *non-match* – *NM*). The Reasoning Code *FR* indicated that a student's reasoning aligned with either a goal or problematic facet from this cluster. The Reasoning Code *NFR* indicated that the student used physics reasoning that was not matched to one of the facets from the given cluster, but that either (a) matched a desirable or problematic facet from a different cluster, or (b) represented other physics reasoning not connected directly to any *Diagnoser* facet. The Reasoning Code *neither* was given for non-physics reasoning or non-reasoning. Multiple utterances by a student answering one question could be given multiple Reasoning Codes. A student was given a Match Code *M* if the student's reasoning matched the facet that was explicitly linked to their answer choice, or *NM* if reasoning did not match. The Reasoning and Match Codes were assigned in independent rounds of coding.

We discuss an example of coding the utterances from two different students for Q3 which was shown earlier in Figure 8.1. Q3 is from question set 1 on *Explaining Constant Speed*. First, one student who chose option [b] (linked to PF70) gave the following utterance:

- "[b] That would also make sense because, once again, the forces on it is moving to the left—I mean to the—the block is sliding to the right, and so it wouldn't have—there would be a greater force to the right rather than the left because it's moving to the right . . ." *This utterance was given* Reasoning Code *FR -PF70 and* Match Code *Match.*

An utterance from another student who also selected option [b] (linked to PF70) was:

- "[b] That actually makes more sense than the previous one because if it's greater than its frictional force, that means it can still be moving . . ." *This utterance was given* Reasoning Code *Non-Facet Reasoning (NFR), and was therefore given* Match Code *Non-Match (NM).*

The first utterance is consistent with the problematic reasoning identified in the facet linked to option [b] PF70: "The student thinks that if an object is moving at constant speed, there must be an unbalanced force in the direction of motion." So this utterance was coded with Reasoning Code *FR* and Match Code *M*. The second student's reasoning does not match any facets in this cluster. In particular, the reasoning does not correspond to the posited problematic facet PF70 linked to selected response [b]. Thus the second utterance was coded *NFR* and *NM*.

Match code data from 60 students who responded to the same QS1 from the cluster *Explaining Constant Speed* is given in the top panel of Figure 8.2. Of 32 students who chose the correct answer (linked to Desired Facet DF00), 22 of them (69 percent) were given Match Codes *M* for reasoning that matched DF00. By contrast, only eight of the 28 students (29 percent) who selected an incorrect answer were coded as matching the problematic facet linked to their response option.

The middle and bottom panels of Figure 8.2 show the Reasoning Codes for question sets QS1 and QS2 from the cluster *Explaining Constant Speed*. A number of different Reasoning Codes were defined to indicate multiple types of reasoning (see Fujii, Haertel, & McElhaney, 2015). For simplicity, the detailed Reasoning Codes were combined into three categories: Desirable Reasoning (*DR*), Undesirable Physics Reasoning (*UR*), and Non-Physics Reasoning (*NPR*). Recall that a student may receive a separate Reasoning Code for each of multiple utterances on a given question. For each question the graphs give the proportion of Reasoning Codes in each of the three categories out of all Reasoning Codes assigned for that question. For each question in QS1, the proportion of *DR* codes was greater than 50 percent, whereas for three of the seven questions in QS2, the proportions of *DR* codes were 40 percent or less.

Summary of Findings and Implications

Cognitive laboratories provide a window on student response processes and allow for an evaluation of the consistency between thinking as reflected in a student's utterances and the posited thinking for questions' facet-linked response options. Data revealed both consistent and inconsistent student reasoning with the *Explaining Constant Speed* facets of thinking, and greater consistency by students who selected the correct response, as compared to students who selected an incorrect response (see Figure 8.2) (Fujii et al., 2015). These findings are preliminary and represent only one of the question sets. Also, greater non-matches for students selecting wrong answers may be confounded with student difficulties in verbally articulating their problematic thinking. That is, students may in fact be influenced by PF70 thinking but may not articulate PF70 ideas well in think-aloud utterances (e.g., see work on recapitulating reasoning by Nisbett & Wilson, 1977; also see Madhyastha & Hunt, 2009).

Empirical Evidence of Diagnoser Validity: Expert Reviews

We discuss two further sources of validity evidence – expert reviews and analysis of scored student responses – to complement and support the student response process data.

Method and Findings

Six expert panelists, selected for collective expertise in physics instruction, science standards, physics content, and cognitive science, reviewed the alignment of the tasks and facet clusters. They

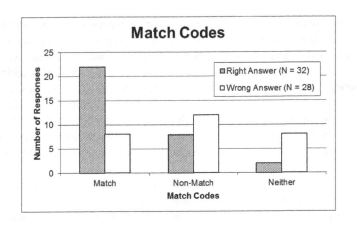

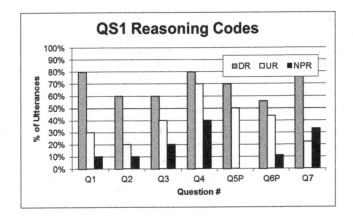

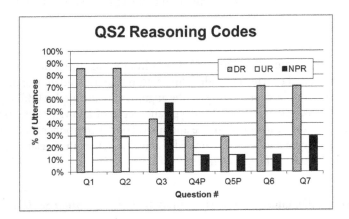

Figure 8.2 Cluster 15, Question Sets 1 and 2 Match and Reasoning Code Summaries

Source: Fujii et al., 2015

Notes

The top histogram summarizes match code data for cognitive laboratory study of *Diagnoser* QS 1 from *Explaining Constant Speed*.

The middle and bottom graphs are for QS1 and QS2, respectively. Each bar gives the proportion of coded utterances that were assigned a particular reasoning code.

A variety of specific reasoning codes were combined into three summary codes: *DR* = desired reasoning; *UR* = undesired physics reasoning; and *NPR* = non-physics reasoning.

These data were taken from a sample of 60 middle school students.

responded separately for each of four judgments: (a) alignment between the facets and *AAAS Benchmarks for Science Literacy* (American Association for the Advancement of Science (AAAS), 1993); (b) extent to which the problematic facets within the 17 clusters were representative of misconceptions as established within physics misconception research and panelists' teaching experience; (c) alignment between each response option and the facet code to which it is linked; and (d) alignment between questions and responses with Type of Knowledge (Li, Shavelson, & White, 2002; Ruiz-Primo, Shavelson, Hamilton, & Klein, 2002) as well as Level of Knowledge (Hess, 2010; Webb, 2002).

Alignment between facet clusters and AAAS Benchmarks. Panelists rated an existing mapping provided by developers and agreed that the benchmarks were assigned appropriately for 11 of the 17 clusters.

Representativeness of Problematic Facets. Across all 17 clusters and three panelists, 88 percent of ratings of representation of problematic thinking were good or very good. One panelist rated only one cluster as poor. For a few clusters, questions were raised about the nature of one of the problematic facets within the cluster.

Alignment Between Question Response Options and Linked Facets. The 17 Force and Motion clusters included 32 question sets with a total of 218 questions or pairs of questions, and 916 response options. For every question and response option, panelists rated the alignment of the facet linked to that option as appropriate (score 2), somewhat appropriate (score 1), or not appropriate (score 0). Eleven of the 32 question sets received alignment scores of 0.80 or more; nine question sets received alignment scores between 0.60 and 0.71, and the remaining 12 question sets received average alignment scores between 0.20 and 0.56. Alignment scoring was relatively consistent across panelists for most question sets (see Fujii et al., 2015 for more details).

Type and Level of Knowledge. The experts found that most questions elicit declarative knowledge and some elicit schematic knowledge. Procedural knowledge was elicited heavily in some question sets and infrequently in others, reflecting the nature of the content. Strategic knowledge was not elicited at all in the questions. All questions were rated Level 1 (recall and reproduction: 202 questions out of 218 – 93 percent) or Level 2 (skills and concepts: 16 questions out of 218 – 7 percent). No questions were rated Level 3 (strategic thinking) or Level 4 (extended thinking).

Implications

These findings bear on cognitive, instructional, and inferential components of validity of the *Diagnoser* assessments, and provide grounding for interpreting the student response process data discussed above. For example, expert ratings of the alignment to normative thinking and forms of problematic thinking, as well as ratings of the type and depth of knowledge elicited by the questions, provide direct evidence about cognitive and instructional components of validity. Acceptability of the ratings of type and level of knowledge must be determined relative to the intended design and interpretive use of the question sets.

Empirical Evidence of Diagnoser Validity: Analysis of Online Question Set Data

We next discuss an analysis of scored student performance data as complementary evidence for interpreting student response process data and for constructing an overall validity argument. We investigated a large online dataset from the *Diagnoser* website. We relate the findings to both the expert review and cognitive laboratory studies.

Diagnoser Student Question Set Performances

In this study we examined an online *Diagnoser* dataset that included more than 317,000 completed question set records from 61,000 students in classrooms of approximately 830 teachers. The large dataset is challenging to interpret, in part because it lacks direct information about the instructional context for *Diagnoser* use. *Diagnoser* is openly and freely available on the web for use by any instructor, and an investigation of use by students within particular classes of given teachers revealed a wide range of patterns of use. For instance, students in some classes completed both question sets of a cluster on the same day. Other class uses were more spaced out, showing a week or more between completions of QS1 and QS2 of a cluster. Spaced use allows at least the possibility that relevant instruction has occurred within that class between the two QS performances. By contrast, responding to both QS1 and QS2 on the same day ensures that there can have been little to no instruction between the two question set performances, implying that any learning that might have occurred between QS1 and QS2 was the result of massed practice on the QS sets along with the inter-item feedback (inter-item feedback is discussed further below) (Gane, Okoroh, DiBello, & Minstrell, 2015).

Student Response Patterns: Effects of Inter-Item Feedback

Diagnoser question sets are designed to be diagnostic, and a strong validity claim is that student selection of particular response options provides an observable indicator of important aspects of student thinking. In particular, beyond right or wrong, selection of a response option linked to a particular facet code is considered evidence for the teacher in favor of the claim that the student used that facet of thinking to make that response. This provides an example, at least in theory, of an assessment whose scoring directly supports a multivariate latent space in which a student may hold one or more problematic facets of thinking to be triggered in particular problem scenarios.

In general, clusters are made up of 4 to 7 problematic facets and QS sets have 7 to 10 questions. For purposes of interpreting QS data, we note that the *Diagnoser* assessments present immediate, inter-item feedback to students after each question. When students answer an item incorrectly, a feedback screen describes the problematic thinking in which they might be engaged. Sometimes students are served a related item immediately, to provide an opportunity to use the prior feedback to answer this item. Thus, the *Diagnoser* assessments mix assessment with dynamic instruction that may support some learning as students complete the assessment.

We examined patterns of use of a small sample of teachers (N = 23) to identify possible proxies for opportunities to learn as a way of qualifying the interpretation of student performance data. We filtered the data to include only classrooms where students completed QS1 before QS2 of a cluster, and identified two groups of such classrooms: group A where students did both question sets within a single burst of 1 to 3 days, and group B where the two question sets were separated in time by more than a week between QS1 and QS2 (multiple bursts).

To interpret student performance, we used analytic methods that take account of correct answers – student proportion correct across a question set – as well as the problematic facets to which any wrong answers are linked. For each facet we computed the student's proportion of questions answered with that facet out of all questions available that included a response option linked to that facet, i.e., out of all affordances of that facet for a given QS.

Figures 8.3a and 8.3b show the mean proportion of times that students endorsed desired and problematic facets on each of QS1 and QS2. In both groups A and B, the mean proportion endorsed of the desired facet is higher on QS2 than on QS1. The difference is larger in the single-burst group (Group A) than in the two-burst group (Group B), consistent with students forgetting over a longer retention interval. After completing QS1 (including inter-item feedback), students endorsed fewer problematic facets and more goal facets when completing QS2. These findings are consistent with an instructional sensitivity pattern.

Experience in working directly with teachers on *Diagnoser* has been that the clusters of desirable and problematic facets of thinking and related diagnostic question sets are formatively useful for teachers. Thus it is worth conducting further cognitive laboratory studies and probing more deeply into the available online data to understand what they reveal in terms of student response processes, relative to aspects of cognitive, instructional, and inferential validity.

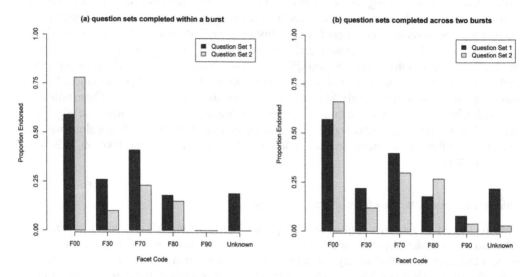

Figures 8.3a & 8.3b Proportion of desired facet (F00) and problematic facets (F30, F70, F80, F90, unknown) endorsed by students for Question Sets 1 & 2 of the cluster "Explaining Constant Speed, Cluster 15"

Notes

Figure 8.3a shows aggregate student data ($N = 66$) from 1 teacher (4 classrooms) in which classes completed both question sets within the same burst of activity (mean days between completions = 0.4 days, $SD = 1.4$ days).

Figure 8.3b shows aggregate student data ($N = 79$) from 2 teachers (7 classrooms) in which classes completed both question sets across two different bursts of activity ($M = 18.0$ days, $SD = 6.4$ days).

Conclusions Regarding Validity Components and the Diagnoser Assessments

Collectively these analyses – (a) student cognitive laboratory studies, (b) expert review and alignment studies, and (c) analysis of scored student performance on question sets relative to patterns of *Diagnoser* online use – benefit our discussion in two ways. They provide convergent sources of evidence about multiple components of validity of the *Physics Diagnoser* diagnostic assessment question sets for formative classroom use, and they ground the examination of student response processes within a fuller validity analysis.

The cognitive laboratory studies showed mixed evidence of consistency between student thinking and the expected facet thinking linked to student responses, with a stronger match for students who selected the right answer, as compared to students who selected wrong answers. Since the diagnosis of student response processes and problematic thinking is central to the *Diagnoser* intended purpose and use, these preliminary findings provide important evidence for revision and improvement of the questions and question sets. Expert reviewers found moderate evidence of alignment to standards and representation of learning goals, and to the problematic student thinking as identified in physics education research. Their findings help ground the analysis of the cognitive laboratory studies. Statistical and model-based analysis of scored student performance data is in very early stages, and will apply diagnostic psychometric models to investigate issues of measurement error and model-data fit.

Concluding Comments

Educational assessment is a complicated enterprise and much of the discussion regarding assessment tends to focus on large-scale standardized tests, especially given their prominent use in the United States for accountability purposes. Relatively little attention has been given to the design and validation of assessments that function close to classroom teaching and learning, with the exception of evaluation studies done by assessment developers as part of their own development efforts. Developers' evaluations are valuable and necessary, but what has been missing is a framework for independent, principled validity analysis that is applied relative to a program's intended purpose and use, as discussed here.

Although assessments currently are used for many purposes in the educational system, a premise of the *Knowing What Students Know* report (Pellegrino et al., 2001) is that an assessment's effectiveness and utility must ultimately be judged by the extent to which it promotes student learning. The aim of assessment should be "*to educate and improve* student performance, not merely to *audit* it" (Wiggins, 1998, p. 7, original emphasis). Because assessments are developed for specific purposes, the nature of their design is constrained by their intended use.

This paper illustrates how a validity argument might be constructed for one type of instructionally supportive assessment, and considers student response processes within the context of overall validity. Meaningful interpretation of student response process data requires a particular lens to determine which aspects of student response processes are most salient and for what reasons. The overall validity framework, consisting of cognitive, instructional, and inferential components, serves as such a lens for interpreting student response process data. In general, validity judgments must be tightly coupled to contextual factors related to students' curricular and instructional experiences as well as teacher practice and intended interpretive use.

As argued throughout, a meaningful interpretation of response process data relies upon deep connections to multiple sources of evidence that are constructed and interpreted within an overall validity argument. Effective teaching and learning depend on alignment between student response processes and an assessment's intended purpose and use. Without an overriding validity framework to help structure and guide data collection protocols and analytic methods as applied to student response processes, teachers will not be able to rely on claims about the interpretation of assessment results. The most frequent use of assessment is in the classroom, and teachers rely on a variety of assessment tools and resources as a part of their everyday practice. Yet much of what they use has limited validity evidence at best. It is time to apply clear standards of validity evidence to such materials and demand that validity analyses be conducted for such assessment materials so that educators and the public know whether assessment materials support or undermine effective practices of teaching and learning. This is especially pertinent given a significant shift in the goals for learning signaled by the Common Core Standards in Mathematics and English Language Arts (Common Core State Standards Initiative, 2010a, b) and the Framework for K-12 Science Education and the Next Generation Science Standards (Achieve, 2013; National Research Council, 2012).

References

Achieve (2013). *Next generation science standards*. Retrieved from www.nextgenscience.org.

American Association for the Advancement of Science (AAAS). (1993). *Benchmarks for science literacy*. New York: Oxford University Press.

Black, P., Harrison, C., Lee, C., Marshall, B., & Wiliam, D. (2004). *Assessment for learning: Putting it into practice*. Maidenhead, UK: Open University Press.

Briggs, D.C., Diaz-Bilello, E., Peck, F., Alzen, J., Chattergoon, R., & Johnson, R. (2015). Using a learning progression framework to assess and evaluate student growth. Boulder, CO: Center for Assessment Design Research and Evaluation (CADRE), University of Colorado; Dover, NH: National Center for the Improvement of Educational Assessment (NCIEA).

Common Core State Standards Initiative (2010a). *English language arts standards*. Washington, DC: National Governors Association and Council of Chief State School Officers. Available from www.corestandards.org/the-standards/english-language-artsstandards.pdf.

Common Core State Standards Initiative (2010b). *Mathematics standards*. Washington, DC: National Governors Association and Council of Chief State School Officers. Available from www.corestandards.org/assets/CCSSI_Math Standards.pdf.

DeBarger, A. H., Feng, M., Fujii, R., Ructtinger, L., Harris, C., & Haertel, G. (2014). *An alignment study of a facets-based formative assessment system for physics instruction*. Menlo Park, CA: SRI International.

DiBello, L. V., Henson, R. A. & Stout, W. (2015). A family of generalized diagnostic classification models for multiple choice option-based scoring. *Applied Psychological Measurement*, 39(1), pp. 62–79.

Duschl, R. A., Schweingruber, H. A., & Shouse, A. W. (Eds.). (2007). *Taking science to school: Learning and teaching science in grade K-8*. Washington DC: The National Academies Press.

Fujii, R., Haertel, G., McElhaney, K., D'Angelo, C., Werner, A., Ructtinger, L., Feng, M., Gong, B., et al. (2015). *The performance of facet-based items: A cognitive analysis study* (Technical Report II). Menlo Park, CA: SRI International.

Gane, B. D., Okoroh, C., DiBello, L. V., & Minstrell, J. (2015, April). *Making sense of big data from classroom assessments: Teacher case studies and facets-based physics assessments*. Paper presented at the American Educational Research Association annual meeting, Chicago IL.

Gordon Commission on the Future of Assessment in Education (2013). *Policy report*. Available from www.gordoncommission.org/publications_reports.html.

Haertel, E. H. & Lorié, W. A. (2004). Validating standards-based test score interpretations. *Measurement*, 2(2), 61–103.

Heritage, M. (2010). *Formative assessment: Making it happen in the classroom*. Thousand Oaks, CA: Corwin Press.

Hess, K. K. (2010). Applying Webb's depth of knowledge levels in science. National Center for the Improvement of Educational Assessment. Retrieved from www.nciea.org/beta-site/publication_PDFs/DOK science_KH11.pdf

Hunt, E. & Minstrell, J. (1994). A collaborative classroom for teaching conceptual physics. In K. McGilly (Ed.), *Classroom lessons: Integrating cognitive theory and classroom practice*. Cambridge: MIT Press.

Jorion, N., Gane, B., James, K., Schroeder, L., DiBello, L., & Pellegrino, J. (2015). An analytic framework for evaluating the validity of concept inventory claims. *Journal of Engineering Education*, 104(4), 454–496.

Kane, M. T. (2006). Validation. In R. L. Brennan (Ed.), *Educational measurement* (4th ed., pp. 17–64). Washington, DC: American Council on Education; Westport, CT: Praeger.

Kane, M. T. (2013). Validating the interpretations and uses of test scores. *Journal of Educational Measurement*, 50, 1–73.

Kilpatrick, J., Swafford, J., & Findell, B. (Eds.). (2001). *Adding it up: Helping children learn mathematics*. Washington, DC: National Academies Press.

Kingston, N., & Nash, B. (2011). Formative assessment: A meta-analysis and a call for research. *Educational Measurement: Issues and Practice*, 30(4), 28–37.

Li, M., Shavelson, R. J., & White, R. T. (2002). *Toward a framework for achievement assessment design: The case of science education*. Stanford CA: School of Education, Stanford University.

Madhyastha, T., & Hunt, E. (2009). Mining diagnostic assessment data for concept similarity. *Journal of Educational Data Mining*, 1(1), Article 3.

Messick, S. (1989). Validity. In R. L. Linn (Ed.), *Educational measurement* (3rd ed., pp. 13–103). New York: Macmillan.

Messick, S. (1994). The interplay of evidence and consequences in the validation of performance assessments. *Educational Researcher*, 23(2), 13–23.

Minstrell, J. (1992). Facets of students' knowledge and relevant instruction. In R. Duit, F. Goldberg, & H. Niedderer (Eds.), *Research in physics learning: Theoretical issues and empirical studies* (pp. 110–128). Kiel, Germany: IPN.

Minstrell, J. (2001). Facets of students' thinking: Designing to cross the gap from research to standards-based practice. In K. Crowley, C. D. Schunn, & T. Okada (Eds.), *Designing for science: Implications for professional, instructional, and everyday science*. Mahwah, NJ: Lawrence Erlbaum.

Minstrell, J., Anderson, R., Kraus, P., & Minstrell, J. E. (2008). Bridging from practice to research and back: Tools to support formative assessment. In J. Coffey, R. Douglas, & C. Stearns (Eds.), *Science assessment: Research and practical approaches*. Arlington, VA: National Science Teachers' Association Press.

Minstrell, J., Anderson, R., & Li, M. (2011). *Building on Learner Thinking: a framework for assessment in instruction*. Commissioned paper for the Committee on Highly Successful STEM Schools or Programs for K-12 STEM Education. Washington DC: NRC.

Mislevy, R. J., & Riconscente, M. M. (2006). Evidence-centered assessment design: Layers, concepts, and terminology. In S. Downing & T. Haladyna (Eds.), *Handbook of test development* (pp. 61–90). Mahwah, NJ: Lawrence Erlbaum.

Mislevy, R. J., Steinberg, L., & Almond, R (2003). On the structure of educational assessments. *Measurement: Interdisciplinary Research and Perspectives, 1*, 3–67.

National Research Council (2003). *Assessment in support of learning and instruction: Bridging the gap between large-scale and classroom assessment.* Washington, DC: National Academies Press.

National Research Council (2012). *A framework for K-12 science education: Practices, crosscutting concepts, and core ideas.* Committee on a Conceptual Framework for New K-12 Science Education Standards, Board on Science Education. Washington, DC: National Academies Press.

Nisbett, R., & Wilson, T. (1977). Telling more than we can know: Verbal reports on mental processes. *Psychological Review* 84(3): 231–259.

Pellegrino, J. W., Chudowsky, N., & Glaser, R. (Eds.) (2001). *Knowing what students know: The science and design of educational assessment.* Washington, DC: National Academies Press.

Pellegrino, J. W., Wilson, M., Koenig, J. & Beatty, A. (Eds.) (2014). *Developing assessments for the Next Generation Science Standards.* Washington, DC: National Academies Press.

Pellegrino, J. W., DiBello, L. V., & Goldman, S. R. (2016). A framework for conceptualizing and evaluating the validity of instructionally relevant assessments. *Educational Psychologist, 51*(1), 59–81.

Ruiz-Primo, M. A., Shavelson, R. J., Hamilton, L., & Klein, S. (2002). On the evaluation of systemic science education reform: Searching for instructional sensitivity. *Journal of Research in Science Teaching, 39*, 369–393.

van der Linden, W. J., & Hambleton, R. K. (Eds.) (1997). *Handbook of modern item response theory.* New York: Springer.

Webb, N. L. (2002). *Alignment study in language arts, mathematics, science, and social studies of state standards and assessments for four states.* Washington, DC: Council of Chief State School Officers.

Wiggins, G. (1998). *Educative assessment: Designing assessments to inform and improve student performance.* San Francisco, CA: Jossey-Bass.

Wiliam, D. (2007). Keeping learning on track: Formative assessment and the regulation of learning. In F. K. Lester Jr. (Ed.), *Second handbook of mathematics teaching and learning* (pp. 1053–1098). Greenwich, CT: Information Age Publishing.

9 Score Processes in Assessing Academic Content of Non-Native Speakers

Literature Review and ONPAR Summary

Rebecca J. Kopriva and Laura Wright

Building on Mislevy (1994) and Kane's (2013) work, Kopriva, Thurlow, Perie, Lazarus, and Clark (2016) outline the dominant conceptual framework this chapter will use as we discuss considering response process data of non-native speakers to validate academic score meaning. Kopriva et al. (2016) assert that valid measurement involves more than: (a) identifying intended assessment content and cognitive demands, (b) proposing consistent claims to infer from the operationalization of constructs, (c) building clear tests that consistently measure these demands, and (d) using evidence and theory to support the proposed interpretations for specific uses. They argue that valid measurement must also include identifying and addressing the test takers, who are as much a part of the testing operation as the content being tested, the testing machinery that presents and delivers the content and responses, and the evaluations of validity and reliability. The authors refer to this as the 'Person Dimension,' which is akin to but more pervasive and inclusive than simply addressing current definitions of fairness. The Dimension involves several aspects of impact. It includes considering student background and abilities not associated with particular test content; past and current experiences that aggravate access to typical test conditions; and how these influences impact how students attend to items in non-standard or unintended ways, how and how well they process, and how they perform on tests. While the aspects have an impact in different ways, the result is they call into question the proper interpretation of the academic test scores for certain students. The Dimension is particularly pertinent when the impact involves the interaction of individual students' characteristics with construct-irrelevant testing attributes within test situations where responses are generated and evaluated. However, the problematic interactions can often be subtle if not well understood. The focus must first be on addressing the construct-irrelevant situations known to act as sufficient barriers to access and measurement of the intended content and cognitive skills, knowing that this is a necessary but not sufficient step in producing defensible score interpretations. For most assessments tied to ongoing learning and the classroom, the impact of the testing situations the test takers experience in assessment situations should be understood and act as catalysts for assessment adaptation at a more nuanced level. Adaptation is accomplished such that the target constructs remain constant across students and score meaning is improved for various individual students. Kopriva et al. (2016) contend that this should be occurring even when the situations do not reach the level of an inaccessible barrier, and that not doing so will decrease the validity of the interpretations. These authors argue that sufficient documentation of evidence and theory associated with the impact of and interaction with the Person Dimension should be a necessary and essential component of validating score meaning for all test takers. For non-native speakers, two particularly pertinent person x test interaction aspects have a direct impact on the quality of score meaning—students successfully comprehending what items are asking, and having access to response situations that allow them to communicate their solution reasonably well. A third, access to internal problem-solving strategies and related skills, is also key but less well understood.

This chapter first reviews salient response process literature associated with these three aspects and then summarizes a promising approach to testing non-native speakers called ONPAR that attempts to improve the validity of the scores by introducing possible solutions to a number of the key problems raised in the literature. For the chapter review, the small-scale response process research that will be reviewed involves the following data collection methods: individual interviews, direct observations using field data retrieval techniques, qualitative inspections of items or other testing features, and small exploratory research studies where data analyses focus on test taker intent and behaviors. Every effort has been made to choose research that appears to be of high quality and uses defensible protocols and systematic analytic procedures. The reviews are not comprehensive but representative of the types of findings available for validation purposes. Using an integrated systems approach to designing items, the purpose of the ONPAR section is to introduce an assessment model that holistically increases points of access, and uses multisemiotic and load-sharing linguistic techniques to improve the validity of score meaning for a variety of non-native speakers. By tackling a number of the problems raised in the response data literature in the first section, the ONPAR methodology research to date summarizes how, when, and why such techniques appear to broaden access to test item questions and provide better evidence of intended score inferences than was evident using primarily traditional approaches.

Review of Relevant Response Process Literature

Comprehending What the Test Items are Asking

Most of the large- and small-scale research to date agrees that without comprehension of what the items are asking, test scores of non-native speakers will tend to remain distorted by their meaning negotiations over languages and diverse demographic, academic, and cultural experiences. For non-native speakers comprehension refers to understanding the target measurement focus of the items, including how meaning is conveyed. Winter, Kopriva et al. (2006) distinguished between full and partial comprehension. English learners (ELs) who fully comprehended what items were asking performed substantially better than those with partial comprehension, where those with partial comprehension understood the gist of the question, but missed the nuanced overlays or more subtle aspects.

Linguistic Features

A distinction is made here between linguistic complexity and cognitive content complexity. Studies have shown that when more-challenging academic content involving greater cognitive content complexity is measured, greater linguistic complexity often becomes a key construct-irrelevant factor impacting content score meaning. This is because the vocabulary, language, and discourse structures used to convey sophisticated concepts, reasoning, and skills are generally also sophisticated. In theory, some may argue that this puts more-challenging content off limits to those with lower language proficiency. However, there is ample empirical literature showing that those who have not yet developed full proficiency in a second (school) language can and do learn complex content (i.e., Gee, 2008; Schleppegrell, 2004). The challenge for teachers and measurement professionals is to utilize the 'work arounds' students use to understand and convey meaning in an assessment while not altering the cognitive demands of the content.

For example, Martiniello (2008) used six state mathematics test items in English and conducted think-aloud interviews with 24 4th grade students whose first language was Spanish and who had been in U.S. schools two or more years. She found that students made errors in sentences that used multiple clauses, long noun phrases, and limited syntactic transparency, and had problems with lower frequency words and those with multiple meanings. Even when students were able to decode and literally comprehend the meaning of the text, expressions were problematic that referenced unfamiliar contexts and cultural references (often subtle and such a part of the U.S. cultural lexicon the problems were not identified in reviews). These findings are generally consistent in other subjects and with students from other language backgrounds (Logan-Terry & Wright, 2010; Logan-Terry, 2011; Noble, Rosebery, Suarez, & Warren, 2014; Noble, Suarez, Rosebery, O'Connor, Warren, & Hudicourt-Barnes, 2012; Wright, 2008; Wolf & Leon, 2009). Winter et al.'s (2006) cognitive lab study with 156 3rd and 5th graders found that phrasal verbs and verb tenses are also problematic for non-native speakers. Such expressions and grammatical forms are rarely found in English glossary accommodations and need to be properly negotiated for non-native speakers, as do atypical and colloquial language (see also Carr et al., 2008).

Prosser and Solano-Flores (2011) conducted cognitive labs with 78 Spanish-speaking and monolingual English speakers. They found that how ELs versus non-ELs acquired their understanding of text-based test items differed in how they interacted with the science and non-science content terms, and how they approached and understood more linguistically challenging sentences. In navigating native and second languages (L2), Solano-Flores and Li's analysis of differential student-level variance (2006) found that, because of specific linguistic, cultural, and localized influences of particular item elements, the Haitian-Creole speakers sometimes performed better with English text and sometimes better with Haitian-Creole text. Roth, Oliveri, Sandilands, Lyons-Thomas and Ercikan (2013) conducted think-alouds with a group of expert translators considering English and French versions of items, and noted differences in the length of French and English versions, syntactic and semantic differences, and differences in the logical structure of item content or form as well as cultural issues.

A few projects have looked at the interaction between linguistic complexity and content complexity. Martiniello (2008) noted that ELs had more problems overall with the language in more difficult content items than in less difficult items. Carr et al.'s (2008) qualitative review of English language traditional and 'access-based' versions of mathematics, science, and social studies items found that the greatest improvement in EL scores across versions was for items measuring more-basic knowledge and skills. Much smaller differences were noted for ELs on the adapted versions vs. the traditional when the items measured more-cognitively-challenging constructs. Carr noted that the language adaptations used in the more-complex content items still resulted in greater linguistic complexity than language changes on the items measuring more-basic abilities, even though relevant static visual and format adaptations were added. Non-text features appeared to be insufficient to provide enough support to successfully offset the increased linguistic complexity. In her discourse analysis of a middle school science classroom, Wright (2008) found ELs tended to use 'muddled' language while in the throes of learning challenging science content even as they demonstrated facility with more-sophisticated academic language in general. She argues that using less sophisticated language and other supports on tests of challenging content may likely provide more valid data on students' science abilities. In their large cognitive lab project Chen and Yi (2005) reported larger effects of traditional vs. language adapted versions in more rudimentary items for elementary ELs than for more-challenging items.

Cultural Features

The interrelationships between home and majority cultures, convergent and divergent expectations, and ongoing experiences in and between these cultures within classrooms and socially are but a few examples of why and how the literature suggests cultural features impact score meaning for non-native speakers (see Basterra, Trumbull, & Solano-Flores, 2011; Gee, 2008). Unfortunately, most of the process studies do not specifically focus on cultural features, but rather look at these features within the context of the linguistic features as discussed above (e.g., Martiniello,

2008; Noble et al., 2014; Noble et al., 2012; Solano-Flores & Li, 2006; Solano-Flores, 2010). In an exploratory systematic language review of differential item functioning (DIF) items by two French-speaking education experts, Ercikan, Roth, Simon, Lyons-Thomas, and Sandilands (2014) note that the nature and frequency of access to the mainstream culture outside of school may contribute to differential score meaning. In her observational analysis of assessment items and answers from majority and minority language speakers in a middle school science classroom, Logan-Terry (2011) found that native English speakers were able to more successfully notice subtle contextualization cues in test item prompts than emergent bilingual students. She noted that culturally-nuanced details of assessments, such as sequencing of questions and cultural understandings of visuals all contributed to miscues by emergent English speakers. Mann and Emick (2006) described findings from interviews with teachers about parents of new, non-English speakers. For those with limited exposure to mainstream U.S. schooling, many parents did not understand the purpose or nature of formal and regular classroom testing in U.S. classrooms or of different question types. Teachers said that parent misunderstandings negatively affected the way a number of their students interacted in at least some of the testing situations, and that the students' confusion negatively impacted their test scores as compared to what the students had exhibited otherwise in the classrooms.

Multisemiotic Features

Multisemiotic communication is the use of multiple communication modes, signs, or representations to convey meaning, rather than relying primarily on the mode of language, especially the language of the majority culture (Peirce, 1977). Most classrooms are inherently multimodal today and the multiple modalities have been considered part of best practice in teaching ELs, especially when more-challenging conceptual and reasoning skills are being learned. A small number of projects have focused on how other modalities might be used together with written text to successfully convey meaning to non-native speakers in assessment. While Wright (2008) and Logan-Terry (2011) found rich multisemiotic communication during teaching, they noted non-text representations, if used at all in assessment, were almost always used in an auxiliary position to language to convey the meaning of concepts and skills. Kopriva et al. (2007) researched the links between item features and EL needs, investigating how specific multi-mode adaptations geared to the students' needs (such as static visuals tied to verb phases and low frequency nouns) affected their performance. They found that student scores significantly increased when they used representations associated with student need, but scores did not significantly change when the alternative modes were not needed. Solano-Flores (2010) and Solano-Flores and Wang (2011) found important cultural differences associated with illustration features for Chinese students. Carr, Kopriva, and Siskind (2008) inspected the features of the visuals in access items, for ELs who performed better, worse, or similarly on the traditional and adapted items, and relative to their peers with learning disabilities (LD), students with hearing impairments (DHH), and control students. While no distinct score patterns emerged for the controls, for ELs, higher scores on specific access items seemed to be associated with the gestalt of the visual features. For the LD, higher scores appeared more related to the clarity of the individual features, and higher DHH scores seemed more dependent on gestures and facial expressions of the people.

Problem Solving and Response Processes

There seems to be very little process literature that focuses in detail on how non-native speakers approach and conduct problem solving during tests, or literature that considers how different response opportunities interact with student needs and preferences. However, there is speculation that these factors impact the validity of inferences.

Problem Solving

Walqui and Heritage (2009), Wright (2015), and others explain that non-native speakers still learning the academic language of the school while also learning challenging content use multimodal systems and meaning representations to acquire and expand their mental learning maps about the content. These internal multimodal structures will often be non-standard, meaning that students tend to use their home language and the language they are taught in, but use them in incomplete language structures that integrate language with a variety of other schematic representations. Some suggest that these non-standard learning internal maps may signal differences in problem-solving strategies in testing (Gee, 2004; Moschkovich, 2014; Santos et al., 2013).

In order to evaluate how selection and application of problem-solving strategies interact with item comprehension and response for ELs and others, Winter et al. (2006) hypothesized that three response process aspects and the score would reflect a recursive chain relationship: apprehension → strategy → application → response. Investigating the probabilities of using an appropriate solution strategy given a level of comprehension, results from 156 cognitive labs indicated that using an appropriate strategy increases sharply as comprehension goes from partial to full for open- and close-ended items, particularly in 5th versus 3rd grade. On the other hand, the relationship between the appropriateness of the strategy used and the accuracy of its application was found to be stronger in 3rd rather than 5th. The recursive regression results indicated that, for both grades, increasing the degree to which students comprehend a task affects the probability that they will select an appropriate solution strategy. Fullness of comprehension also mediated the correctness of the application of that strategy. These distinctions between partial and full comprehension and their relationships to the subsequent processes were particularly strong for ELs versus non-ELs in both grades, and were evident in how ELs responded in their labs to both basic and adapted items. Based on her observations in classrooms, Wright (2008) suggested that traditional text-laden methods of testing may actually inhibit problem solving, or at least inhibit students' use of their problem-solving skills in items presented in this way. She observed that the middle school science teachers often provided multisemiotic learning opportunities while they were teaching, and that these methods not only facilitated learning but also seemed to act as catalysts to deepen or encourage more-sophisticated reasoning and problem-solving skills. She noted that when ELs were asked to explain their thinking they frequently used multiple representations to get their points across to their teachers and peers. On the other hand, when these same students took traditional text predominant tests in English, their responses and scores did not reflect the reasoning and skills they had previously exhibited in class.

Response

Based on their observations Wright (2008) and Wright, Staehr-Fenner, and Moxley (2013) noticed what they felt was a causal link when items more closely mirror how students are making meaning in classrooms. For ELs with low- through mid-level English language proficiency, this seemed to include allowing non-standard formats and multiple sign systems. When there was a dissonance between how students made meaning during learning and on traditional text-based assessment, she observed this resulted in lower scores (as students translated their non-standard learning and process maps into English text).

In their cognitive labs, Chen and Yi (2005) investigated how elementary ELs interacted with traditional multiple-choice and constructed-response (CR) math items and their adapted accessible counterparts. They highlighted problems in responding to traditional multiple-choice options because of the difficulties of properly interpreting what amount to English 'shorthand' option phrases. The adapted versions were sometimes able to minimize the shorthand language problems but not always, particularly when the criteria for adapting items did not include a close look at the language of English over and above addressing the literacy level. The researchers also reported that lower, mid-level and some higher-English-proficient ELs more often used non-standard response methods to fully explain what they knew in responding to CR items than did native speakers. The methods included use of mixed home and majority text, home language conventions or phonetics applied to their written English, and greater use of manipulatives, diagrams, and drawings to express themselves.

Using a draft of a CR scoring guide designed to interpret EL responses (Kopriva & Sexton, 1999), Kopriva and Lara (1997) investigated the effects of the document and a one-hour training integrated into the traditional NAEP scorer training for hand-scoring CR responses. After training, the participants, about 15 monolingual English-speaking scorers not involved in the initial scoring, blindly rescored responses from mostly higher proficient ELs and a random sample of non-ELs to a set of middle school NAEP science items. Comparing the scores from this study with the original scores of the same responses, the researchers found that the scores for ELs from this study were generally higher than their original scores; they also noted score differences for some native speakers. In interviews conducted at the end of scoring, participants said training prompted them to read and analyze the quality of the responses more carefully and to not prematurely judge responses based on their non-standard presentation methods (e.g. interspersing language and drawing or graphical devices, responses having 'organization issues', or responses they referred to as 'colloquial').

Discussion

To date, what does this literature suggest about how to improve intended inferences for this population? As Kopriva et al. (2016) argue, the processes for evaluation of score meaning and producing assessments useful for non-native speakers rest in framing argument paths and collecting sufficient empirical and argument-based evidence linking tests with particular features and conditions that facilitate valid meaning to profiles of students who benefit from these features or conditions. The profiles not only specify needs and levels but also strengths that can be drawn upon to enable valid meaning. The literature above suggests that this process starts with understanding what traditional methods are insufficient, why, and for whom, and when and how the methods lead to distortion of score meaning. It also provides some clues about how to mitigate these problems. These include what kinds of parameters and evidence are necessary to, first, improve the intended inferences of scores for non-native speakers and, second, to improve a constant score meaning over native and non-native students with varieties of profiles.

Much of the literature outlined above has focused on problematic native language linguistic features and the impact on intended meaning to and from the students. To some degree, non-native speaking students from different languages and cultures share native linguistic challenges and the need to negotiate between their home languages and cultures as they are taught in the majority language. In general, second-language acquisition tells us that receptive and productive skills associated with learning more challenging coursework lags behind their understanding and expression of more-basic knowledge and skills. These challenges seem to heighten their compensatory strengths to make meaning in and out of school that in turn allows them to learn more-challenging and more-cognitively complex content than their current levels of native language proficiency might suggest. The students are also heterogeneous, extending beyond their various home languages and cultures to their own temperaments, personal strengths, challenges, interests, and experiences. As they navigate their learning, different preferred compensatory methods and strategies are encouraged or inhibited in a dynamic fashion over time and content areas.

For test developers and classroom teachers, these aspects, as well as others, begin to suggest a framework for improving score meaning and better understanding of the knowledge, skills, and abilities of non-native speakers. First, for purposes of assessing content, linguistic and content-cognitive complexity need to be de-coupled as much as possible. Non-native speakers are learning challenging content—we need to better document how to build assessment opportunities that mirror their successes. Second, it is important to develop parsimonious but representative student profiles that capture the key student characteristics associated with assessing the content-related concepts, reasoning, and other skills of those students. The profile criteria should include both strengths and challenges, and differ in detail for test developers and teachers. Third, students are dynamic learners of both content and the native language, and preferred assessment methods will change over time, over items, probably over content areas, and at different ages. This, coupled with different student profiles, suggests that assessment should have a more fluid, multi-method and flexible quality of presenting and accepting communication to and from students within established constraints of maintaining defensibility. Assessment defensibility over students requires that what is being measured be held constant, and that retention of the same targets needs to be supported by evidence over profiles and for smaller as well as larger components of tests, for instance items. Varying features and conditions should be designed explicitly to impact non-target aspects of the items and not cue responses or lower the complexity of the construct targets across some variations. Finally, improving score meaning for non-native-speaking students means that there is an ongoing need for projects that will begin to apply what we know to date about how to improve assessment opportunities for non-native speakers. This includes process studies that contribute, refine, research, and communicate aspects of viable and valid assessment frameworks, profiles, and assessment methodology that works and leads to improved score meaning. In large part, this means that ongoing work should focus on how these and other aspects dynamically interrelate, for summative and formative assessment opportunities, and in ways that are feasible, accessible, and available.

An illustration: ONPAR

Below is a brief explanation of one promising measurement approach developed to explicitly improve academic score meaning of non-native speakers as well as others. Built from the ground up as a way to embrace and address the differentiated needs of students, it seeks to respond to a number of the problems summarized above, the recent literature associated with needs of various students, and needs to broaden assessment item types that better measure today's challenging coursework in a systematic way. This methodology, called ONPAR, has demonstrated success in using technology-based multisemiotic representations that include but are not limited to native speaker text in order to improve the validity of score meaning to and from students. This approach is discussed here for two reasons. First, ONPAR seeks to mitigate many of the problems raised in process studies for non-native speakers such as those summarized above. In so doing the findings in this section respond to this literature and outline how well one set of solutions seem to work to address some of these concerns. Second, critical evaluations of the new techniques using response process studies are outlined here as well, in an effort to expand the focus of methods involved in the ongoing validation discourse going forward.

Developed over the course of three federally funded research grants and private funds, the assessment items and tasks simultaneously use multiple modalities on screens to broaden the inclusion of students who differentially utilize different sign systems in different situations to access meaning. Drawing from linguistics and semiotic theory (e.g., Jewitt, 2008; Kress, 2003; Kress, 2010; Kress & van Leeuwen, 2001), ONPAR capitalizes on the affordances of different modalities to create a multisemiotic 'grammar' of assessment design that may allow developers to better communicate to test takers and hear from them in novel ways. In general, the questions ONPAR focuses on are ones that measure a variety of skills and depth of knowledge conventionally assessed through tasks requiring substantial language. To convey what questions are asking students to do, the items and tasks utilize representations such as simulations, animations, image rollovers, sound, interactive sequences, and some L1 and L2 text and oral support as needed for precision. Depending on the nature of the questions, students are asked to respond by building, modeling, assembling, categorizing, or producing relational or inferential explanations using screen stimuli. To date approximately 20 different types of response spaces are used. Supportive elements include the standardization of several aspects of screens within and across tasks undergirding the novel presentation and response screens without overwhelming or confusing students. For instance, consistent color hues and layouts, placement of screen elements, novel onscreen assists, and accessible dashboards are used as well as animated and static visuals, oral English and L1, and various directional non-text rollovers that support text without cueing any particular response. Additional techniques that facilitate communication rely on careful placement of interactive buttons, target questions, and response spaces, pacing, and task introduction (approach and length). Underlying algorithms capture and score responses, conceptual threads, and screen interactive processes and strategies in real time and individualized student reports are available immediately. Readers are encouraged to visit the website at www.iiassessmnt@wceruw.org for more information.

The research and feasibility studies investigated the validity of methodology for measuring challenging mathematics and science in elementary, middle school, and high school, for ELs, students with higher and lower abilities in the content areas, native English speakers, and students with learning and other communicative and attention disabilities. Across studies 161 cognitive labs (of focal and control students) researched when and how variations in language and other representations can be integrated within and across sign systems to achieve effective and efficient communication to and from students (Wright and others, 2009, 2011, 2013). Three experimental (Kopriva et al., 2011; Kopriva et al., 2013; Kopriva et al., in press) and a correlational study (Carr & Pfaffinger, 2013) found that, controlling for content ability in most cases, the focal groups (ELs, low income, and others with literacy, processing, and attention issues) generally scored significantly higher and in preferred rank orderings using ONPAR as compared to traditional testing methods measuring the same content. Control groups scored more similarly using both methods, which the researchers suggest, underscore that this approach does not artificially inflate scores, and that it reflects a viable and valid method for measuring challenging concepts for these students as well. Two new grants are researching formative ONPAR methodology within classroom-embedded settings.

ONPAR Comprehension

The ONPAR labs typically focused on accessing comprehension of test items and providing accessible response spaces. In examining comprehension, the researchers found that even low English proficient students could access the nuanced meaning of most ONPAR items. The labs confirmed that the consistent ordering of task screens and careful placement of information across screens aided students in expecting certain types of information and comprehending the flow of information. Further, non-native and native students in general approached visual representations and animations by themselves and as part of a gestalt with other semiotic elements such as movement, language, or interactive engagement in a similar way as they would read text (left to right, top to bottom). Non-text stimuli were largely successful in serving in a primary position to substantively convey meaning, especially in introduction and problem-building screens. Native speakers and higher-English-proficient ELs more often asked for English text in addition to the multi-modal stimuli to confirm what they were seeing, especially in high school. The lab investigators reported that the semiotic quality of involving virtual movement in items (on the screen versus movement of the test takers themselves) seemed effective in conveying substantive meaning denoting action sequence explanations or over time changes as relevant and germane to the context or target question. Additionally, the lab researchers reported that frequent interactive opportunities were useful in keeping students focused throughout the tasks, keeping them involved in and curious about solving cognitively challenging tasks with substantial content demands that sometimes unfolded over a number of screens. Items that allowed students the opportunity to interact early on, through moving screen stimuli or asking simple questions, were particularly useful. When the meaning of visual representations was not clear, the labs found that written text, serving as anchorage on the screen, was often a sufficient way to constrain the context or communicate a precise meaning. Text labels of the visual stimuli, usually an individual word or a noun or verb phrase, were sometimes adequate; otherwise, full simple sentences in English worked best (e.g. 'This is a number machine').

The first set of labs examined characteristics of written English text in the target questions per se for elementary and middle school science items (Wright & Kopriva, 2009). By systematically varying the amount of written English text used in the questions while holding all other parts of the ONPAR items the same, researchers found that low English proficient students and others on the whole performed best with full, complete, succinct sentences using precise content language as relevant, and with context-relevant, target irrelevant, words or phrases supported by other semiotic representations. Succinct questions were most often possible when the meanings of non-target language were 'learned' on prior problem-building screens. Support rollovers of non-target verb and sometimes adjectival and adverbial phrases, versus individual words were found most useful as opposed to word-by-word supports. To retain the precision of the item questions, the native language option was added on these screens, and generally found not to be necessary on other screens, even for lower-proficient ELs. One benefit of less language is less to translate, greatly reducing translation error and allowing for multiple language translations of the questions (provided in ONPAR). Overall, lower- and mid-level English proficient elementary and middle ELs sometimes used oral L1 to make meaning of ONPAR item questions, sometimes they relied more heavily on non-text modes, and sometimes they used oral and/or written English. High English proficient ELs also seemed to benefit from these features in high school more so than in lower grades.

ONPAR Problem Solving and Response

Problem Solving

The 161 labs investigated some strategies students used to address the ONPAR items, but the two current projects will focus more heavily on assessing these processes. In one strand of data gathered in the earlier labs, researchers noticed that students linked understanding of ONPAR items to substantive, pertinent knowledge, procedures, and reasoning they learned in and outside the classroom. Further, the level of quality and relevance of such knowledge or procedures was generally consistent with the quality of their responses. Students more often reported that the higher quality understanding of the prior knowledge also seemed to stimulate and activate strategies they would use to build upon for solving the problems, if they knew how to do so. Their repertoire included not only describing different data organization and interpretation methods learned in their classes, but the ability to link the methods with the content specified in the item, and place and use this information within the larger problem-solving context as it was required to reach a solution.

For students who did not know the target content, their links to the prior knowledge and skills, while relevant, seemed vague and ill-formed, and their strategies seemed to follow suit. Poorly constructed response spaces sometimes further confused these students but did not appear to usually be the cause of their incorrect answers. In addition, the investigators reported that more and less knowledgeable students used roundabout logic, incorporating outside experiences and related concepts, skills, and knowledge; others were more direct. Logic streams also differed but not by content ability—some began conceptually while others began more procedurally. On the other hand, ELs with little knowledge and using primarily guessing or trial and error to respond were most often unsuccessful.

Response

As noted above, some authors argue that the key to improving the validation of non-native speaker scores can be traced back to the multisemiotic ways they express meaning in the content classrooms. ONPAR's varied response environments range from capturing more-basic answers to responses conveying more in-depth conceptual, reasoning, or multi-step integrative or interpretive concepts and skills. Many of the response screens use open as compared to hotspot technology and are scored algorithmically so reports are available immediately. Categories of response types include (a) demonstrating concept knowledge by manipulating screen elements; (b) assembling models, or using diagrams or other symbolic forms to represent systems and meta-systems relationships; (c) drawing; (d) manipulating and/or creating graphs; (e) categorizing; (f) filling-in basic to more-complex structures, including basic to complex relational and causal chains; (g) predetermined or choice-based statement frames where visuals, symbols, and supported item-irrelevant language are placed in syntactic relationships to form explanations or articulate reasoning, from simple to complex; and (h) open-response environments with numerical, pictorial, symbols, and/ or language-response elements students can use to create proofs or otherwise capture their thinking. Most screens are designed so guessing is at a minimum.

It is easy to overcrowd response spaces and interviewers found a number of students, but particularly those with language, literacy, or processing challenges, very sensitive to this dynamic. Rollovers de-clutter response screens, as does the use of symbolic forms 'learned' from and connected to meaning in earlier screens. Standardized placement of different response aspects have been found to be important, as has access to work results from prior screen(s) and the ability to go back and forth. In the lab reports Wright and others found that many but not all of the ONPAR response spaces and features were effective. For instance, investigators reported that demonstrated responses, where students move visual response elements to provide evidence about what they know, were generally found to be successful for both native and non-native English speakers. Student difficulties with this response type mostly seemed to reflect the difficulty of the task, not the difficulty of the response space. Many of the screens use rollovers of non-target symbols, words, phrases, or other screen stimuli, and the researchers noted that different types of students, including lower-proficient ELs seemed to use these in order to hear or see meaning expressed in a different semiotic form. Most fill-in response spaces were found to be clear for native and non-native speakers, even when the screen requested several different responses. This was because the screens used standardized symbols, colors, or shapes. The biggest drawback to the fill-in screens was if the response contexts were confusing, or if unclear visuals, language, or symbols were used. As long as the screens were well formatted researchers reported that non-EL and ELs at different English proficiency levels could still readily navigate more-complex screens, such as those requiring relational responses and causal chains with greater and fewer parameters.

Statement frames, where students explain, reason, or interpret using text as well as visuals and symbols, are designed to provide more or less 'syntactic' structure and direction. Use of conjunctions constrained some sentences; sometimes students choose among different frames to respond. Success of the frames depended largely on clarity of the frames relative to the question, the response elements, and the non-target text supports. Some statement frames used color-coded spaces to signal object or verb positions, which tended to be very useful for less fluent English learners. When graphics or symbols were used to convey meaning across response types, their success was largely due to their universality of meaning. This universality was generally more important than the context in which it was found, and overall students responded well to novel and familiar contexts when the symbols were understood. Numbers and mathematical symbols were the easiest form of symbolic notation for students to recognize. The broad uses of symbols in tech-based applications outside of ONPAR have standardized more and more symbols, increasing ONPAR's repertoire and their success in items. Arrows were reported to be the most easily misunderstood, as often their meaning had to be inferred by students from their embedded contexts. Researchers have called for more standardization of arrows on ONPAR screens, probably by function and purpose.

Closing Thoughts

Used correctly, ONPAR methods appear to be viable tools to improve score meaning for many non-native speakers, and results from random trials in all studies, as well as the response process data outlined above, have largely supported this. In general, the data demonstrate that multiple signs can and do carry substantive academic meaning, and the signs are used to communicate meaning primarily or with equal weight alongside language. They demonstrate that non-text representations can carry more-cognitively challenging meaning to and from students, and online screens can flexibly make use of multiple symbols targeting the same concept or skill as well, enabling students with various preferences and needs to be accommodated at the same time without being overwhelming or confusing.

ONPAR, however, is only one approach, and there is still much to do to properly understand this and other novel methodologies. Critical response process evaluations of the ONPAR techniques have suggested a number of the techniques work, but future studies need to better understand when and for whom? The usefulness of student profiles and what information populates them remains an ongoing question to be addressed by small response studies designed to defensibly distinguish which multi-faceted needs and strengths are essential. Specific validation queries related to the interaction of new methods and students with different profiles need to be hypothesized during design and empirically addressed. The objective of summarizing this one novel approach here is to get this discourse started.

References

Basterra, M. R., Trumbull, E., & Solano-Flores, G. (2011). *Cultural validity in assessment: Addressing linguistic and cultural diversity*. New York: Routledge.

Carr T. G. & Pfaffinger, S. (2013). Psychometric interrelationships among item types. Internal report 348, Institute for Innovative Assessment. Madison, WI: University of Wisconsin. Retrieved from http://iiassessment.wceruw.org/research.

Carr, T. G., Kopriva, R. J., & Siskind, T. (2008). Distractor analysis as a tool to identify items that differentially impact English learners and students with disabilities: Results from the Achieving Accurate Results for Diverse Learners (AARDL) Project. Presentation at the CCSSO National Conference on Student Assessment, Orlando, FL.

Chen, C. S. & Yi, M. (2005). Cognitive lab report. In R. J. Kopriva & R. Mislevy, *Final research report of the Valid Assessment of English Language Learners Project* (C-SAVE Rep. No. 259). Madison, WI: University of Wisconsin, Center for Innovative Assessment.

Ercikan, K., Roth, M., Simon, M., Lyons-Thomas, J., & Sandilands, D. (2014). Inconsistencies in DIF detection for sub-groups in heterogeneous language groups. *Applied Measurement in Education, 27,* 273–285.

Gee, J. P. (2004). *Situated language and learning: A critique of traditional schooling*. Melbourne: Common Ground.

Gee, J. P. (2008). Literacies, identities, and discourses. In M. Schleppegrel & C. Colombi (Eds.), *Developing advanced literacy in first and second languages: Meaning with power* (pp. 159–175). New York, Routledge.

Jewitt, C. (2008). Multimodal classroom research. *Review of Research in Education, 32,* 241–267.

Kane, M.T. (2013). Validating the interpretations and uses of test scores. *Journal of Educational Measurement, 50*(1), 1–73.

Kopriva, R.J. & Lara, J. (1997). Scoring English language learners' papers more accurately. In Y.S. George and V.V. Van Horne (Eds.), *Science education reform for all: Sustaining the science, mathematics and technology education reform* (pp. 77–82). Washington, DC: American Association for the Advancement of Science.

Kopriva, R.J. & Sexton, U. (1999). *Guide to scoring LEP student responses to open-ended science items.* Washington, DC: Council of Chief State School Officers.

Kopriva, R.J., Emick, J.E., Hipolito-Delgado, C.P., & Cameron, C.A. (2007). Do proper accommodation assignments make a difference? Examining the impact of improving decision making on scores for English language learners. *Educational Measurement: Issues and Practice, 26*(3), 11–20.

Kopriva, R.J., Carr, T.G., Gabel, D., & Cameron, C. (2011). Improving the validity of mathematics results for students with learning disabilities in reading and other SwDs who struggle with language and literacy: Findings from the ONPAR elementary and middle school mathematics experimental study. Madison, WI: Institute for Innovative Assessment, University of Wisconsin-Madison. Retrieved from http://iiassessment.wceruw.org/research.

Kopriva, R.J., Winter, P.C., Triscari, R., Carr, T.G., Cameron, C., & Gabel, D. (2013*). Assessing the knowledge, skills, and abilities of ELs, selected SwDs and controls on challenging high school science content: Results from randomized trials of ONPAR and technology-enhanced traditional end-of-course biology and chemistry tests.* Madison, WI: Institute for Innovative Assessment, University of Wisconsin-Madison. Retrieved from http://iiassessment.wceruw.org/research.

Kopriva, R.J., Thurlow, M.L., Perie, M, Lazarus, S.S., & Clark, A. (2016). Test takers and the validity of score interpretation. *Educational Psychologist, 5*(1), 108–128.

Kopriva, R.J., Wright, L., & Triscari, R. (in press). Examining a multisemiotic approach to measuring challenging content for English learners and others: Results from the ONPAR elementary and middle school science study. *Educational Assessment.*

Kress. G. (2003). *Literacy in the new media age.* London: Routledge.

Kress, G. (2010). *Multimodality: A social semiotic approach to communication.* London: Routledge Falmer.

Kress, G. & van Leeuwen, T. (2001). *Multimodal discourse: The modes and media of contemporary communication.* New York: Oxford University Press.

Logan-Terry, A. (2011). *Achievement, assessment, and learning: A study of emergent bilinguals. Students in mainstream content classrooms.* Doctoral dissertation, Georgetown University, Washington, DC.

Logan-Terry, A. & Wright, L.J. (2010). Making thinking visible: An analysis of English language learners' interactions with access-based science assessment items. *AccELLerate! 2*(4), 11–14.

Mann, H. & Emick, J. (2006). *Language liaisons: A novel accommodation for new ELLs.* Paper presented at the annual meeting of the American Educational Research Association, San Francisco, CA.

Martiniello, M. (2008). Language and the performance of English-language learners in math word problems. *Harvard Educational Review, 78*(2), 333–368.

Mislevy, R.J. (1994). Evidence and inference in education assessment. *Psychometrika, 59*(4), 79–85.

Moschkovich, J. (2014). Mathematics, the common core, and language: Recommendations for mathematics instruction for ELs aligned with the common core. Retrieved from http://ell.stanford.edu/sites/default/files/pdf/academic-papers/02-JMoschkovich%20Math%20FINAL_bound%20with%20appendix.pdf.

Noble, T., Suarez, C., Rosebery, A., O'Connor, M.C., Warren, B., & Hudicourt-Barnes, J. (2012). "I never thought of it as freezing": How students answer questions on large-scale science tests and what they know about science. *Journal of Research in Science Teaching, 49*(6), 778–803.

Noble, T., Rosebery, A., Suarez, C., & Warren B. (2014). Science assessments and English language learners: Validity evidence based on response processes. *Applied Measurement in Education, 27*(4), 248–260.

Peirce, C.S. (1977). *Semiotics and significs.* Charles Hardwick (Ed.). Bloomington IN: Indiana University Press.

Prosser, R. & Solano-Flores, G. (2011). *Examining problem solving strategies on multiple-choice science items among English language learners through cognitive interviews.* Paper presented at the Annual Conference of the American Educational Research Association, New Orleans, Louisiana, April 7–11.

Roth, W.-M., Oliveri, M.E., Sandilands, D., Lyons-Thomas, J., & Ercikan, K. (2013). Investigating sources of differential item functioning using expert think-aloud protocols. *International Journal of Science Education, 35*, 546–576.

Santos, M., Darling-Hammond, L., & Cheuk, T. (2013). Teacher development to support English language learners in the context of Common Core State Standards. Retrieved from http://ell.stanford.edu/sites/default/files/pdf/academic-papers/10 Santos%20LDH%20Teacher%20Development%20FINAL.pdf.

Schleppegrell, M. (2004). *Language of schooling: A functional linguistics perspective.* Mahwah, NJ: Lawrence Erlbaum.

Solano-Flores, G. (2010). *Vignette illustrations as a form of testing accommodation for English language learners: A design methodology for use in large-scale science assessment.* Paper presented at the Annual Conference of the National Council of Measurement in Education, Denver, Colorado, April 29–May 3.

Solano-Flores, G. & Li, M. (2006). The use of generalizability (G) theory in the testing of linguistic minorities. *Educational Measurement: Issues and Practice 25*(1), 13–22.

Solano-Flores G. & Wang, C. (2011). *Conceptual framework for analyzing and designing illustrations in science assessment: Development and use in the testing of linguistically and culturally diverse populations.* Paper presented at the Annual Conference of the National Council on Measurement in Education, New Orleans, LA, April 7–11.

Walqui A. & Heritage, M. (2009). *Instruction for diverse groups of English language learners.* Stanford, CA: Understanding Language: Language, Literacy, and Learning in the Content Areas. Retrieved from http://ell.stanford.edu/sites/default/files/pdf/academic-papers.

Winter, P., Kopriva, R. J., Chen, S., & Emick, J. (2006). Exploring individual and item factors that affect assessment validity for diverse learners: Results from a large-scale cognitive lab. *Learning and Individual Differences, 16,* 267–276.

Wolf, M. K. & Leon, S. (2009). An investigation of the language demands in content assessments for English language learners. *Educational Assessment, 14*(3), 139–159.

Wright, L. J. (2008). Writing science and objectification: Selecting, organizing, and decontextualizing knowledge. *Linguistics and Education, 19*(3), 265–293.

Wright, L. J. (2015). Inquire to acquire: A discourse analysis of bilingual students' development of science literacy. D. Molle, T. Boals, E. Sato, & C. A. Hedgspeth (Eds.), *Multilingual learners and academic literacies: Sociocultural contexts of literacy development in adolescents.* New York: Routledge.

Wright, L. J. & Kopriva, R. J. (2009*). Using cognitive labs to refine technology-enhanced assessment tasks and ensure their accessibility: Insights from data collected to inform ONPAR elementary and middle school science task development.* Madison, WI: Institute for Innovative Assessment, University of Wisconsin-Madison. Retrieved from http://iiassessment.wceruw.org/research.

Wright, L. J. & Staehr-Fenner, D. (2011). *Results from ONPAR mathematics cognitive labs.* Retrieved from http://iiassessment.wceruw.org/research.

Wright, L. J., Staehr-Fenner, D., & Moxley, K. (2013). *Exploring how diverse learners interact with computerized, multi-semiotic representations of meaning: Highlights from cognitive labs conducted with ONPAR end-of-course biology and chemistry assessment tasks.* Retrieved from http://iiassessment.wceruw.org/research.

10 Assessment of Students with Learning Disabilities

Using Students' Performance and Progress to Inform Instruction

Gerald Tindal, Julie Alonzo, Leilani Sáez, and Joseph F. T. Nese

Introduction

Understanding test score meaning for students with (learning) disabilities (SWD) is both complex and understudied. By definition, SWD bring non-typical processing to their learning, and therefore, their performance on any particular academic assessment. In particular, SWD are presumed to have difficulty in the acquisition and use of listening, speaking, reading, writing, reasoning, or mathematical skills (National Joint Committee on Learning Disabilities, 1990) that not only affect their ability to learn but also to demonstrate what they know. In addition, for SWD, proficiency measurement is no longer considered merely a general indication of achievement, but rather, a call to action. For example, a response-to-intervention (RTI) delivery model now systematically combines the use of formative assessment results and performance interpretations to directly guide instruction for SWD and their underperforming peers.

The combination of RTI and formative assessment, particularly curriculum-based measurement (CBM), provides an explicit system for better understanding and validating instructional decision-making using student responses. RTI entails "student-centered assessment models that use problem-solving and research-based methods to identify and address learning difficulties in children [through] high-quality classroom instruction, universal screening, continuous progress monitoring, research-based interventions, and fidelity of instructional interventions" (Berkeley, Bender, Peaster, & Saunders, 2009, p. 86). This system depends heavily upon assessment results to both inform the need for intervention and to reflect learning over time so that targeted interventions are either vindicated or changed to optimally support identified learning needs.

For Wanzek and Cavanaugh (2012), fully developed RTI models combine general and special education to identify and integrate school resources in providing effective instruction and intervention. Such implementation relies on scientifically based evidence to develop effective instruction, including the intensity of instruction (e.g. time, frequency, duration, and instructional group size). Because of the complex consequences of test score meaning in today's RTI assessments, we argue in this chapter that understanding score meaning for SWD requires more than a singular perspective on how the examinee responds to test items (e.g., through inspection of strategies, knowledge, or item engagement). We contend that it also necessitates an examination of teacher responses as used in a RTI model, interpreting score meaning in a more contextual manner for understanding what SWD know and can do.

Curriculum-Based Measurement

Curriculum-based measurement (CBM) began with a series of studies on measurement of reading, spelling, and writing at the University of Minnesota with the Institute for Research on Learning Disabilities (IRLD). The initial goal of the research was to identify and validate simple measures that teachers could use in the classroom to better evaluate the effects of instruction being delivered for students with disabilities. Typically, CBM has consisted of brief one-to-three minute indicators of proficiency in a particular academic skill (Deno, 2003), although this time limit has been extended for more-complex domains, such as reading comprehension, and mathematics. Over the past three decades, researchers have implemented planned studies and analyzed large data sets to provide important evidence on the technical adequacy of CBM measures for screening and monitoring students' instructional progress over time. This research has been synthesized in both reading and mathematics. For example, in a special issue of *The Journal of Special Education*, Wayman, Wallace, Wiley, Tichá, and Espin (2007) provide a literature synthesis that addresses the extensive research on reliability, validity (primarily criterion-related), and growth of CBM in reading. Likewise, considerable research has been summarized on the technical adequacy of curriculum-based measures in mathematics (Foegen, Jiban, & Deno, 2007).

Such studies, however, fail to provide essential insights into the challenges that practitioners face when using CBM to guide their instructional decision-making. Moreover, such studies, in focusing on "average" student performance and general case examples, may miss nuances important to understanding the validity of such measures for improving learning outcomes for SWD. This gap in the literature prevents any testable verification that SWD respond to test items in the intended manner, a requirement for establishing evidence of construct validity (American Educational Research Association et al., 2014). Therefore, we explicitly use three guiding principles behind the use of CBM in a response-to-intervention system (RTI) to frame our case study.

The first principle is that student responses need to be based on *psychometrically adequate measures* and be consistently noticeable using graphic displays so teachers can use slope (rate of change) and variation of student responses to adjust instruction as needed. Tindal (2013) has summarized this research for a variety of measures that have been systematically investigated over the past 30 years in reading, mathematics, and writing, as well as content areas in secondary settings. In reading, fluency is considered important so attention can be given to comprehension and contextual cues; in mathematics, fluency in basic operations is needed to focus on problem solving. However, more-complex assessments of reading and math are also needed with accuracy of responding to individual problems serving as the key to understanding what and how to teach. In the case study, measures are based on (oral reading) fluency as well as accuracy in responding to multiple-choice questions using easy CBM (Alonzo, Tindal, Ulmer, & Glasgow, 2006).

The second guiding principle is that *teacher responses need to be individualized* and *iteratively developed* to maximize student success. Even though various educational interventions have research behind them, most of this research is based on research designs with outcomes averaged and comparisons made for groups, controlling for various confounds. These designs are typical in educational research, providing a strong empirical basis for validating interventions in general, and are certainly a good place to begin searching for possible interventions (for example, see the *What Works Clearing House* at http://ies.ed.gov/ncee/wwc). However, such group effects cannot be applied to individuals with any certainty. Not only are there uncertainties dealing with comparability of populations (of students in the studies) but positive outcomes are attained for the distribution of students with a wide array of effects (negative to positive). Using the legal mandates of Individualized Educational Programs (IEPs), teachers for students with disabilities are required to complete long-range goals, short-term objectives, along with interventions unique to the student being served. Often these goals and objectives are framed with loosely defined measurement systems that are not technically adequate. However, if simple measures are available for teachers to use in framing goals and objectives (e.g., CBM), it is possible to individually evaluate educational programs. Our case study illustrates specialization of instructional programs for a student with a learning disability who had specialized instruction over many years with adjustments made over time.

The third guiding principle is that teachers' *interventions should lead to improved student responses* and when this is not the outcome, further interventions are warranted until success is achieved. Because interventions are best-guess hypotheses that need to be evaluated, teachers can use single case designs with successive interventions compared using a technically adequate measurement system to document improved student performance. This perspective is built off the logic of Popper (1963) in which conjectures are made but need to be refutable and refuted through the collection of evidence. For example, teachers might use the best evidence to date for selecting an intervention, but it is incumbent upon them to collect data that either verifies or refutes its effects. In essence, it is the teacher's response to the student's response that provides the essential validation evidence. Our case study presents this perspective for a single student learning to read over his entire elementary schooling experience so we include information on successive teachers' interventions overlaid on graphed CBMs with varying levels of success.

Given our framework of RTI and CBM, we focus our discussion on the need for a dual-level examination of response processes. Student responses to interventions form the first level, with teacher responses (decision-making) forming the second level. We begin with some background, both in terms of measurement assumptions and existing practices, followed by a case study example to illustrate the potential opportunity for examining response processes from both a student and teacher perspective, and end with directions for future work in this area.

Promoting Learning Gains through Student and Teacher Response Processes

In considering validation of score meaning, we focus on three components: *measurement sufficiency* (type, frequency, and appropriateness of assessments used are sufficient), *instructional adequacy* (instruction provided to students promotes change in performance on the CBM measures and documents learning), and *decision-making* (educators use the information from the CBMs to appropriately introduce, maintain, and end interventions, as data indicate)—see Figure 10.1. Individual components are not as critical as their intersections (*N.B.* the time series is important in making causal arguments in which time proceeds from left to right). As teachers collect data

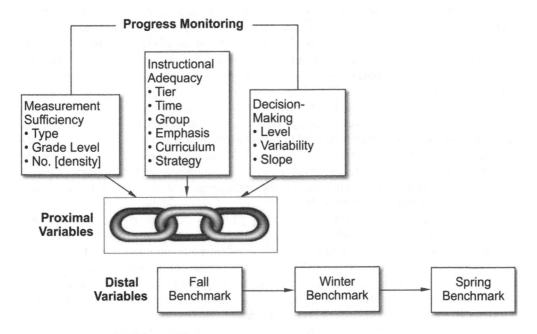

Figure 10.1 The Inter-linked Aspects Important to Consider

(from benchmark to decisions of risk and monitoring of progress), data used to inform decisions need to be sufficient, directed toward instruction, and adjusted as needed.

Given the general principles above, we focus on student responses while being measured with CBMs. In particular, we enhance the overall paradigm of screening and benchmarking (norm-referenced perspective at one point in time) and progress monitoring (individual referenced at multiple points in time) by addressing specific responses from both teachers and students (criterion-referenced perspective that is diagnostic and skill/strategy-specific). The critical components are the use of sufficient measurement to inform and adjust instruction as well as monitor developmental trajectories over time (within and across years). Measurement sufficiency should lead to instructional adequacy, including level of support (tier), amount of time, grouping of students, deployment of resources, use of an enacted curriculum, and choice of specific instructional strategies. Finally, with interventions being implemented over time, decision-making becomes important by examining student responses and analyzing through changes in level, slope, and variability.

The three main areas we highlight (measurement sufficiency, instructional adequacy, and decision-making) provide potential opportunities for greater exploration of both student and teacher response processes for acquiring greater test score meaning. In the next section, we use case study data to illustrate the deeper understanding of validation to be gained by looking more deeply at the use of CBM for a student with learning disabilities in actual practice.

Case Study Example: Larry

In general, the results from universal screening assessments represent a quick way for a teacher to understand the status of each student in the class on a variety of general outcomes. Broad inferences can then be drawn about a single student's performance relative to the entire classroom or a normative sample. Our case study student, whom we have named Larry, was in fifth grade at the time of our data harvesting, although he had been identified as early as first grade with problems in reading. The youngest of three children from an intact family with both parents working in professional fields, Larry offers some interesting insights on measurement sufficiency, instructional adequacy, and decision-making that are illustrated in his reading and mathematics progress monitoring. For example, issues arise about (a) consistent use of measures that may not be sensitive and therefore appropriate for progress monitoring, (b) discrepancies from year to year, (c) the lack of progress without consequent interventions, and (d) a possible restriction in both assessment and instruction.

We begin with an examination of Larry's benchmark performance on three easy CBM measures of reading competency: Vocabulary, Reading Comprehension, and Passage Reading Fluency. We explore how his normative performance led to particular inferences about his instructional needs in reading. This normative performance is displayed in the graphs as percentile rank (PR) bands connecting fall, winter, and spring performance on screeners administered to all students. In these graphs, the lowest band represents the 10th PR, the next up represents the 20th PR, the next is the 50th PR, and the highest line is the 90th PR.

Next, we examine Larry's progress-monitoring performance to more-closely inspect his response processes to test items, and those of his resource teacher, Ms. Karn, to his test scores. We focus on her decision-making, including the instructional interventions implemented in response to his identified "needs" (based on his CBM scores), and assessment strategy for tracking Larry's reading skills development over time. Incorporating the response process of both Larry and the teacher reveals Larry's approach to solving items (e.g., read words or compute math answers) as well as Ms. Karn's approach to shaping his instruction.

RTI is a formalized model used to deliver instruction for students with disabilities; it is particularly effective in integrating general and special education programs for students with learning disabilities. Often, students are screened, and those identified for Tier 1 instruction are taught in a general education environment with strategic instruction. As students fail to respond to interventions, they are moved to Tier 2 and provided with targeted instructional programs. Finally, if responsiveness is not forthcoming, Tier 3 instructional programs are implemented, representing highly individualized instruction, sometimes in special education settings. In this way, the response process guides instruction, as Larry's knowledge and competencies and approach to assessment items reveal his strengths and deficiencies in relation to curriculum standards, which validates the purpose of CBM in judging the effects of instruction.

CBM Benchmark Performance

When we met Larry, he was a fifth-grade student at a local school implementing an RTI approach for provision of instruction. He was receiving special reading services, having been initially identified for services in first grade. Larry's fifth-grade universal screening (raw) scores for the Vocabulary, Reading Comprehension, and Passage Reading Fluency measures in the fall were 12 (of 20) on Vocabulary, 10 (of 20) on Reading Comprehension, and 78 words correct per minute on Fluency (compared to the grade-level normative averages of 135 words correct); these scores are difficult to interpret in isolation but do indicate some areas of concern. However, when we compare them to a normative sample, it is clear that in all reading domains, Larry scored around the 10th percentile rank (PR) coming into fifth grade. Given district policy, his performance qualified him for small group instructional services focused on building these skills.

According to his historic benchmark scores, as a first-grade student, Larry showed average or above-average proficiency in Phoneme Segmenting, below grade-level proficiency in Letter Sounds Fluency, and far below grade-level proficiency in oral reading fluency, as measured by both Word and Passage Reading Fluency measures. Larry's performance in Vocabulary was slightly better than his performance on fluency measures, with scores well below the 10th percentile rank in third grade, the first year he was assessed in this construct, nearing the 30th percentile rank by the end of fourth grade, and then dipping back to just below the 10th percentile rank on the fifth-grade measures.

Larry's performance on the mathematics measures provides rather convincing evidence of a specific learning disability in reading, rather than simply low performance and achievement more generally. In math, he began the year with low performance, but ended each year performing at or above grade-level expectations on the benchmark assessments. Beginning in Grade 1, Larry's performance was near the 20th percentile (at the risk cut point) on the National Council of Teachers of Mathematics (NCTM) measures, but ended the year near the 90th percentile. The same outcomes occurred in grades 2 and 3, showing low initial performance with high end of year performance. In grade 4, Larry's teachers began using the Common Core State Standards (CCSS) Reading Comprehension measures, and Larry's performance began and ended near the 30th percentile; this same pattern reoccurred in grade 5. Although the change in math measures may have caused his slight drop in performance or improvement, the teachers were not alarmed and did provide targeted or differentiated math instruction. In summary, with annual progress over successive years (in grades 1–3) and only slightly lower performance and progress with the switch to new measures (in grades 4 and 5), the academic problems for Larry appear to be specific to reading.

CBM Progress Monitoring

Larry's teacher initially began progress monitoring his beginning reading skill development using a Letter Sound Fluency measure, but after two scores that neared the 30th percentile rank (based on national norms), his progress monitoring was altered to focus solely on oral reading fluency, despite repeated scores well below the 10th percentile rank. Monitoring progress with only oral reading fluency mirrors trends in CBM research and has predominated over all other CBM measures. Yet, based on a discussion with both Larry and his current fifth-grade teacher, this may not have been the best strategy for a student displaying Larry's particular academic needs. Recall that in Larry's district, scores below the 20th percentile are considered in need of Tier 2 targeted instruction, which may have influenced the decision to move away from measurement of Letter Sounds Fluency, despite clearly insufficient passage reading fluency. Over the years, teachers responded to Larry's performance somewhat inconsistently, in part because he was often accurate in his reading (just not fluent) and he was often able to interact with teachers on the meaning of the text he was reading.

Figure 10.2 displays Larry's performance on the first-grade Word Reading Fluency (WRF) progress measures in grade 1; Figure 10.3 displays his performance on the first-grade Passage Reading Fluency (PRF) measures. Despite improving his raw score on the measures (from a low of 1 CWPM in the fall of grade 1 on WRF to a high of 14 or 13 even later, on that measure in the spring. He did not improve, however, in passage reading fluency (PRF) from 13 CWPM in the fall of grade 1 to 11 CWPM in the spring, Larry's performance actually stayed the same. The WRF interventions (Figure 10.2) are more clearly articulated: Tier 2 included scheduling reading instruction four times per week and focus on letter sounds and blending using the Treasures curriculum; Tier 3 indicated scheduling Larry for 30 minutes two times per week in a group of 1:2 teacher to student ratio using the Read Well curriculum while emphasizing WRF; these Tier 2 and 3 labels are also reflected in the PRF graph (Figure 10.3).

Larry's progress-monitoring graphs for Passage Reading Fluency in grades 2–5 showed a similar pattern, though we have focused only on Larry's progress-monitoring graphs for PRF in grade 3 (see Figure 10.4) and grade 5 (see Figure 10.5). The pattern indicated slow growth in oral reading fluency while continuing to fall further behind peers across subsequent years even with a concerted focus on trying to meet his needs in Tier 3 that targeted instruction two times per week for 30 minutes using Read Naturally. Later, this intervention included the Learning Center four times per week for 30 minutes using the Triumphs to focus on fluency and comprehension.

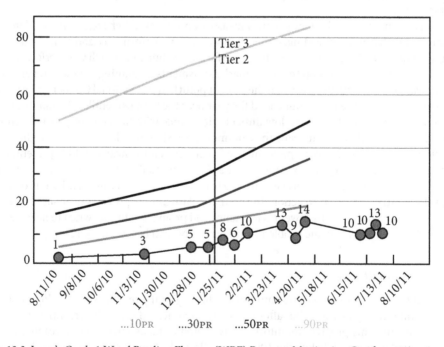

Figure 10.2 Larry's Grade 1 Word Reading Fluency (WRF) Progress Monitoring Graph

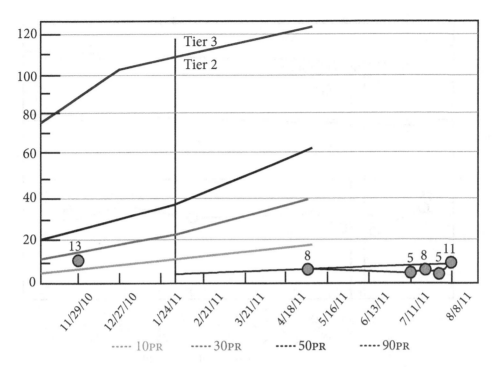

Figure 10.3 Larry's Grade 1 Passage Reading Fluency (PRF) Progress Monitoring Graph

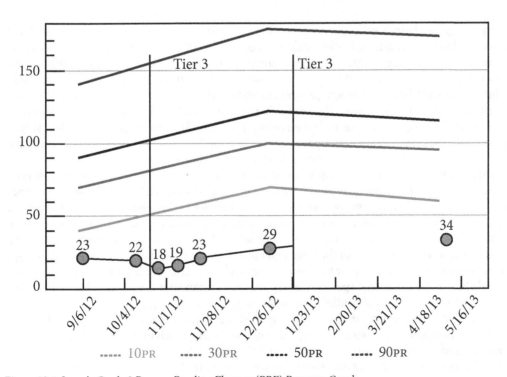

Figure 10.4 Larry's Grade 3 Passage Reading Fluency (PRF) Progress Graph

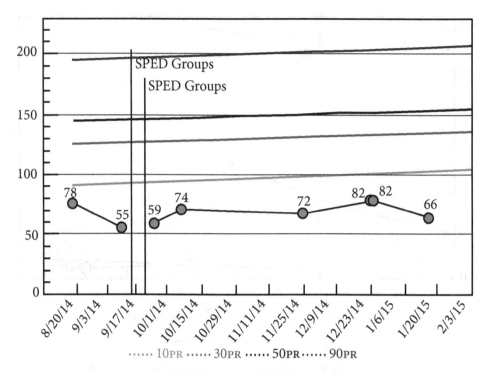

Figure 10.5 Larry's Grade 5 Passage Reading Fluency (PRF) Progress Graph

By 5th grade, Larry's schedule for targeted reading instruction includes work in the small group (2:1) in the Learning Center with the teacher, meeting daily (five times per week) for 40 minutes using a direct instruction curriculum (Corrective Reading), as well as drilling and practicing on Dolch words (220 most common words and 95 nouns). Another change is added in which Larry attends an after-school program three times per week for 30 minutes, operated by a certified teacher who pre-teaches the lesson, focusing on decoding skills integrated with a direct instruction spelling curriculum with the reading program (Spelling Mastery). Finally, Larry is placed into a special education group that meets daily for 30 minutes, with the teacher using the Triumphs curriculum to integrate fluency decoding and comprehension.

Larry's current teacher, in discussing his academic skills, was quick to refer to his poor performance on oral reading fluency measures and to note that he does much better in math. "Larry tries hard, he comes from a very supportive and intact family, where his siblings and parents have all done very well academically. Larry has a strong vocabulary and is well behaved, easy to get along with in the classroom. When it comes to reading out loud, though, he often substitutes words in a passage for words that start with the same letter but make no sense in the context of the passage. These substitutions do not appear to follow any particular pattern. He isn't consistent in the words he substitutes, even in a single passage." Larry's teacher demonstrated good insights into her student's skill deficits and solid familiarity with his progress-monitoring data.

When asked what interventions or strategies had been tried, Larry's teacher explained that he had been in interventions emphasizing oral reading fluency, including repeated reading, pre-reading, and choral responding. She explained that when the instructional focus shifted away from fluency, Larry's oral reading fluency scores seemed to decrease. She also said that use of color overlays appeared to help him focus better, although no significant improvement appeared in scores on the ORF measures, with or without the use of color overlays as a testing accommodation. Ms. Karn's response to his scores through a sustained focus on oral reading fluency (that provided the input for evaluating Larry's reading proficiency) is consistent with Larry's performance and progress.

However, a broader diet of reading assessment and intervention is not as noticeable, possibly due to this repeated use of a fluency assessment. Certainly, the current teacher's qualitative assessment of Larry was that he was a very capable student; he just could not read well. But with that in mind, an expanded focus on vocabulary and context clues for comprehension may have provided an intervention capable of transferring to more fluent reading. And with this expanded intervention, she could have concurrently used assessments of Larry's fluency, vocabulary, and comprehension to triangulate the problem and test further hypotheses for intervening, particularly because fluency had not improved much over several years.

Student Response Processes on CBM Tasks

We interviewed Larry about his thinking while completing both reading and easy mathematics CBM tasks. In general, despite his demonstrated weak oral reading skills, Larry appeared comfortable discussing the importance of reading. "If we didn't have books," he explained, "we wouldn't know anything." When he was asked to explain his approach to reading, Larry shared that he, like his teacher, thought that color overlays on the text helped him be a better reader, although his performance when reading indicated a continued struggle with accuracy when reading aloud.

Reading

When reading a passage, Larry appeared to focus on saying words aloud without reflecting on whether what he read made any sense. Although not timed (as he would be for an assessment of his passage reading fluency), Larry clearly needed an extended length of time to get through the short grade-level text. Despite his slow speed and nearly complete inaccuracy, his comprehension was fairly strong, when not dependent on successful decoding. For example, Larry was able to answer explicit questions about the passage, talk cogently about his answer choices, and demonstrate a good general understanding of the narrative. However, he often read words incorrectly, which influenced his answers. Larry correctly read initial sounds, but appeared to randomly generate medial and final sounds, often generating new words. At times, this did not affect his understanding—for example, substituting "house" for "home." More often, however, this strategy led him to a different word that affected the story in a meaningful way (e.g., substituting "thirty" for "thirteen"), or resulted in a substitution that did not make sense (e.g., substituting "concares" for "concerts") or precluded proper comprehension (e.g., substituting "anyone could" for "everyone would"). Larry's reading fluency, which Ms. Karn estimated to be about two grades below grade level, was the target focus of his reading intervention. However, the response process revealed that Larry would benefit from additional, different decoding instruction.

Vocabulary

Engaging Larry in one-to-one administration revealed much more information than his scores represent. Although Larry scored around the 10th percentile on Vocabulary, his conversational language was robust. He was able to identify synonyms of many grade-level words and correctly identify word definitions given minimum context. Thus, with a low score on his screening assessments in Vocabulary and his consistent low performance on fluency, his informal (social) language may be an instruction lever to improve both his fluency and his vocabulary. With Larry nearly ending his elementary years and moving into middle school, time has nearly run out for exclusively teaching him to read. Using both vocabulary and fluency, a broader response-to-intervention could be developed, with each (vocabulary and fluency) supporting the other through his relatively rich informal social vocabulary.

Math

Larry's responses to math items revealed several strategies that he uses for solving problems and responding to test items. For example, Larry often relied on visual representations of data to answer items, capitalizing on his strength in this area. Similar to his approach to reading comprehension, in which he returned to the text to answer explicit passage comprehension items, Larry performed well on math items that required interpretation of a visual representation of a math concept. Two examples are shown in Figure 10.6. The first depicts five dice, each showing five dots on their face. Familiar with the principles of multiplication, Larry answered correctly, giving the equation represented by the picture, not the product. The second item depicts a word item that he answered correctly without applying division, rather eliminating the answer choices that were in the wrong unit, as those "were not money."

Larry also performed well on multiplication items without visuals, as evidenced by his process and response to the first item that involved applying the concept of order of operations (Figure 10.7). The process he took in responding to the math items showed that he readily knew some multiplication, but had knowledge gaps, and his process was not automatic. Larry correctly answered the second item below by using a strategy to capitalize on his existing knowledge. He knew 8 x 2, but not 8 x 3; so from 8 x 2 = 16, he counted on this fingers 8 times to reach 24. This is represented to the left of the item, with notes from the assessor, not Larry.

Larry's problem-solving process documented in the margins of the first item, however, revealed a skill deficit in division (incorrectly dividing 84 by 14) that is confirmed in the adjacent division item, a straightforward division item presented in a common format. Larry's conceptual

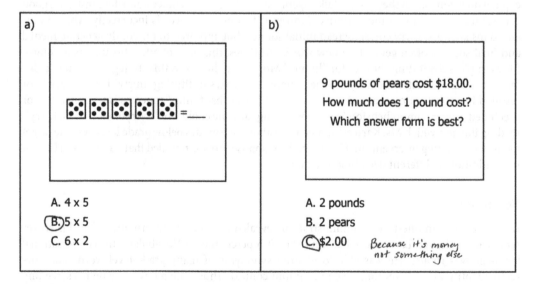

Figure 10.6 Larry's response to multiplication math items

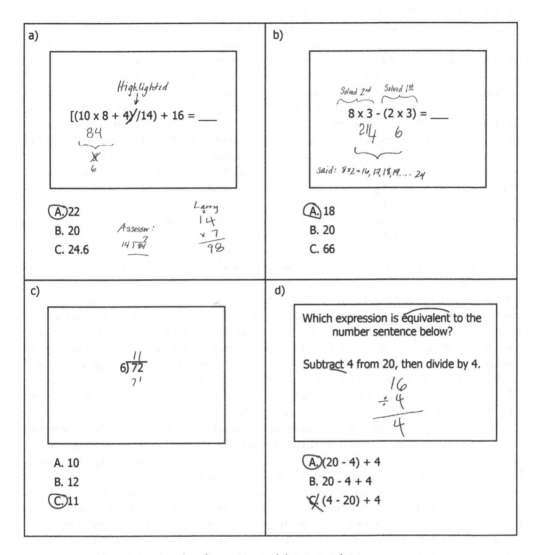

Figure 10.7 Larry's response to order of operations and division math items

mathematical understanding is depicted in the fourth item (d), but his problem-solving process highlights his misconception of division: He writes 16 ÷ 4 vertically, rather than as it is represented and taught in the classroom (i.e., $4\sqrt{16}$).

Summary

Analysis of Larry's response process yielded rich information about his knowledge and competencies in reading and math, information beyond the total scores of his universal screening measures. Larry's performance on grade-level universal reading assessments (i.e., vocabulary, comprehension, and fluency) demonstrated what had been evident since Grade 1: Larry is not a fluent reader with sound alphabetic skills. His response process revealed that he has difficulty decoding novel and multisyllabic words, as he does not have the skills to approach and decode these words. This deficiency, of course, affects his reading comprehension, despite his robust conversational vocabulary and mechanisms he applies to adapt despite his difficulties.

Larry's teachers persevered with progress monitoring using oral reading fluency measures (initially, Word Reading Fluency, and later Passage Reading Fluency) throughout first through fifth grades. His progress-monitoring graphs reflect that, even with a variety of interventions, little progress has been made. Although Larry has become somewhat more fluent in his reading, with raw scores moving from 13 words correct per minute (WCPM) in first grade to about 70 WCPM in fifth grade, his standing relative to same-grade peers has not changed much. When assessed using grade-level reading passages, Larry's performance has never advanced beyond the 10th percentile rank in oral reading fluency. And, despite a lack of progress, his oral reading fluency has continued to be assessed every few weeks throughout the year, not just in one grade, but in all grades first through fifth (see Figures 10.2–10.5). Clearly, he has not successfully responded to interventions, and another approach is likely to be needed. This new approach may be to broaden the intervention being targeted (decoding and fluency building) as well as the skills being assessed (to more than fluency). This new approach may use other skill areas such as vocabulary and context (for comprehension) to complement fluency. Furthermore, given Larry's somewhat natural proclivity to use language in social interactions, this combination is likely necessary sooner than later, particularly given his passage into middle school.

Larry displayed reasonably sufficient math skills; however, his universal screening scores suggest he was somewhat at risk for poor math outcomes, and his response process revealed specific strengths and weaknesses. Although he was able to utilize information presented in items with visual representations, produce some multiplication facts, and apply concepts such as order of operations, his foundational multiplication knowledge was incomplete and not automatic, and his division facts and skills were deficient. As math materials advance and accelerate, Larry may fall further behind if instruction does not address automaticity to provide him with the necessary skills and foundational principles needed in middle school.

In summary, our case study suggests that although a large number of curriculum-based measurement (CBM) assessments were administered to Larry over the course of his elementary school career, his scores reflect a lack of instructional responsiveness, despite repeated changes and perhaps a need for an expanded focus on different CBM assessment data to inform instructional decision-making. Larry's progress-monitoring graphs clearly document a teaching staff committed to collecting assessment data and providing interventions to students who struggle academically. They illustrate substantial time and resources dedicated to meeting a struggling student's needs. Unfortunately, they also suggest that despite these good intentions and the willingness to embrace CBM as a guide to instruction, the CBM data have not resulted in improved standing in grade-level groups.

If, as the basic premise of CBM suggests, CBM score *meaning* goes beyond measurement of a construct to focus on instructional adequacy and improved decision-making, both of which are to lead to improved student learning, a focus on student responses—or lack of responses—can provide important insights into the validation of score meaning in this area. And, as measurement and instructional decisions are aligned with the interpretations of score meaning, a greater understanding of decision-making (response processes) is sorely needed in real school time. With frequent measurement afforded by CBM and a focus on growth over time, it is possible to see the effect of this decision-making directly in time to iteratively inform subsequent decisions. Indeed, the response-to-intervention paradigm is designed to interactively connect teachers to students' responses as conjectures and refutations (Popper, 1963).

Implications for Future Research

Despite a long history of research and widespread practice, scant evidence of curriculum-based measurement response processes is available, which weakens the implicit assumptions that underlie CBM use concerning score meaning and domain fluency because little examination of the processes' and strategies' underlying performance exists (Leighton & Gierl, 2007). Particularly for students with disabilities, aligning student responses and test performance with teaching allows teachers to make empirical judgments for individuals, using norm, criterion, and individual references.

Critically, we note that current uses of CBM warrant a dual perspective about the need to examine strategies, knowledge, and process for understanding score meaning. Although rich information about student response processes for test taking is sorely needed, so too, is information about teacher response processes for interpreting score meaning within the complicated context of RTI. The consequences of poor data-based decision-making strategies, knowledge, and process can thwart the learning trajectory for SWD, creating an element of meaning that is less about the student and more about the context within which s/he is provided the opportunity to learn (as our case study example shows). Therefore, the same types of questions that can be posed for understanding how students respond to test items can also be posed for understanding deeper score meaning to extend beyond a particular test administration.

Cognitive interviews, think-aloud protocols, and analysis of error response patterns can all reveal the ways in which SWD respond to test items. However, both cognitive interviews and think-aloud protocols suffer from an "off-line" effect in that, when fluency is measured, neither can be examined during the process of performance without influencing (i.e., slowing) performance. Although analysis of error patterns is useful, some CBM items may not avail themselves well to this type of inspection. Thus, innovative approaches for effectively obtaining student response process data using CBM fluency measures are needed.

When thinking beyond student-level evidence, a number of potential considerations are necessary for examining teacher-level response processes. For example, the meaning of a test score may vary as a function of the breadth and depth of item representation. For most teachers (and developers), CBM scores reflect a simple number without consideration of the type of measure and the point within skill development at which administration occurs. Furthermore, the role of instructional adequacy on score meaning warrants greater attention (i.e., how tier, instructional time or content, and grouping impact what has been largely perceived as inherently a student response process issue). Finally, we do not yet fully understand the extent to which particular strategies or competencies are utilized in the interpretation of score meaning, and consequently the "responsiveness" to student needs. Combined, these issues bring the concept of test responding full circle by capturing "hidden" influences on student performance that seemingly begin with the student's thinking, but reach back further into the instructional and decision-making process loop in which CBM is currently situated. Especially for SWD, for whom CBM is purported to indicate not only their performance level, but also the growth of their learning, a broader perspective for evaluating CBM score meaning is necessary and overdue.

The most significant implication of a response-to-intervention system using CBM is that the validation process changes in the development of next-generation assessments. Rather than focusing on measures, the focus is on decision-making, which can be considered at two levels. At the student level, when presented items and tasks that form the initial assessment base, their responses can be analyzed and diagnosed with hypotheses generated on how they "think" about or orient and organize their response. This analysis is rich and full of potential for developing appropriate interventions. But they are merely conjectures and need to be refuted, which is where the second level of analysis enters. As teachers test their hypotheses about what works and why, they continue to collect student responses to verify (or refute) their own responses. This analysis is designed to be explicit and based on the science of learning, with rigorous analysis of student data and interventions with empirical support. Together, this dual focus on students' responses concurrently with teachers' responses appropriately anchors the development process for next-generation assessments.

References

Alonzo, J., Tindal, G., Ulmer, K., & Glasgow, A. (2006). *easyCBM online progress monitoring assessment system*. Eugene, OR: Behavioral Research and Teaching.

American Educational Research Association, American Psychological Association, & National Council on Measurement in Education (2014). *The Standards for Educational and Psychological Testing*. Washington DC: Author.

Berkeley, S., Bender, W., Peaster, L., & Saunders, L. (2009). Implementation of response to intervention. *Journal of Learning Disabilities, 42*(1), 85–95.

Deno, S. L. (2003). Developments in curriculum-based measurement. *The Journal of Special Education. 37*, 3, 184–192.

Foegen, A., Jiban, C., & Deno, S. (2007). Progress monitoring measures in mathematics: A review of the literature. *Journal of Special Education, 41*, 121–139.

Leighton, J. P., & Gierl, M. J. (2007). Defining and evaluating models of cognition used in educational measurement to make inferences about examinee's thinking processes. *Educational Measurement: Issues and Practice, 26*, 2, 3–16.

National Joint Committee on Learning Disabilities (1990). Learning disabilities: Issues on definition. Available at www.ldonline.org/njcld.

Popper, K. (1963 [1945]). *Conjectures and refutations: The growth of scientific knowledge*. New York: Routledge.

Tindal, G. (2013). Curriculum-based measurement: A brief history of nearly everything from the 1970s to the present. *ISRN Education, 2013*, 1–29.

Wanzek, J., & Cavanaugh, C. (2012). Characteristics of general education reading interventions implemented in elementary schools with reading difficulties. *Remedial and Special Education, 33*(3), 192–202.

Wayman, M. M., Wallace, T., Wiley, H. I., Tichá, R., & Espin, C. (2007). Literature synthesis on curriculum-based measurement in reading. *The Journal of Special Education, 41*, 85–120.

11 Validation of Score Meaning in Multiple Language Versions of Tests

Guillermo Solano-Flores and Magda Chía

Introduction

Examining the influence of language on the ways in which students interact with tests is critical to ensuring valid and fair testing for linguistically diverse student populations (Winter, Kopriva, Chen, & Emick, 2006). In multilingual assessment contexts, in which the same test is administered in different languages, examining differences in response processes across students who are given different language versions of the same test is particularly important in identifying potential threats to validity. Languages encode meaning differently, therefore, there is no avoiding error associated with test translation (Solano-Flores, Backhoff, & Contreras-Niño, 2009). As a consequence, construct equivalence and the equivalence of the cognitive demands of tasks across languages are major concerns in multilingual assessment contexts (Arffman, 2013; Hambleton, 2005; Sireci, 1997; van de Vijver & Hambleton, 1996).

Ensuring validity in multilingual assessment contexts entails much more than test translation. Attention to response processes in different language versions of a test and in students from different linguistic groups allows test developers and researchers to determine whether and how the constructs measured by tests are different across language versions. For example, information on response processes can be used to account for and resolve differential item functioning or to formatively evaluate the process of test translation (Allalouf, 2003; Ercikan, Arim, Law, Lacroix, Gagnon, & Domene, 2010; Solano-Flores, Chía, Shavelson, & Kurpius, 2010).

This chapter discusses and illustrates the challenges of examining response processes in multiple language versions of tests that stem from both the complexity of linguistic groups and the limitations of current assessment practices. One of these multilingual assessment contexts is international test comparisons such as PISA (Programme for International Student Assessment) and TIMSS (Trends in Mathematics and Science Study). A second multilingual assessment context is that of the national assessment programs in the U.S. in which English language learners (ELLs) or emergent bilingual students participate. These students are developing English as a second language while they continue to develop their first language mostly in English-only instructional contexts (see García & Kleifgen, 2010).

The first section examines the diversity of multilingual assessment contexts and the correspondence between the language in which tests are administered and several student language background variables critical to examining response processes. The second section offers a systemic view for examining response processes in multilingual assessment contexts. This systemic view allows identification of the ways in which current assessment practices may limit the ability of researchers and test developers to properly examine response processes among students tested with translations of tests. The third section discusses experience on the design of pop-up translation glossaries embedded in computer-administered tests with the intent to support ELL students in the U.S. in their understanding of words or terms identified as likely to be linguistically challenging.

Characterizing Multilingual Assessment Contexts

We distinguish two types of linguistic groups, reference and focal. A *reference linguistic group* is a group of examinees in whose language a test is originally created; a *focal linguistic group* is a group of examinees into whose language a test is translated. In PISA and TIMSS, tests are developed in English and then translated into different languages.[1] Native English users are the reference group; the users of other languages are the focal groups. Likewise, in national assessment programs in the U.S., tests are also developed in English and, in some cases, translated into the first languages of different groups of ELLs. Thus, non-ELL students are the reference group and the groups of ELLs students are the focal groups.

Table 11.1 shows the correspondence between the language in which a test is administered and students' language background. The table shows that this correspondence is only partial for focal groups, especially for ELLs in U.S. national assessment programs. Examination of response processes for focal groups needs to be sensitive to the instances in which this correspondence does not exist. For example, in PISA, TIMSS, and officially-recognized multilingual societies such as Canada (Gierl, 2000; Mullis, Martin, Ruddock, O'Sullivan, Arora, & Eberber, 2005; TIMSS & PIRLS International Studies Center, 2006), the language in which focal group students are tested is the language in which they receive instruction. In contrast, in U.S. assessment programs that offer partial or full translations, focal linguistic group students are tested in a language that in many cases is not the language in which they receive instruction, given that instruction is often in English. Recognizing this important difference between focal linguistic groups across assessment systems is critical to properly obtaining information on response processes (e.g., designing cognitive labs) that are sensitive to the characteristics of the student populations.

Table 11.1 Correspondence of the Language of Testing and the Students' Linguistic Background in Characteristics of Multilingual Assessment Contexts

Assessment context	Linguistic Group	Characteristics of the Language Version. The language in which the test is administered is . . .		
		the language in which students receive instruction	the predominant language in which students live	the language in which the test was developed originally
International test comparison (e.g., PISA, TIMSS)	Reference: Students in English-speaking jurisdictions tested in English (the original version of the test)	yes	yes	yes
	Focal: Students in non-English speaking jurisdictions tested with a translation of the test	yes	mostly[a]	no
U.S. national assessment program	Reference: Students who are native users of English tested in English (the original version of the test)	yes	yes	yes
	Focal: ELL students tested with a translation of the test	rarely[b]	yes	no

Notes

a In some jurisdictions, the test is administered in more than one language (see Grisay et al., 2007). The number of speakers and the power and social status of those languages is not necessarily the same.

b In spite of the fast growing number of ELL students in the U.S., the percentage of ELLs in bilingual programs is low (Zehler et al., 2003)

It is important to keep in mind that what counts as *the language in which the test is administered* admits to a wide range of interpretations (see Solano-Flores, 2012). For example, the full text of a test in the source language may be replaced entirely by its translation; or the test may have a format in which both the original language version and the translated version of the test are displayed next to each other; or only partial translations consisting of glossaries with translations of certain terms or words are offered.

Attention to the correspondence of the language in which tests are administered and the students' language background is critical to determining the aspects in which construct equivalence across languages may be threatened and, therefore, the aspects on which examination of response processes should focus.

A Systemic View on Response Processes and Validity

Language Versions of Tests

We contend that, in order to produce information relevant to the validity of tests in different languages, response processes need to be examined systemically, in relation to the components in the process of test development. These components are activities completed or outcomes reached at three main stages in the process of assessment development: conceptual, test development, and try-out/test administration (Figure 11.1).

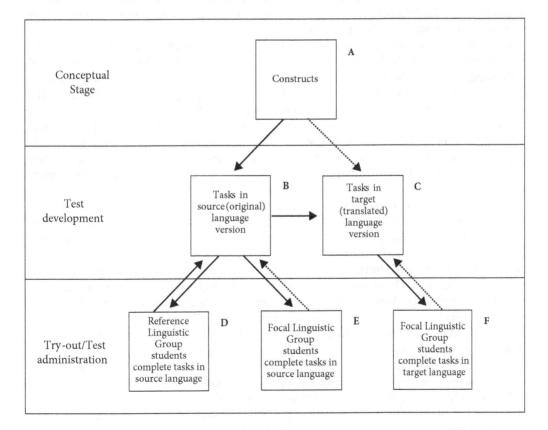

Figure 11.1 Assessment development process in multilingual assessment contexts

Note
Boxes indicate activities or outcomes; arrows indicate relationships between these components. Solid arrows indicate relationships typically addressed by current assessment practices; dotted arrows indicate relationships rarely or never addressed by current assessment practices.

The outcome of the conceptual stage is the formalization of a series of constructs to be assessed (Figure 11.1, Box A). These constructs may be documented in assessment frameworks, standards documents, and item specification documents. Typically, in large-scale assessment programs, in the development stage, a test is created in the original, source language based on those constructs and documents (Box B). In contrast, the translation of tests (Box C) is created from the tasks in the source language, not based on the constructs or the documents.[2] In their translated versions, tests address the constructs indirectly, through the tests created in the original language version.

This asymmetric relationship between language versions has serious potential validity implications. A great deal of the process of developing a test has to do with refining its tasks' textual and visual characteristics (e.g., wording, structure, layout) based on knowledge of the students' characteristics. This process of review and revision does not take place for a translated test. As a result, even the best possible translation of a test may not be as sensitive to the characteristics of the focal linguistic group as the original language version is to the characteristics of the reference linguistic group.

Alternative approaches have been investigated in which, rather than translating a test from one language into another, two language versions of the same test are developed simultaneously (Solano-Flores, Trumbull, & Nelson-Barber, 2002; Tanzer, 2005). In these approaches, teams of test developers develop different language versions of the same test concurrently, from scratch. The teams of test developers interact continuously, so that any modification on the characteristics of the tasks are negotiated and agreed upon. Also, draft versions of tasks are tried out with samples of students from the different linguistic groups of interest and the results of these try-outs inform the process of development of the test in the two languages.

Available empirical evidence shows that concurrent development allows identification of subtle but important ways in which different languages interact with the nature of the knowledge and skills assessed (Solano-Flores et al., 2002). However, its implementation is costly and time consuming, which makes it unlikely to be adopted by assessment programs in the near future. The importance of the concurrent development approach is conceptual.

According to Figure 11.1, in existing test development practices, tasks in the original language are tried out with samples of students from the reference linguistic group (Box D). These tasks may be refined by examining pilot students' response processes, such as transcriptions of cognitive interviews. This dynamic relationship is indicated by a double, solid arrow between components B and D.

In U.S. assessment programs, the tasks in the original language should also be tried out with focal linguistic group students (Box E). Yet typically, information on ELL students' response processes is rarely collected during the process of test development. As a consequence, the tasks in the source language version are not refined based on information collected from the focal linguistic group students (which is indicated by the solid arrow from B to E and the dotted arrow from E to B).

A similar scenario can be observed for students who are given the translation of a test (Box F). In a fair assessment development process, the translation of a test should be refined based on experience trying it out with focal linguistic group students. Unfortunately, this is not done routinely (which is indicated by the solid arrow from C to F and the dotted arrow from F to C). The current version of the standards for educational and psychological testing (American Educational Research Association et al., 2014) recognizes the importance of establishing the comparability of test scores across languages. However, the document does not refer explicitly to response processes and the need to try out translations of tests with samples of students of focal linguistic groups.[3] Moreover, the document implies statistical power as a condition for examining equivalence across test language versions[4]—which dismisses cognitive labs and other methods for examining response processes that typically use small samples of students due to time and cost restrictions. A study with a crossed design in which four coders coded all the transcriptions of verbal answers given by 124 students to four open-ended questions about their interpretation of a mathematics item, required a total of 19 days of coding (see Solano-Flores & Li, 2009). This experience illustrates the complexities of examining response process with large samples of students.

Language Mode and Language in which Students Provide Information

The language (source or target language) in which students provide information on the ways in which they interpret tasks and respond to them and the language modes (oral or written) in which they provide this information are important factors to consider in investigating response processes. These factors should be thought of as independent of the language in which students take a task. For example, an ELL student may be given a task in their first language but be interviewed in English about the reasoning they use in completing the task. While, typically, students are asked to provide information verbally, written reports may also be appropriate, especially when it is important to collect information from many students in a cost-effective manner. Figure 11.2 shows the response of an ELL student native Chinese speaker to the same problem in two languages. The student used different notation and problem-solving strategies across languages (Solano-Flores, Lara, Sexton, & Navarrete, 2001). These differences would have been impossible to identify through conventional interviews or by examining the students' responses given to items administered in either English or their first language.

Of utmost importance concerning the language used in obtaining information on response processes is the notion that confining ELL students to using either English or their first language to report their thinking may affect their ability to solve problems. ELL students engaged in collaboratively solving mathematics problems may switch languages both between and within sentences. Code-switching allows them to optimize different language functions, such as arguing, expressing disagreement, or referring to concepts learned during formal instruction. Optimal problem solutions emerge when ELLs are allowed to use fully the linguistic resources they possess in both their first language and their second language (Moschkovich, 2000).

A gum ball machine has 100 gum balls; 10 are yellow, 30 are blue, and 50 are red. The gum balls are well mixed inside the machine.

Jenny gets 10 gum balls from the machine. What is your best prediction of the number that will be red?

In English:	In Chinese (English translation):
5. *Because 100 ÷ 10 = 10* *If he get 10 out than mean 50÷10=5 and that is why I chose this number.*	*Because 50 = 50/100, 30 = 30/100, 20 = 20/100.* *If we minimize the, it will become 5/10, 3/10 and 2/10.*

Figure 11.2 Responses of a Grade 4 native Chinese speaker to an item from a mathematics test administered in English and in Chinese on different occasions

Source: NCES (1996): based on Solano-Flores, Lara, Sexton, & Navarrete (2001)

The researcher's or test developer's readiness to use either English or the ELL students' first language appears to be a critical factor for successful data collection. For example, the interviewer needs to be able to conduct a cognitive lab as planned even if the interaction does not take place in the language anticipated by the interviewer, or if the student switches back and forth between languages during the interview.

The researcher's sensitivity to each individual ELL student's language preferences is also critical to interacting successfully with students in a cognitive lab. In principle, it is reasonable to assume that students may feel more comfortable with an interviewer who can speak their first language. However, assuming that a student classified as ELL is more proficient in their first language than in English in the school context may be erroneous. Moreover, when their first language has a low social status, ELL students may not be comfortable using it in the school (see Brisk, 2006).

In sum, in many cases, it may be difficult to anticipate when the interaction with an ELL during a cognitive interview will take place in either language or in both. The research team's linguistic resources allowing, it is always desirable that the researcher who interacts with ELL students be proficient in the student's first language. At the same time, overestimating the researcher's proficiency in the student's first language may lead to obtaining inaccurate data (e.g., due to the student discomfort produced). For some ELL's first languages (e.g., languages with few users), researchers with any level of proficiency may simply not be available. There is some evidence that the majority of ELLs have the minimum command of spoken English they need to participate in cognitive labs, or at least to indicate the parts of the text of items they do not understand or the ways in which a certain accessibility resource helps them to understand the text of items (Prosser & Solano-Flores, 2010). However, the extent to which these findings can be generalized to all ELL students is uncertain. As with many language issues, successfully investigating response processes in multilingual assessment contexts depends on the researchers' ability to be ready to deal with uncertainty and linguistic heterogeneity.

Cognitive Labs and the Use of Glossaries in ELL Assessment

Accessibility Resources in Multiple Languages

As part of perhaps the most ambitious project in history involving multiple languages in the context of national large-scale assessment, the Smarter Balanced Assessment Consortium—one of the two Race to the Top assessment consortia—offers full-stacked translations in Spanish and partial, glossary translations in ten languages plus dialects: Spanish (Puerto Rico, Mexico, El Salvador), Vietnamese, Arabic, Filipino (Tagalog, Ilokano), Cantonese (standard, simplified), Mandarin (standard, simplified), Korean, Punjabi (Eastern, Western), Russian, and Ukrainian (Smarter Balanced Assessment Consortium, 2014b). Other language supports are projected to be added to the set of languages supported. The percentage of ELLs in the U.S. who speak a particular language as a first language is not the only criterion to determine which languages are to be supported. Other variables, such as the extent to which a given linguistic group is historically underrepresented are taken into consideration to determine the languages to support (Solano-Flores, Shade, & Chrzanowski, 2014). In fact, the consortium has piloted translating mathematics test directions into Haitian-Creole, French, Hmong, Japanese, Somali, Dakota, Lakota, and Yup'ik.

The delivery of translated glossaries is possible due to the fact that Smarter Balanced tests are computer-administered. On the computer screen, in the text of the item, a faint dotted line above and below a given term indicates that a translation is available for that term. When a student places the cursor over the term, it is automatically highlighted. Clicking on the highlighted term produces a pop-up window containing the text (Figure 11.3). For any given item, several terms may be glossed. Each gloss consists of a semantic space, a set of different translations sensitive to dialect differences but semantically equivalent.

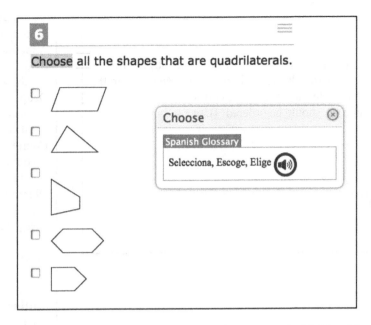

Figure 11.3 Smarter Balanced mathematics training test item showing an embedded Spanish pop-up glossary with three dialects and the audio icon

Source: Smarter Balanced (2014a)

In addition to embedded pop-up English glossaries in mathematics and English language arts tests, Smarter Balanced makes available pop-up translation glossaries to ELL students in its mathematics tests. Furthermore, a student may opt to have access to the English glossary, translated glossary, or both the English and translated versions of the test. The pop-up translated glossaries also include audio recordings of the translated text that students can access. The audio component supports students who may not be literal in their first language but can understand a term if heard. These glossaries are item-specific, grade-appropriate translations of construct-irrelevant terms used in the text of items to provide contextual information.

Designing Pop-Up Translated Glossaries

This current final version of the pop-up glossaries is the result of a long development process. For example, initially, the auditory modality of the translations did not exist. Also, multiple forms of displaying the translated glossaries were tried out before deciding to display pop-up glossaries as semantic spaces. This process of development was shaped by conceptual considerations, empirical evidence from cognitive labs, and practical constraints.

Smarter Balanced attempted to conduct cognitive labs throughout the process of development of mathematics items (Figure 11.4). Initial efforts focused on the design of the interface. These cognitive labs were conducted with the intent to gather in-depth qualitative data on how students react to different types of items and formats, and how they interact with the interface (American Institutes for Research, 2013). One of the cognitive lab protocols specifically sought to examine the impact of translated glossaries embedded within the computer test administration system. Cognitive labs aimed to determine whether translated glossaries were a fair and appropriate way to support ELL students with language needs in mathematics assessments.

1. A roller coaster has a large rise and drop followed by a complete circle. The following diagram shows measurements for the track. An extra 20 feet are needed for cutting and welding. How many feet of track should be ordered? (Use $\pi = 3.14$) A. 280 feet B. 407 feet C. 415.6 feet D. 1,537.4 feet	**Roller coaster** montaña rusa **Rise** subida **Drop** bajada caída **Complete** completo entero **Diagram** diagrama esquema gráfico **Track** vía riel **Cutting** cortar **Welding** soldar

Figure 11.4 Example of a mathematics item with contextual glossary for all item terms

Source: American Institutes for Research (2013)

The cognitive labs included two sets of mathematics items that were parallel in difficulty and administered to Spanish-speaking ELL students. The first set of items contained no glossaries; the second set of items contained glossaries (American Institutes for Research, 2013). As students talked aloud as they interacted with the items, the interviewer took notes on what they said, focusing on terms that were difficult for the students, each individual's ability to interact with the pop-up glossary interface, and the overall student interaction with the interface. Upon completion of all items, the interviewer posed the same set of questions to each student. Students were asked to share whether the glossaries were helpful, the interface was useful, and if they preferred to have the glossaries or the plain text of the test. The interviewer noted if the student did not understand a word and if the glossary helped them access the word or the sentence of which the word was part.

The experience conducting the cognitive labs provided valuable information on the ways in which students should be instructed in order for them to benefit from the accessibility resource and, more specifically, about the way in which glossed terms were highlighted (with a dotted line above and below). Yet, the most valuable information had to do with the limitations of the accessibility resource. First, it became evident that, text-based translations were not helpful for all ELL students. Consistent with the notion that each ELL is a bilingual individual with a unique set of strengths and weaknesses in each language and each language mode (Grosjean, 1985), many ELLs are not bi-literate—they are not able to read in their first language because their schooling experience is predominantly in English. It became evident that an audio component providing audio glossaries would be more helpful for these students. Thus, in the current version, the translated glossaries include an audio component by which a student can hear a human voice read the translation if they click the audio button on the corresponding word or term.

Second, results brought to light the need for clear guidelines for systematically identifying the words and terms that are most likely to be challenging to ELL students. This realization led, later on, to the development of a framework for designing accessibility resources and the establishment of a set of theoretically defensible principles for identifying candidate terms for glossing (see Solano-Flores et al., 2014).

Further, practical lessons were learned concerning the organization of cognitive labs. Challenges experienced during these cognitive labs resurfaced in subsequent attempts to conduct research throughout test development addressing language supports. Recruiting students turned out to be one of the most difficult activities. Not wanting to impact students' opportunity to learn, cognitive labs were scheduled to take place after school and during the summer. Recruitment occurred through states' departments of education, local community groups, and national organizations. Students were offered financial compensation and parents/guardians funds to address travel expenses. However, fewer students than those originally planned were able to participate. Whereas it was possible to work with Spanish-English bilingual students, it was not possible to recruit, during the summer, students whose first language was any of the other languages supported by Smarter Balanced (Vietnamese, Arabic, Tagalog, Ilokano, Cantonese, Mandarin, Korean, Punjabi, Russian, and Ukranian).

There is no doubt that, in order to be able to make proper generalizations across languages and linguistic groups, cognitive labs should be conducted with samples of students who are users of different first languages. However, a design including all first languages of interest could not be attained due to the limited availability of qualified personnel. Finding Spanish-English bilingual and bi-literate adults was challenging but doable. Finding and training interviewers who were bi-literate in both English and the student's first language was considerably more challenging. Moreover, it was seldom that schools or research organizations had an appropriately trained adult who would speak and write both in English and in any of the other languages supported by Smarter Balanced.

Based on these lessons, Smarter Balanced was better able to implement another round of cognitive labs almost two years after the initial cognitive labs took place. These new cognitive labs sought to examine students' familiarity with specific aspects of computer-based testing. Specifically, the cognitive labs examined the interaction of ELL students (and other students with special needs) with embedded and with external keyboard types on tablets. One of the main findings from these cognitive labs is that students' keyboard type preferences appeared to be determined by cognitive style rather than ELL status, school grade, or access to computers or tablets. These findings speak to the value of evidence on response processes as critical to validly and fairly assessing linguistic minority student populations.

Summary and Conclusions

Examination of response processes is critical to developing, translating, and adapting tests, and to making meaningful interpretations of test scores in multilingual assessment contexts—assessment contexts involving multiple language versions of tests and multiple linguistic groups. Translation should not be assumed to preserve the properties of test items. Serious threats to validity and fairness in the testing of multiple linguistic groups may arise due to the fact that the process of development of tests in the original language and the process of development of translated tests are very different. Response processes are critical to identifying such potential threats. Unfortunately, response processes in multilingual assessment contexts have not received the attention they have received in monolingual assessment contexts—a lag of research that reflects assessment programs' limited effectiveness in dealing with linguistic diversity.

This chapter has made the argument that, in order to support meaningful score interpretations in multilingual assessment contexts, response processes have to be interpreted systemically, in terms of their relation to the main components of the process of assessment. The experience with evaluating the effectiveness of glossaries in computer-administered mathematics assessment speaks to the practical challenges of attaining, in large-scale assessment involving linguistically diverse students, designs in which information on response processes is collected from sufficient numbers of students, for all the languages supported, and by adequately trained interviewers.

There is considerable room for innovative research on response processes in multilingual assessment contexts. Theory and methodology for future research need to recognize and address the complexity of language and linguistic groups and the complex relationship between language and cognition as critical to making meaningful, valid interpretation of test scores. Also, researchers and test developers need to recognize and address the systemic and practical constraints that may pose a threat to validity when multiple language versions of tests are used.

Notes

1 In PISA, tests are translated from both English and French versions with the intent to provide more resources for translators to examine whether meaning is preserved across languages (see OECD, 2012).
2 Ideally, translators and test translation reviewers should be provided with all the documentation supporting the tests they translate, including assessment frameworks, standards, etc. (Solano-Flores, 2012). Even if this condition is met, the process of development of an assessment in the original language and in a target language is different.
3 For example, Standard 3.12 states: "Evidence of validity may include empirical studies and/or professional judgment documenting that the different language versions measure comparable or similar constructs and that the score interpretations from the two versions have comparable validity for their intended uses" (p. 69).
4 Standard 3.12 also states: "*Where sample sizes permit*, evidence of score accuracy and precision should be provided for each group" (p. 29, emphasis added).

References

Allalouf, A. (2003). Revising translated differential functioning items as a tool for improving cross-lingual assessment. *Applied Measurement in Education, 16*(1), 55–73.

American Educational Research Association, American Psychological Association, & National Council on Measurement in Education (2014). *Standards for educational and psychological testing*. Washington, DC: American Educational Research Association.

American Institutes for Research (2013). *Cognitive laboratories technical report*. Smarter Balanced Assessment Consortium. Washington, DC: American Institutes for Research.

Arffman, I. (2013). Problems and issues in translating international educational achievement tests. *Educational Measurement: Issues and Practice, 32*(2), 2–14.

Brisk, M. E. (2006). *Bilingual education: From compensatory to quality schooling* (2nd ed.). Mahwah, NJ: Lawrence Erlbaum.

Ercikan, K., Arim, R. G., Law, D. M., Lacroix, S., Gagnon, F., & Domene, J. F. (2010). Application of think-aloud protocols in examining sources of differential item functioning. *Educational Measurement: Issues and Practice, 29*, 24–35.

García, O., & Kleifgen, J. A. (2010). *Educating emergent bilinguals: Policies, programs, and practices of English language learners*. New York: Teachers College Press.

Gierl, M. J. (2000). Construct equivalence of translated achievement tests. *Canadian Journal of Education, 25*(4), 280–296.

Grisay, A., de Jong, J. H. A. L., Gebhardt, E., Berezner, A., & Halleux-Monseur, B. (2007). Translation equivalence across PISA countries. *Journal of Applied Measurement, 8*(3), 249–266.

Grosjean, F. (1985). The bilingual as a competent but specific speaker-hearer. *Journal of Multilingual and Multicultural Development, 6*, 467–477.

Hambleton, R. K. (2005). Issues, designs, and technical guidelines for adapting tests into multiple languages and cultures. In R. K. Hambleton, P. F. Merenda, & C. D. Spielberger (Eds.), *Adapting educational and psychological tests for cross-cultural assessment* (pp. 3–38). Mahwah, NJ: Lawrence Erlbaum.

Moschkovich, J. N. (2000). Learning mathematics in two languages: Moving from obstacles to resources. In W. Secada (Ed.), *Changing faces of mathematics, Vol. 1: Perspectives on multiculturalism and gender equity*. Reston, VA: National Council of Teachers of Mathematics.

Mullis, I. V. S., Martin, M. O., Ruddock, G. J., O'Sullivan, C. Y., Arora, A., & Eberber, E. (2005). *TIMSS 2007 assessment frameworks*. Boston, MA: TIMSS & PIRLS International Study Center, Lynch School of Education, Boston College.

National Center for Education Statistics (1996). *The nation's report card: 1996 assessment mathematics public release*. Washington, DC: National Assessment of Educational Progress.

OECD (2012). *PISA 2009 technical report*. PISA OECD Publishing. http://dx.doi.org/10.1787/97892641 67872-en

Prosser, R. R., & Solano-Flores, G. (2010). *Including English language learners in the process of test development: A study on instrument linguistic adaptation for cognitive validity*. Paper presented at the Annual Conference of the National Council of Measurement in Education, Denver, Colorado, April 29–May 3.

Sireci, S. G. (1997). Problems and issues in linking tests across languages. *Educational Measurement: Issues and Practice, 16*(1), 12–19.

Smarter Balanced Assessment Consortium (2014a). Grades 3–5 Mathematics Training Test: Grade 3, math claim 1 item. http://sbac.portal.airast.org/practice-test

Smarter Balanced Assessment Consortium (2014b). Usability, accessibility, and accommodations guidelines. Prepared with the assistance of the National Center on Educational Outcomes. March 9, 2015. www.smarter balanced.org/wordpress/wp-content/uploads/2014/08/SmarterBalanced_Guidelines.pdf

Solano-Flores, G. (2012). *Translation accommodations framework for testing English language learners in mathematics*. Developed for the Smarter Balanced Assessment Consortium (SBAC). www.smarter balanced.org/wordpress/wp-content/uploads/2012/09/Translation-Accommodations-Framework-for-Testing-ELL-Math.pdf

Solano-Flores, G., & Li, M. (2009). Generalizability of cognitive interview-based measures across cultural groups. *Educational Measurement: Issues and Practice, 28*(2), 9–18.

Solano-Flores, G., Lara., J., Sexton, U., & Navarrete, C. (2001). *Testing English language learners: A sampler of student responses to science and mathematics test items*. Washington, DC: Council of Chief State School Officers.

Solano-Flores, G., Trumbull, E., & Nelson-Barber, S. (2002). Concurrent development of dual language assessments: An alternative to translating tests for linguistic minorities. *International Journal of Testing, 2*(2), 107–129.

Solano-Flores, G., Backhoff, E., & Contreras-Niño, L. A. (2009). Theory of test translation error. *International Journal of Testing, 9*, 78–91.

Solano-Flores, G., Chía, M., Shavelson, R. J., & Kurpius, A. (2010). *Cognitive labs guidelines*. Assessment of Higher Education Learning Outcomes Generic Strand. Document GS.37. New York: Council for Aid to Education.

Solano-Flores, G., Shade, C., & Chrzanowski, A. (2014). *Item accessibility and language variation conceptual framework*. Submitted to the Smarter Balanced Assessment Consortium (October 10). www.smarter balanced.org/wordpress/wp-content/uploads/2014/11/ItemAccessibilityandLanguageVariationConcep tualFramework_11-10.pdf

Tanzer, N. K. (2005). Developing tests for use in multiple languages and cultures: A plea for simultaneous development. In R. Hambleton, P. Merenda, & C. D. Spielberger (Eds.), *Adapting educational and psychological tests for cross-cultural assessment*. Hillsdale, NJ: Lawrence Erlbaum.

TIMSS & PIRLS International Studies Center (2006). *TIMSS: Trends in Mathematics and Science Study*. Boston, MA: Lynch School of Education, Boston College. www.timss.org

van de Vijver, F. J. R., & Hambleton, R. K. (1996). Translating tests: Some practical guidelines. *European Psychologist, 1*(2), 89–99.

Winter, P. C., Kopriva, R. J., Chen, C.-S., & Emick, J. E. (2006). Exploring individual and item factors that affect assessment validity for diverse learners: Results from a large-scale cognitive lab. *Learning and Individual Differences, 16*(4), 267–276.

Zehler, A. M., Fleischman, H. L., Hopstock, P. J., Stephenson, T. G., Pendzick, M. L., & Sapru, S. (2003). *Descriptive study of services to LEP students and LEP students with disabilities. Volume I: Research Report*. Arlington, VA: Development Associates.

12 Commentary II

The Value of Response Process Studies to Evaluate Score Meaning

Suzanne Lane

Introduction

The use of examinee response process data to validate score meaning in educational testing has evolved from studies using protocol analysis to more-recent studies that evaluate log files to infer the strategies and processes examinees use when solving tasks. Methodological advances have also been made within individual procedures, such as protocol analysis, to ensure the validity of the information obtained about students' cognitive processing. Beginning in the 1970s both cognitive psychologists and psychometricians were studying the cognitive processes, knowledge, and strategies that underlie item performance. It was not enough to know whether an examinee responded correctly or incorrectly, researchers wanted to understand what cognitive processes and strategies were used by examinees when solving items and what item features, and consequently processes and strategies, affected item difficulty. In his seminal chapter on validity, Messick (1989) discussed approaches that were emerging for studying processes underlying item performance as well as linking these processes with item difficulty, including protocol analysis, computer modeling, analysis of reasons, analysis of eye movements, and analysis of systematic errors. Some of these methods for studying response processes are discussed in the chapters in this section.

Sources of Response Process Evidence

The purpose of response process studies has evolved from the quest to understand the processes students use as they engage in the solution of tasks to informing the design and validation of assessment and scoring systems. The *Standards for Educational and Psychological Testing* (American Educational Research Association, American Psychological Association, & National Council on Measurement in Education, 2014) identifies evidence based on response processes as an essential aspect of the validity argument for an assessment when claims are made about the processes used by examinees when solving items. In addition to examining the response processes of examinees, the response processes of those who interpret examinee performance, such as raters and scoring algorithms, need to be evaluated to ensure the validity of their inferences and decisions regarding examinee performance. As indicated by Bejar (2012), not only does the degree of structure in the intended response need to be considered in the delineation of the scoring criteria, but rater cognition should also be considered because it is essential that raters not only understand the rubrics and internalize the criteria at each score level, but also accept and accurately implement the rubrics. Construct representation, and the extent to which the assessment is measuring not only the intended construct but also some other irrelevant construct, is affected by the raters' interpretation and implementation of the scoring rubric as well as features specific to the training of the raters, including training materials and procedures (Lane & Stone, 2006; Lane & Depascale, 2016).

As we move away from human raters to automated scoring algorithms to evaluate student responses, we need to study the meaning of scores generated by such scoring algorithms. Scores generated from automated scoring algorithms can, in part, reflect construct-irrelevant variance if the scoring procedures do not encompass important features of proficiency and instead attend to irrelevant features (Bennett, 2006). As indicated by the *Standards for Educational and Psychological Testing* (American Educational Research Association et al., 2014), when automated scoring algorithms are "used to score complex examinee responses, characteristics of responses at each score level should be documented along with the theoretical and empirical bases for the use of the algorithms" so as to allow for the linking of scores to the targeted cognitive processes (p. 91). To evaluate scoring algorithms, Bennett and Zhang (2016) suggest posing the following question: "are the model's features related to one another empirically in theoretically meaningful ways, and do the features and their weighting fully capture the rubric and construct definition?" (p. 160). With respect to writing assessments, they argue that evidence needs to support whether the scoring model is a direct measure of the writing skill instead of just being a correlate of it. The development of an automated scoring algorithm should be integral to the design of the assessment, and the development of the scoring algorithm should be based on a deep understanding and thorough delineation of the construct. Further, if human scores are a basis of validation for automated scoring models a better understanding of rater cognition is needed so that validity evidence encompasses all methods that provide meaning to scores derived from the assessment of students.

Response Process Studies in Test Design and Validation

The extent to which examinee response process data can be used to validate score meaning is dependent on the assessment design procedures. The use of an argument-based approach to validity provides a foundation for assessment design considerations (Kane, 2006, 2013). The interpretive argument explicitly links the inferences from performance to conclusions and decisions, including the actions resulting from the decisions, and therefore the choices made in test design have direct implications for the validity of score meaning. The validity argument provides a comprehensive framework for obtaining evidence to support the claims put forth in the interpretive argument. Claims about the response processes used by examinees are an integral component to the interpretive argument and the collection of evidence to support or refute those claims is embodied by the validity argument.

Principled approaches to test design, such as evidence-centered design (ECD) (Mislevy, Steinberg, & Almond, 2003), have the potential to generate response process data that provide rich information on the extent to which the processes used by examinees are aligned with the claims. In the ECD framework, an evidentiary assessment argument is formed that connects claims about student thinking and knowing, evidence, and supporting rationales. The premise of principled approaches to test design is that evidence observed in student performance on tasks that have clearly articulated cognitive demands is used to make claims about student thinking and knowing. The explicit delineation of the cognitive processes that should be assessed provides guidance on what types of items are needed to allow for evidence to support the claims about student achievement and learning. Cognitive models about student cognition based on theory and empirical evidence, however, are not fully developed in many areas and are supplemented by expert opinion. The development of cognitive models typically is iterative and requires ongoing programs of validity research. Explicit delineation of the claims and evidence can help minimize construct-irrelevant variance and help ensure that the intended skills are sufficiently represented. Task and scoring models that delineate the intended response processes will afford both accuracy and consistency of the measurement of such responses.

Principled approaches to test design in conjunction with universal design procedures will help ensure that all students have access to the assessment and that the targeted cognitive skills are being evoked by the students. The Center for Applied Special Technologies (2011) identified three principles for universal design for learning: Multiple means of representation, multiple means of action and expression, and multiple means of engagement. Multiple means of representation include providing options for perception; language, mathematical expressions, and symbols; and comprehension. Multiple means of action and expression include providing options for physical action, expression and communication, and executive functions (e.g., support for planning and strategy development). Multiple means of engagement include providing options for recruiting interest, sustaining effort and persistence, and for self-regulation. The use of these principles in assessment design will better allow for all students to engage in the intended cognitive processes when solving assessment tasks.

Because subgroups of examinees may respond differently to tasks by engaging in different cognitive processes or strategies, the potential differential use of response processes by subgroups should be considered in the design of assessments and response processes should be evaluated at the subgroup level to inform any potential differences in score meaning across subgroups. Subgroups may include English language learners, students with disabilities, and cultural and racial subgroups in addition to subgroups formed based on different learning styles of students and how students approach and solve problems.

Discussion of Chapters 6–11

This set of chapters elaborates on different ways of using examinee response process data to provide validity evidence in support of score inferences and uses across different assessment contexts. It could be argued that evidence of examinee response processes has become even more essential with the call for the assessment of more-complex thinking for all students, the increased use of automated scoring algorithms, and the increased use of more innovative and performance-based task formats. The assessment of complex thinking however poses design, psychometric, and validity challenges that need to be considered initially as the assessment is being conceptualized (Lane & Stone, 2006; Lane & Depascale, 2016). As suggested by many of the chapter authors, the delineation of a validity argument and the use of principled approaches to test design, such as ECD, will help ensure the design of assessments that measure the intended response processes.

In Chapter 6, Nichols and Huff address the assessment of complex thinking and the use of studies of response processes to provide validity evidence for score meaning in light of the next generation of standards in mathematics, science, and English language arts. They discuss three types of studies of response processes, verbal reports (i.e., think alouds, protocol analysis), eye movements, and log files, with particular attention to verbal reports. The value of both concurrent and retrospective verbal reports is discussed as well as the use of such reports in providing validity evidence to support the assessment of argumentation in the AP World History Exam. The authors also lay out a validity argument using the network of claims for this exam, which was designed using ECD, and provide information on how think-aloud protocols from both examinees and raters were used to obtain data on the cognitive response processes used in both responding to the prompt and scoring student responses in support of the claims. The study they describe provides an excellent example of obtaining validity evidence for not only students' response processes but also raters' response processes when they are evaluating student reports. As self-reports, consideration needs to be given to the completeness and accuracy of verbal reports provided by examinees and raters as well as how reporting affects examinees' cognitive processing which in turn can threaten the validity of the reported information.

In Chapter 7, Bejar discusses threats to the validity of score meaning in automated scoring of writing with respect to construct representation and construct-irrelevant response processes. Although automated scoring may increase efficiency and allow for reporting of scores in a timely manner, it needs to do so without threatening the validity of score meaning. Evidence of the validity of score meaning is discussed by Bejar in terms of the features that are identified for depicting examinee performance and the synthesis of the evidence across the features to produce a score;

both feature extraction and evidence synthesis can threaten the meaning of scores. Score meaning will be negatively affected if the construct is not fully represented, because features are not fully identified such as the failure to capture a feature that reflects argumentative skills in a writing assessment of argumentation. A common procedure that is used to determine the set of features that should contribute to the score involves evaluating the predictive power of identified features using human scores as a criterion. As discussed by Bejar, the validity of this approach is affected by the accurate representation of the features, validity of the human scores, and restriction in the score scale range due to regression to the mean. To ensure score meaning in automated scores, the scoring engine should be an integral aspect in the assessment design process so as to ensure that choices in the design of task features allow for the design of scoring algorithms that capture the intended cognitive skills and knowledge. An inherent conflict will exist between assessing complex thinking skills and knowledge and the design of a scoring algorithm that produces both accurate and reliable scores.

In Chapter 8, DiBello, Pellegrino, Gane, and Goldman elaborate on how examinee response processes contribute to the validity argument and analyses for instructionally supportive assessments. A validity framework is proposed for examining the validity of score inferences from an assessment system that is designed to be both sensitive to instruction and to inform instruction. The validity framework not only includes cognitive and inferential components, but also instructional components so as to reflect a comprehensive system of standards, curriculum, instruction, and assessments that serve unique purposes. They propose that response processes provide evidence for each of these validity components, and therefore response processes need to be examined with respect to their coherency across the components. The cognitive component addresses whether the cognitive skills that a student engages in when responding to a task are assessing relevant rather than irrelevant skills; the instructional component addresses the extent to which response processes are aligned to the curricula and instruction, and the inferential components addresses the extent to which interpretations of scores accurately reflect the response processes, how well the scoring rubrics and scores capture the response processes, and the level of measurement error in scores. Using the *Diagnoser* System for Middle School and High School Physical Science they provide examples of validity evidence for response processes using cognitive laboratory studies, expert reviews, and quantitative analyses of scored student performance for each of the validity components. As they indicate, "a meaningful interpretation of response process data relies upon deep connections to multiple sources of evidence that are constructed and interpreted within an overall validity argument" (p. 103).

In Chapter 9, Kopriva and Wright discuss a conceptual framework for evaluating response processes in the assessment of academic content of non-native speakers. The framework is based on the premise that assessment design and score interpretation involves an evaluation of the interaction of construct-irrelevant conditions experienced by examinees in the testing situation where responses are generated (such as production skills), and the conditions that are barriers in accessing the intended content and processes. The authors identify a number of barriers to students in accessing the construct such as linguistic features, cultural features, multisemiotic features (communication mode), and they delineate how these barriers can affect the cognitive skills used when non-native speakers undertake a problem-solving task. They discuss the evaluation of a system that allows examinees to use multiple modalities (non-text) on screens, allowing for better access for students who use different sign systems to communicate their knowledge and understanding. Allowing multiple means for communicating task information as well as for examinees to communicate their knowledge and skills allows for a more valid assessment of non-native speakers' complex thinking. Careful attention to universal design principles as they have outlined will help ensure the assessment of the intended cognitive skills for all students.

In Chapter 10, Tindal, Alonzo, Sáez, and Nese discuss the use of curriculum-based assessments in response-to-intervention systems for student with disabilities. A primary goal of these assessments is that they provide meaningful information about student performance and progress, and that this information informs instruction. They review studies that examined whether students with disabilities progressed differently than students in general education and whether monitoring students with disabilities systematically showed greater progress. The authors argue that the use of curriculum-based measures for screening and monitoring students' instructional progress allows for both measurement sufficiency and instructional adequacy and decision making. Evidence of response processes underlying performance for curriculum-based assessments however is limited and many of these assessments do not assess complex thinking skills. Research is needed to examine the knowledge, skills, and processes underlying performance on these assessments to better understand score meaning as well as to examine the response processes used by teachers for interpreting score meaning to inform their decisions about instructional interventions. Studies of response processes that use cognitive interviews, think-aloud protocols, and analysis of reasons and error patterns would provide much-needed evidence to support the validity of interpretations and uses of scores derived from curriculum-based assessments.

In Chapter 11, Solano-Flores and Chía provide a systematic framework for examining and delineating response processes in defining the assessment construct, developing assessment design procedures, and piloting assessments in multilingual assessment contexts. The authors discuss how response process studies can help inform assessment design procedures, shed light on the results of differential item functioning studies, and be used to evaluate the assessment translation process. As they suggest, instead of translating an assessment from one language to another, a better approach is to develop two language versions of the same assessment simultaneously. This would make explicit how languages interact differently with the cognitive skills and knowledge being assessed. They argue that in any assessment context to ensure valid score interpretations and uses, multilingual students need to have the opportunity to respond in both their first and second languages and, when evaluating response processes, cognitive lab interviewers need to be flexible in the language they use and to encourage flexibility in the language the student uses. It is apparent that to ensure multilingual students have ample opportunity to display their skills and knowledge, careful consideration needs to be given to the design, implementation, and scoring procedures of assessments and related studies that provide evidence to support score meaning and use.

Concluding Comments

Assessments that measure complex thinking require a systematic evaluation of the extent to which the intended processes and strategies that underlie student performance are consistent with the intended claims. Response process studies should be an integral component in the design of educational assessments, especially those designed to measure complex thinking. The experiences of students during an assessment, and consequently their performances, are affected by a complex interaction of test characteristics (such as academic content, test language, item type, and scoring), and their cultural, language, economic, and educational histories (Solano-Flores, 2008; Solano-Flores & Trumbull, 2003).

To evaluate the extent to which the targeted construct is being assessed in the same way across subgroups of students, measurement invariance studies that examine the comparability of the internal structure of the test across subgroups are needed to ensure the validity and fairness of score interpretations and uses. When measurement invariance studies suggest that the internal structure of an assessment is not comparable across subgroups of students, response process studies can help uncover why such differences occur. As an example, when the presence of differential item functioning (DIF) is identified through field-testing, both the content of the item and the student responses should be analyzed to potentially detect reasons for DIF and to help inform future task and scoring rubric design efforts. In a relatively early study, the potential reasons for gender related DIF on a mathematics performance assessment were examined (Lane, Wang, &

Magone, 1996). Through a systematic analytic analysis of student responses and rationales to items that were flagged as DIF, the authors found that male students in middle school as compared to female students were not complete in showing their solution processes and provided limited conceptual explanations for their answers. Using think-aloud protocols, Ercikan and colleagues (2010) examined whether characteristics of items that were identified by expert reviews as sources of DIF were supported by empirical evidence from examinee think alouds for the English and French versions of a Canadian national assessment. Their results indicated only moderate agreement between experts and examinee-reported response processes with the protocols suggesting types of linguistic differences that may lead to differences in student engagement in cognitive thinking and their performances in multilingual assessments.

In addition to protocol analyses, advances in other methodologies will allow us to better understand the cognitive processes and strategies students use when solving complex tasks and consequently will allow for the design of assessments and scoring systems that are capable of eliciting the targeted response processes. To better understand responses of examinees to mathematics problem-solving tasks, Zhu and Feng (2015) modeled eye movements using social network analysis. Their results suggest that there are common general transition patterns among students. However, high-performing students as compared to low-performing students use more strategic transitions and connect multiple sources of information to solve complex mathematics problems. Low-performing students tended to consider isolated pieces of information when responding to the tasks. Deane and Zhang (2015) examined the feasibility of characterizing writing performance using process features derived from a keystroke log. Their results indicated that there is considerable inconsistency of keystroke log features across assessment occasions, but the features that are most stable have moderate to strong prediction of human essay scores and are generalizable across prompts within a genre. Analyzing eye-movement patterns when examinees are solving problems, and keystroke logs when examinees are responding to an essay, can provide valuable information on how examinees engage with tasks, and have the potential to inform the design of tasks that assess complex thinking. The future holds promise for the design of assessments that will capture complex response processes giving rise to score meaning, and advances in technology will provide rich information on the extent to which assessments capture these processes.

References

American Educational Research Association, American Psychological Association, National Council on Measurement in Education (2014). *Standards for educational and psychological testing.* Washington, DC: American Educational Research Association.

Bejar, I. I. (2012). Rater cognition: Implications for validity. *Educational Measurement: Issues and Practice, 31*(3), 2–9.

Bennett, R. E. (2006). Moving the field forward: Some thoughts on validity and automated scoring. In D. M. Williamson, R. J. Mislevy, & I. I. Bejar (Eds.), *Automated scoring of complex tasks in computer-based testing* (pp. 403–412). Hillsdale, NJ: Lawrence Erlbaum.

Bennett, R. E. & Zhang, M. (2016). Validity and automated scoring. In F. Drasgow (Ed.). *Technology and testing: Improving educational and psychological measurement.* New York: Routledge.

Center for Applied Special Technologies (2011). *Universal Design for Learning Guidelines version 2.0.* Wakefield, MA: Author.

Deane, P. & Zhang, M. (2015). Exploring the feasibility of using writing process features to assess text production skills. *Research Report Series, 2015*(2), 1–16.

Ercikan, K., Arim, R., G., Law, D. M., Lacroix, S., Gagnon, F., & Domene, J. F. (2010). Application of think-aloud protocols in examining sources of differential item functioning. *Educational Measurement: Issues and Practice, 29*(2), 24–35.

Kane, M. T. (2006). Validation. In R. L. Brennan (Ed.), *Educational measurement* (4th ed., pp. 17–64). Washington, DC: American Council on Education; Westport, CT: Praeger.

Kane, M. T. (2013). Validating the interpretations and uses of test scores. *Journal of Educational Measurement, 50*(1), 1–73.

Lane, S. & Stone, C.A. (2006). Performance assessments. In B. Brennan (Ed.), *Educational measurement* (4th ed., pp. 387–432). Washington, DC: American Council on Education; Westport, CT: Praeger.

Lane, S. & DePascale, C. (2016). Psychometric considerations for alternative forms of assessments and student learning objectives. In H. Braun (Ed.), *Meeting the challenges to measurement in an era of accountability.* New York: Routledge.

Lane, S., Wang, N., & Magone, M. (1996). Gender related DIF on a middle school mathematics performance assessment. *Educational Measurement: Issues and Practice, 15*(4), 21–27, 31.

Messick, S. (1989). Validity. In R. L. Linn (Ed.), *Educational measurement* (3rd ed. pp. 13–104). New York: American Council on Education, and Macmillan.

Mislevy, R. J., Steinberg, L. S., & Almond, R. G. (2003). On the structure of educational assessments. *Measurement: Interdisciplinary Research and Perspectives, 1*(1), 3–62.

Solano-Flores, G. (2008). Who is given tests in what language by whom, when and where? The need for probabilistic views of language in the testing of English language learners. *Educational Researcher, 37*(4), 189–199.

Solano-Flores, G. & Trumbull, (2003). Examining language in context: The need for new research and practice paradigms in the testing of English-language learners. *Educational Researcher, 32*(2), 3–13.

Zhu, M. & Feng, G. (2015). *An exploratory study using social network analysis to model eye movements in mathematics problem solving.* Proceedings of the Fifth International Conference on Learning Analytics and Knowledge, New York.

Contributors

Volume Editors

Kadriye Ercikan is the Vice President of Statistical Analysis, Data Analysis, and Psychometric Research (SADA&PR) at the Educational Testing Service and Professor of Education at the University of British Columbia. Her research focuses on language and cultural issues in measurement, psychometrics, assessment of history learning, and the contribution of different research paradigms to creating knowledge and making generalizations in education research.

In 2000, Ercikan received an Early Career Award from the University of British Columbia and in 2010 she received the AERA Division D Significant Contributions to Educational Measurement and Research Methodology Award for her co-edited volume *Generalizing from Educational Research: Beyond Qualitative and Quantitative Polarization* (Routledge). She has been a member of the National Academy of Education Committee on Foundations of Educational Measurement and has served as an elected member of the NCME Board of Directors. She is currently Vice-President for AERA's Division D.

James W. Pellegrino is Liberal Arts and Sciences Distinguished Professor and Co-director of the Learning Sciences Research Institute at the University of Illinois at Chicago. His research and development interests focus on children's and adults' thinking and learning and the implications for assessment and instructional practice. He has published over 300 books, chapters and articles and chaired several National Academy of Sciences study Committees, including the Foundations of Assessment, Defining Deeper Learning and 21st Century Skills, and Developing Assessments of Science Proficiency in K-12. He served on the Board on Testing and Assessment of the National Research Council and is a member of the National Academy of Education and the American Academy of Arts and Sciences.

Contributors

Julie Alonzo holds an associate research professor position at the University of Oregon, where she co-directs the Behavioral Research and Teaching research unit. A National Board certified teacher, Dr. Alonzo specializes in the study of multi-tiered systems of support with an emphasis on teacher decision making and assessment development. She has served as a PI or Co-PI on numerous federal grants and provides professional development to school districts throughout the United States. She also served as a consultant on a US Aid project assisting the Republic of Georgia in the development of their first national literacy and mathematics assessments.

Isaac I. Bejar is interested in improving methods of testing by incorporating advances in psychometric theory, cognitive psychology, natural language processing, and computer technology. Dr. Bejar was a member of the editorial board and advisory board of Applied Psychological

Measurement from 1981 to 1989, and was awarded the Educational Testing Service's Research Scientist Award in 2000. He published *Cognitive and Psychometric Analysis of Analogical Problem Solving* (Springer-Verlag) and more recently co-edited *Automated Scoring of Complex Tasks in Computer-Based Testing* (Erlbaum). He is a Principal Research Scientist with Educational Testing Service in Princeton, New Jersey (USA).

Magda Chía's research addresses validity and fairness in assessments across diverse student populations including ELs, students with disabilities, and ELs with disabilities. She specializes in the relationship between cultural and linguistic diversity and assessment development, implementation, data use, and classroom instruction. Her work has been funded by numerous organizations, including the OECD, NSF, and the U.S. Department of Education. She has led efforts across multiple disciplines to produce summative, interim, and formative assessments that support all students. Chia received her doctorate at the University of Colorado, Boulder, has a master's from New York University, and was a Fulbright scholar in Peru.

Louis V. DiBello is a research professor in the Learning Sciences Research Institute at the University of Illinois at Chicago. As a researcher and product developer within the testing industry, he played an international leadership role in bringing psychometric research on cognitive diagnostic assessment into development and practice. His research interests include psychometrics, cognitive assessment, assessment design and development, assessment validity, and links among assessment, cognition, teaching, and learning.

Brian D. Gane's primary research interests center around the research and development of learning environments, including the design of assessments, instruction, and curriculum within those learning environments. He focuses on how technology affords novel interactions that promote learning and the measurement of that learning. Recently, his work has concentrated on the development and validation of assessments for engineering and science disciplines, particularly with respect to "multi-dimensional learning" as described in the Next Generation Science Standards. In addition, Dr. Gane is involved in on-going teacher education, especially around enacting instruction and assessment that allows students to productively use their knowledge.

Susan R. Goldman is co-director of UIC's Learning Sciences Research Institute, and a distinguished professor of psychology and education in UIC's College of Liberal Arts and Sciences. She conducts research on subject matter learning, instruction, assessment, and on roles for technology, especially in literacy and mathematics. Goldman is widely published in discourse, psychology and education journals. She has been elected to the National Academy of Education, named a Fellow of the American Educational Research Association and of the Society for Text and Discourse, and selected as the Inaugural Outstanding Alumnus of the Learning Research and Development Center. Goldman serves the field through a number of editorial appointments, including executive editor for *Cognition & Instruction* and associate editor for *Journal of Educational Psychology*. She sits on the editorial board of *Reading Research Quarterly, Journal of the Learning Sciences* and *Educational Psychologist*. Goldman is a board member and of the International Society of the Learning Sciences and served as its president from 2011 to 2012. She also has served as president of the Society for Text and Discourse, and vice-president for Division C of the American Educational Research Association.

Joanna Gorin, Vice President of Research at the Educational Testing Service, is responsible for a comprehensive research agenda to support current and future educational assessments for K–12, higher education, global, and workforce settings. Gorin's own research has focused on the integration of cognitive theory and psychometric theory as applied to principled assessment design and analysis. With a publication record that includes articles in top-tier educational assessment journals and chapters in numerous edited volumes, her recent publications have focused on the role of cognitive and psychometric models, methods, and tools to support improved measurement of complex competencies, including literacy and the Next Generation Science Standards.

Kristen Huff is Vice President, Assessment and Research at Curriculum Associates. Her work focuses on ensuring the coherence of assessment design, interpretation, use, and policy to advance equity and high-quality education for all students. Previously, she has worked on designing state-wide tests used for accountability as well as college placement and admission tests. Kristen received her Ed.D. in Measurement, Research and Evaluation Methods from the University of Massachusetts Amherst in 2003, and her M.Ed. in Educational Research, Measurement, and Evaluation from the University of North Carolina at Greensboro in 1996.

Yue Jia is currently a psychometric director in the Research and Development Division at ETS in Princeton, NJ. Yue received a Ph.D. degree in statistical science in 2007 and a M.A. degree in statistical science in 2004—both from the Southern Methodist University. Yue's current work at ETS focuses on directing the design, analysis, psychometrics, and research work, under the ETS contract, of the National Assessment of Educational Progress (NAEP). Yue's research interest is around applying developments in statistics, psychometrics and technology to practical problems in educational survey assessments.

Michael Kane has been the Messick Chair in Validity at the Educational Testing Service since 2009. He served as Director of Research at the National Conference of Bar Examiners from 2001 to 2009, and as a professor in the School of Education at the University of Wisconsin from 1991 to 2001. Prior to 1991, Dr. Kane served as VP for research and development and as a senior research scientist at American College Testing (ACT) in Iowa City, as Director of Test Development at the National League for Nursing in New York, as a professor of education at SUNY, Stony Brook, and as Director of Placement and Proficiency Testing at the University of Illinois, Urbana-Champaign. His main research interests are validity theory and practice, generalizability theory, licensure and certification testing, and standard setting. Dr. Kane holds a Ph.D. in education and an M.S. in statistics from Stanford University, and a B.S. and M.A. in physics from Manhattan College and SUNY, Stony Brook, respectively.

Deirdre Kerr's research focuses on determining methods of extracting information about student understanding and performance from low-level log data from educational video games and simulations. Publications include *Identifying Key Features of Student Performance in Educational Video Games and Simulations through Cluster Analysis, Identifying Learning Trajectories in an Educational Video Game*, and *Automatically Scoring Short Essays for Content*.

Rebecca J. Kopriva is a senior research scientist at the University of Wisconsin Madison. Author of many books, chapters and articles, Dr. Kopriva investigates improving how we assess knowledge and skills in K-12 large-scale and classroom academic assessments when traditional methods prove problematic. Most recently her team developed and researched a successful approach to using technology-based multi-semiotic game-like methods, novel responses environments, and sophisticated scoring algorithms to immediately provide an individualized diagnostic profile of achievement, why students might be struggling, and what teachers might do to address further learning. The methodology is especially effective for diverse students and in measuring more challenging concepts.

Suzanne Lane's scholarly interests are in educational measurement and testing, with a focus on design, technical, validity and policy issues in large scale testing. She has published in the *Journal of Educational Measurement, Applied Measurement in Education, Educational Assessment, and Educational Measurement: Issues and Practice*. She was the President of

NCME (2003–2004), Vice President of Division D-AERA (2000–2002), member of the Joint Committee for revising the Standards for Educational and Psychological Testing (1993–1999). She has served on the Editorial Boards for the *Journal of Educational Measurement*, *Applied Measurement in Education*, *Educational Assessment*, *Educational Researcher*, *and Educational Measurement: Issues and Practice.*

Jacqueline P. Leighton is a registered psychologist and professor in the School and Clinical Child Psychology (SCCP) Program at the University of Alberta, accredited by the Canadian Psychological Association (CPA). She earned her doctorate and postdoctoral training at the University of Alberta and Yale University. She is past Chair of the Department of Educational Psychology and director of CRAME. Her research interests include think-aloud and cognitive lab methodologies and socio-emotional correlates of assessment performance for enhancing formative feedback to students. She is a past winner of the 2009 AERA Division D Significant Contribution to Educational Measurement and Research Methodology Award.

Robert Mislevy is the Frederic M. Lord Chair in Measurement and Statistics at ETS and Emeritus Professor at the University of Maryland. His research applies developments in technology, statistics, and cognitive science to practical problems in educational assessment. His work includes an evidence-centered assessment design framework and, with the Cisco Networking Academy, simulation-based assessment. Publications include books on Bayesian psychometric modeling, Bayesian networks in educational assessment, psychometrics for game-based assessment, and the chapter on cognitive psychology in *Educational Measurement* (4th Edition, American Council on Education). He has received career contributions awards from AERA and NCME, and is past president of the Psychometric Society.

Joseph F. T. Nese is a Research Assistant Professor at Behavioral Research and Teaching at the University of Oregon. He received his Ph.D. in school psychology from the University of Maryland in 2009, and his B.A from the University of California at Santa Barbara in 2002. His research involves educational assessment and applied measurement, focusing on using statistical methods to measure and monitor student growth, and developing and improving systems that support data-based decision making by using advanced technologies.

Paul Nichols is currently a Senior Director and Distinguished Research Scientist in the Research Division of ACT, Inc., where Dr. Nichols supports principled assessment and product design, the development of validity arguments and the use of methods such as protocol analysis and eye movement tracking. Dr. Nichols' research integrates the most recent findings from research in learning science, assessment and measurement and technological innovations with best practices in applied studies and the design of assessments and other products.

Andreas Oranje is a principal research director in ETS' Research division. As principal research director he oversees research centers focused on the development and validation of generalizable assessment capabilities. His scope of responsibility includes groups conducting research on psychometric models applied to automated scoring, new scoring and modeling tools, natural language and speech processing, dialogic and multimodal processing, cognitive science, scenario- and game-based assessments and various assessment and assistive technologies. He also serves as Project Director for Design, Analysis, and Reporting under the ETS contract of the National Assessment of Educational Progress (NAEP 2013–2017).

Leilani Sáez is a Research Assistant Professor at the University of Oregon. She received her Ph.D. in Educational Psychology from the University of California, Riverside, and has 15 years of experience working in applied learning settings (early childhood, K-12 schools, and university). Her research focuses on the early identification of learning difficulties through a cognitive-behavioral-academic perspective to help teachers make effective instructional decisions. Leilani publishes and presents in the areas of reading, working memory, learning disabilities, and assessment, and develops innovative technological tools and curricula to support children's learning needs.

Guillermo Solano-Flores is Professor of Education at the Stanford University Graduate School of Education. He specializes in educational assessment and the linguistic and cultural issues that are relevant to both international test comparisons and the testing of cultural and linguistic minorities. His research is based on the use of multidisciplinary approaches that use psychometrics, sociolinguistics, semiotics, and cognitive science in combination. He has conducted research on the development, translation, localization, and review of science and mathematics tests. He is the author of the theory of test translation error, which addresses testing across cultures and languages.

Gerald Tindal is currently the Castle-McIntosh-Knight Professor in the College of Education, University of Oregon, and Director of Behavioral Research and Teaching (BRT), a research center funded by grants and state contracts. His research focuses on integrating students with disabilities in general education classrooms using curriculum-based measurement for screening students at risk, monitoring student progress, and evaluating instructional programs. Dr. Tindal conducts research on large scale testing and alternate assessments, investigating teacher decision-making on test participation, test accommodations, and extended assessments of basic skills. Finally, he has taught courses on assessment systems, data driven decision-making, research design, and program evaluation.

Lauress L. Wise has worked as a psychometrician and test developer for over 40 years. He recently served as President of the National Council on Measurement in Education and previously served as a co-chair of the committee that wrote the 2014 edition of Standards for Educational and Psychological Testing and as chair of the National Academy of Science Board on Testing and Assessment. Prior to joining HumRRO, he directed research and development for the Armed Services Vocational Aptitude Battery. He also held the position of Director of Research for the American Institutes for Research, where he directed Project TALENT among other activities.

Laura Wright holds a Ph.D. in linguistics from Georgetown University, specializing in sociolinguistics and discourse analysis. She has been working with English learners and diverse students for more than 20 years in a variety of capacities including classroom instruction, curriculum and assessment development, and research. Dr. Wright's research has focused on how students express conceptual understanding through discourse in complex learning environments and how language development and conceptual understanding are interrelated in academic contexts.

Index

Note: italic page numbers refer to figures and tables; numbers in brackets preceded by *n* are chapter endnote numbers.

Taylor & Francis eBooks

Helping you to choose the right eBooks for your Library

Add Routledge titles to your library's digital collection today. Taylor and Francis ebooks contains over 50,000 titles in the Humanities, Social Sciences, Behavioural Sciences, Built Environment and Law.

Choose from a range of subject packages or create your own!

Benefits for you

» Free MARC records
» COUNTER-compliant usage statistics
» Flexible purchase and pricing options
» All titles DRM-free.

Benefits for your user

» Off-site, anytime access via Athens or referring URL
» Print or copy pages or chapters
» Full content search
» Bookmark, highlight and annotate text
» Access to thousands of pages of quality research at the click of a button.

REQUEST YOUR **FREE** INSTITUTIONAL TRIAL TODAY

Free Trials Available
We offer free trials to qualifying academic, corporate and government customers.

eCollections – Choose from over 30 subject eCollections, including:

Archaeology	Language Learning
Architecture	Law
Asian Studies	Literature
Business & Management	Media & Communication
Classical Studies	Middle East Studies
Construction	Music
Creative & Media Arts	Philosophy
Criminology & Criminal Justice	Planning
Economics	Politics
Education	Psychology & Mental Health
Energy	Religion
Engineering	Security
English Language & Linguistics	Social Work
Environment & Sustainability	Sociology
Geography	Sport
Health Studies	Theatre & Performance
History	Tourism, Hospitality & Events

For more information, pricing enquiries or to order a free trial, please contact your local sales team: www.tandfebooks.com/page/sales

 Routledge
Taylor & Francis Group

The home of
Routledge books

www.tandfebooks.com